Future of Business and Finance

The Future of Business and Finance book series features professional works aimed at defining, analyzing, and charting the future trends in these fields. The focus is mainly on strategic directions, technological advances, challenges and solutions which may affect the way we do business tomorrow, including the future of sustainability and governance practices. Mainly written by practitioners, consultants and academic thinkers, the books are intended to spark and inform further discussions and developments.

Horacio Falcão • Rodrigo Gouveia •
Hervé Lamarque

Pharma, Prices and Power

Reshaping Pharmaceutical Pricing Negotiations for a Healthier Future

Springer

Horacio Falcão
INSEAD
Abu Dhabi, United Arab Emirates

Rodrigo Gouveia
Value Negotiation
Blonay-St-Légier, Switzerland

Hervé Lamarque
Celigny, Switzerland

ISSN 2662-2467 ISSN 2662-2475 (electronic)
Future of Business and Finance
ISBN 978-3-031-93935-8 ISBN 978-3-031-93933-4 (eBook)
https://doi.org/10.1007/978-3-031-93933-4

This Springer imprint is published by the registered company Springer Nature Switzerland AG
The registered company address is: Gewerbestrasse 11, 6330 Cham, Switzerland

"A must-read for anyone seeking to better understand the complexities of healthcare systems and the multiple perspectives present. On a foundation of win-win negotiation excellence the authors are leading us through dilemmas and trade-offs before finally leaving us equipped and inspired to collaboratively drive greater value in healthcare."
—Caroline Kaas Kristiansen, *Head of Global Market Access Network & Excellence*

"I really enjoyed this book. As a professional in pharmaceutical industry for 20 years, I deeply understand the importance to achieve a win-win negotiation in P&R negotiations for the healthy development of this industry. This book explained the challenges behind government and biopharma and also the challenges in P&R negotiation. Especially, when win-lose is the predominant strategy in P&R negotiations, it will be hard to create safe environment, not mentioning value creation. To negotiate win-win and to improve everyone's satisfaction, we should always increase the pie and have an absolute success mindset, which means my win is independent of your win. In the execution level, this book even gives some vivid, step-by-step examples on how to do a P&R negotiation. A win-win strategy means to create a safe environment to share information so the parties can collaborate to enhance the odds of increasing the value of the deal, and also means to make power moves unnecessary throughout the negotiation. This book gave me another angle to understand this toughest type of negotiation."
—Jessie Sijing Xiong, *Strategy and Investment Director of WuXi Biologics*

"This is a crucial resource for those engaged in pharmaceutical negotiations, providing a comprehensive view that reflects the complexity and significance of the process. It underscores the collaborative efforts required to promote public health goals while tackling the challenges and opportunities of a constantly changing industry. It emphasizes that despite technical and economic factors, the primary responsibility is toward patients and the community. Highly recommended!"
—Catarina Costa, *Market Access and Public Affairs Professional at Novo Nordisk, formerly Pharmaceutical Technician at INFARMED* (the Portuguese Medicine Agency)

"I run dozens of negotiations with health authorities and payors in Italy, France, Spain, Portugal, Germany and England and the implementation of concepts developed by the authors such as the importance of "legitimacy," of "separating relationship from substance," of moving from a "bargaining" approach to "value creation" working jointly to find solutions that serves both parties "interests and goals" made it possible to radically change the dynamic of those negotiations unlocking many complex reimbursement discussions and bringing innovative health solutions to patients across Europe."
—Valentino Confalone, *Presidente Novartis Italia*

"*Pharma, Prices, and Power* is a must-read and is a very meaningful and insightful contribution to helping stakeholders find better ways of working together. Health systems are in transition with huge opportunities and strains with new technologies and demographic changes—rethinking how health works is more important now than ever, and no one stakeholder can do it all. The authors share great insights about the role that negotiations can play in navigating complex sets of incentives in health care and in identifying innovative ways to share information and interact differently to improve health value creation."
—Stephen Chick, *Professor and Academic Director, INSEAD Healthcare Management Initiative*

"I met Horacio Falcão, a prominent Professor during a course on Leadership and Negotiation that I took at Insead, Singapore, in November 2011. Bright! Now, I come across this important book, which is also authored by Rodrigo Gouveia and Hervé Lamarque, an expert in the Biotech and Pharma industry.

The title of the book already says a lot and encourages us the reading of this important work—Pharma, Prices, and Power: Reshaping Pharmaceutical Pricing Negotiations for a Healthier Future.

The Pharma Companies has enormous power over people's health and lives, impacting people's budgets and governments' budgets. There is continued research and development to discover new drugs that bring safety and efficacy to the population that needs medicines.

However, it is quite clear that the course taken by the drug industry and with this unbridled and growing cost of medicines, we will not be able to maintain equity in their use. People and governments will not bear this cost.

The authors show us, in an objective, thought-provoking, and encouraging language, narrating in the different chapters of the book, how this evolution was and show ways for everyone to have the win-win. The pharmaceutical industry operates in a trillion-dollar economy. Evolving pricing models is critical for sustainable health, because it profoundly affects global health systems.

The analyses made by the authors are intriguing and fundamental for us to have better days in health systems. They show the players involved, how negotiations take place and create paths and strategies, including sharing risks. The authors solidify the importance of ethics, transparency, values, and so many other principles that should guide our lives. Like me, everyone who reads this book will be delighted and will get to know this pharmaceutical market even more.

Congratulations to the authors and thank you very much for providing us with this excellent masterpiece."
—Florentino Cardoso, MD, Brazil, *Oncological Surgeon and President of the Brazilian Medical Association* (2011-2017)

Foreword

In the "good old days," bringing a new medicine to market was a relatively straightforward process. You conducted your research, demonstrated effectiveness and safety, obtained market authorization, set a price, and hoped that the medical value of your product would be recognized. I admit this is a gross oversimplification, but the process was outcome-oriented, with the goal of providing better treatments for existing health problems.

Since the 1970s, pharmaceutical pricing has attracted increasing political attention and become a target of "cost-containment" efforts. Quietly, healthcare had grown into the largest identifiable economic sector in many economies, often financed directly from public or semi-public budgets.

While political interventions have successfully driven down the prices of off-patent drugs—such as generics and branded generics—they have also led to unintended consequences like unstable supply chains and drug shortages. In contrast, prices for new, patented medicines remained largely untouched—and soared.

That changed in the early 21st century, when health system administrators found themselves unable to pay the high prices being asked for new medicines. Governments began demanding lower prices as a condition for reimbursing new drugs. While they framed this as seeking a fair balance between quality, value, and cost, others interpreted it more cynically—as a case of "we want innovation, but we don't want to pay for it."

Whereas effectiveness and safety were once the main criteria for market approval, efficiency has now become the key to successful market entry. In this environment, rationing has effectively become part of the real-world access strategy for new medicines.

While both justification and criticism of this new reality are valid, the system—or rather, the systems, since we are talking about many countries with different approaches—has grown extraordinarily complex. The process begins with the conflicting expectations of stakeholders and is further strained by the demands of patients and healthcare professionals who may be desperately awaiting the arrival of a new drug.

Negotiations in this space are complicated by legal constraints, public expectations, political objectives, and pressure from patient and professional organizations and—not to forget— shareholders eager for a return on their investment.

The work of Horacio Falcão, Rodrigo Gouveia, and Hervé Lamarque—"Pharma, Prices, and Power: Reshaping Pharmaceutical Pricing Negotiations for a Healthier Future"—offers valuable guidance for navigating this minefield. Through systematic analysis and practical approaches, they chart a path toward a common goal: enabling access to meaningful innovation that improves medical diagnosis and therapy, while preserving a profitable environment capable of delivering the medicines we need. Such guidance is both timely and essential.

Secretary General of the World Medical Association Otmar Kloiber
Ferney-Voltaire, France

Preface

Healthcare workers and researchers in the biopharma industry mostly choose to enter this industry because of the positive difference they can make to improve or even save patients' lives. They then dedicate their professional lives to demanding, high-impact jobs under great government and media scrutiny and enormous pressure to innovate and make sustainable profits in a highly competitive industry while doing their best to stick to their dreams and mission of helping others. Meanwhile, these professionals must have tremendous technical knowledge at the vanguard of science, resilience against frequent experiments and commercial failures, and determination to work daily to improve our lives.

Besides the scientific work of creating new therapies and the scientific work of curing patients sits the mysterious and highly complex world that this book covers. This middle world decides which therapies are allocated or not, to whom, why, when, and at what price, and thus, it has a tremendous yet somewhat invisible impact on all our lives, be it our health or wealth. While this in-between world is trying to become increasingly more scientific, fair, and sustainable in a few parts of the world, for the most part, it is one where power, politics, and human conflict play a considerable role.

We co-wrote this book based on our decades-long collaboration to improve worldwide negotiation performance between Pharma and Payers. We saw how proper negotiation training enabled several Pharma and Payer negotiators to understand their ingrained problems and how to fix them to create more efficiency, positive dynamics, and ultimately more value. Superior negotiation skills also allowed them to anticipate the multiple ways a negotiation could go wrong, correct it early on, and thus secure much better and more sustainable outcomes.

From our collective experience, seven years ago, Hervé came up with the idea for this book: to contribute to those of us who sit between pharma researchers and healthcare workers (e.g., Pharmaceutical executives, Payers, and others) and want to excel at our jobs, for those on the outside who also wish to contribute directly to improving this world in the middle, or just by becoming better-informed citizens able to voice their qualified opinions on such matters within their communities, media, or civil societies.

In response to the goal above, we wrote a detailed pharmaceutical negotiation manual (now summarized as Chapter 6 here). In that process, we realized that the negotiations and main decisions in this healthcare middle world had contextual and historical factors that we needed to explore to answer our core question of how to improve Pharma-Payer negotiations. We ended up investing seven years in creating a thorough negotiation analysis of the context and dynamics of the Pharma and Payers so that our readers could understand how the world in the middle of healthcare really works.

Our research and analysis showed the tremendous impact of negotiation and power on all healthcare stakeholders and how a better negotiation approach, whether top-down or bottom-up, could dramatically improve this impact.

We thank you for your interest in this book. We hope that you enjoy reading it, that it helps you better understand this complex world, that you become more motivated to invest in your negotiation skills, and that it ultimately empowers you to bring impactful benefits to those around you and for those you work for.

Abu Dhabi, UAE — Horacio Falcão
Blonay-St-Légier, Switzerland — Rodrigo Gouveia
Celigny, Switzerland — Hervé Lamarque

Acknowledgments

The authors would like to thank the many clients and colleagues in the pharmaceutical industry who have shared their negotiation problems with us and allowed us to advise them on how to turn them into more collaborative negotiations without caving in.

Individually, we would also like to thank:

Horacio:

I would like to thank my wife Camila, my two sons Luca & Mateus, and my parents Horacio & Evangelina. The microcosm of our negotiations has been the seed of my passion for the field. I would also like to thank my co-authors and friends Rodrigo & Hervé for their commitment to excellence and our many win-win interactions when discussing our many ideas for this book. Finally, I want to thank my friend Sharmilah. Without your collective support and patience, my contribution to this book would not have been possible or as enriching.

Rodrigo:

I would like to thank my parents, Alfredo and Maria de Lurdes, my grandparents Alfredo and Maria Cristina, my sister Mariana, and Maria, for their support and inspiration in my life.

I would also like to thank my co-authors and friends Horacio and Hervé for the wonderful joint work in this book, their creative ideas and writing. Thinking together on how to create a better world has been awesome.

I would also like to thank my girlfriend Fernanda Stukart for always believing in me and for the very stimulating conversations.

Hervé:

I extend my deepest gratitude to my wife, Isandre, whose unwavering support and belief in me fuel my drive; to my parents, Simone and Gérard, for instilling in me their ingenuity; to my children, Antoine, Elise, and Ingrid, whose playfulness reminds me of the power of curiosity and creativity; and to my brilliant co-authors, Horacio and Rodrigo—whom I proudly introduce as the sharpest minds I've had the privilege to collaborate with.

Competing Interests The authors have no competing interests to declare that are relevant to the content of this manuscript.

Contents

About the Authors

Horacio Falcão (Ph.D., MBA, Masters, and LL.M.) has been bringing Win-Win to the world for the past 25 years. In 2010, he created the method and book Value Negotiation: How to Finally Get the Win-Win Right, building on the early knowledge passed on by his mentor Roger Fisher, as well as his many years advising businesses across all types of negotiations and researching Negotiation.

In his effort to disseminate how to implement Win-Win correctly, Horacio has been voted the Best Elective Professor of the Year at INSEAD 21 times and has co-founded Value Negotiation (a negotiation advisory company), VN Tech (a Negotiation SaaS), Qinect (AI EdTech in negotiation), and the INSEAD Negotiation and Conflict Management Collaborative (NCMC).

Since 2013, Horacio and Rodrigo have advised several pharmaceutical companies to improve their negotiations and relationships with Payers.

Rodrigo Gouveia (Ph.D.) has advised many clients across different geographies and industries on how to overcome their diverse negotiation challenges through Win-Win. He is a Partner at Value Negotiation and teaches Negotiation at INSEAD as a visiting professor.

Since 2013, Rodrigo and Horacio have advised several pharmaceutical companies to improve their negotiations and relationships with Payers around the world. In some, this involved enabling their internal negotiation processes, negotiation culture, and skills to Win-Win.

Rodrigo has helped strategize and support negotiations for dozens of pharmaceutical products, across 25 countries and has taught Market Access Win-Win negotiation to more than 400 people in the pharmaceutical industry.

Hervé Lamarque is a seasoned expert in the Biotech and Pharma industry who has overseen the negotiations of more than 20 pharmaceutical products (including several blockbusters) in its Market Access Leadership positions in AstraZeneca, Bristol Myers Squibb, and Incyte Biosciences. Inw these roles, Hervé has overseen negotiations with most European national authorities, where he has implemented Win-Win—that he first learned from Horacio when taking the executive MBA at INSEAD in 2006.

Across more than 250 negotiations, Hervé has implemented Win-Win in Pharma and understood the details and difficulties of succeeding in the current very tense climate between European Healthcare authorities and Pharmaceutical Companies.

Introduction 1

1.1 Why Drug Price Negotiations Matter

The pharmaceutical industry—if it were a country of its own—would have a GDP of roughly US$1 trillion (Mikulic 2020)—which would rank it as one of the top 20 economies in the world. Among its over 4000 member companies, US$170 billion is spent annually on R&D (Investopedia 2022), a full 10% of the total R&D spend of all industries in the world combined. There are many good things about the pharmaceutical industry, as it works to invest in making people healthier and saving lives, for now and in the future. For instance, according to one study, between the years 1990 and 2005, a full year of increased life expectancy—35% of the total increase—can be attributed to the innovation brought about by the pharmaceutical industry (Migliara 2020). During the COVID-19 pandemic, pharma, as the financial publication *Barron's* writes, "invested their own money to develop patented manufacturing technologies in record time" (Glassman 2021). And yet, despite all the positive impact, pharmaceutical companies have a negative reputation among the public, as exemplified by the widespread anti-vaccine sentiment. Besides the huge suspicion, there is frequent criticism regarding conflicts of interest, harmful products with understudied or undisclosed side effects, questionable business practices (Valet 2018), or unfair or unethical behavior that can seriously harm people's lives.

Some pharmaceutical companies have been accused of promoting products with dubious value, hiding data about toxicity (Wikipedia Contributors 2019), misrepresenting drugs to doctors to increase sales (Van Zee 2009), and even pushing millions of people into serious drug addiction (e.g., the opioid crisis, resulting in 399,000 deaths in the USA as of 2022) (National Institute on Drug Abuse 2024). These misdeeds have had huge repercussions and have contributed to Pharma's negative reputation (Gallup 2007). Some see pharma as a greedy and unscrupulous actor. Others think that some of this negative behavior is driven by the pressure on pharmaceutical companies to maximize profits and shareholder value to the detriment of other health-related objectives and that malpractices are limited and too often

H. Falcão et al., *Pharma, Prices and Power*, Future of Business and Finance,
https://doi.org/10.1007/978-3-031-93933-4_1

generalized. Some negative behaviors may be reinforced as pharma companies negotiate with many aggressive healthcare stakeholders who act in self-interested and shortsighted ways that give way to more poor behaviors and escalate the problem further.

Our contention is that pricing and reimbursement (P&R) negotiations—that is, the negotiations that define the conditions, patient populations, and prices of pharmaceuticals—could become a major factor in leading us to a better global healthcare system for all. While numerous books cover broad political questions around healthcare (Dawes 2020; Kapur and Chalil 2020), few if any dive deep into these negotiations and recognize their importance.

Despite genuine efforts by regulatory agencies and pharma researchers alike, when a drug reaches the market, it still carries some uncertainties that make its price negotiation hard. There are uncertainties within several parameters, such as long-term efficacy, market size, long-term side effects, and degree of adequacy with local practices or data requirements. While diligent and partially technically based, the negotiation process between authorities and company representatives can strongly erode the value of the research and development process. Success or failure—for a particular drug but perhaps also for the entire company behind it—is determined at this moment, including the fates of the potential patients and the impact on a country's healthcare budget.

P&R negotiations only happen after regulatory agencies like the European Medicines Agency (EMA) authorized the drug's usage based on demonstrated efficacy, safety, and quality of production. These negotiations are not only about a drug's price, but also about its market access—the extremely important decision about whether to allow or reject entry of a specific drug into a particular country, and about *optimizing* its use locally by following safe and scientifically defined recommendations.

We, the authors of this book, have been successfully working together on P&R negotiations for a decade. We have joined our theoretical expertise as academics devoted to the study of win-win negotiations with the executive and advisory experience from dozens of P&R negotiations on all continents to find that there are better ways to handle the value-destroying P&R negotiation challenges of today. We have developed an approach that has already led to some more effective and successful negotiations where all stakeholders emerged better off, achieving results that satisfied demands on all sides, faster, and with less conflict than before.

We believe that this book will fulfill the purpose of educating readers on the challenges of P&R negotiations and the possibilities for change. We rely here on modern negotiation theory, namely, the Value Negotiation system, as the lens through which to understand the challenges and to provide suggestions for improvement. This book makes the theory and the practice accessible to all readers, those with or without prior knowledge of negotiation theory or experience in the pharmaceutical industry.

1.2 Where Healthcare Currently Stands

It is helpful, as we begin this book, to level-set, both in terms of what is currently happening with regard to P&R negotiations around the world as well as to lay out our utopian vision of what a well-functioning healthcare market ought to look like. This vision informs and motivates everything we propose in the pages to come.

We want to be clear that we know this vision is far-fetched and idealistic, and a vision not for tomorrow but rather aimed further into the future. We know it is open to interpretation, but as we set out to move toward a particular target in this book, we wanted to at least articulate the goal at the start.

We believe that patients should have the most effective access to drugs, considering the politically acceptable balance between efficacy and affordability. We want a world that sustainably maximizes drug innovation benefits to patients while distributing the rewards based on the value generated and not negotiation power or wrongful tactics.

We believe that healthcare systems, public or private, should pay a price for the value of such drugs that creates sustainable incentives for pharmaceutical companies to invest in new cures and therapies. We also believe that the pharmaceutical companies should receive a fair profit for their efforts, so that together with their shareholders they are motivated to continue their investment in our health. From a cost perspective, we believe in a broader sharing of the burden of innovation between countries to maximize worldwide health, wealth, and happiness.

We also believe that the rules of the system, and the interaction between Payer (e.g., the one who buys and ultimately pays for pharmaceutical products, often the Government in universal care systems) and Industry, should be set in a way where misleading or abusive behavior is penalized effectively and to the extent that it discourages such misbehaviors.

How do we get there? Many argue that healthcare can become better, cheaper, and faster through technological advancements. However, as just one example, Haven, a company founded in 2018 by an alliance of tech leaders and billionaires Warren Buffett, Jeff Bezos, and Jamie Dimon, whose goal was to revolutionize healthcare, went bust two years later for failing to appreciate the non-technological complexities of healthcare (Hiltzik 2021). They realized that prices matter, along with defined incentives. These shape our healthcare (Yaşar 2009). And what specifically defines these prices is the large politically influenced P&R negotiations we discuss in this book.

An unfortunate reality is that a significant obstacle to pain-free, longer lives is an ignorance of how local P&R negotiations have been negatively shaping the global healthcare industry. In the search for the perfect short-term solution on a local level, each country and pharma company has been a consistent contributor to and victim of the tragedy of the commons—how we as self-interested individuals or institutions, when distrusting each other, or failing to communicate, almost inevitably behave against our collective interests when attempting to reap the most personal benefit from any given common resource available to us (Ostrom 2009). When honest and high-quality communication is not the rule (as happens between healthcare stakeholders), pursuing self-interest ends with both companies and governments making their problems worse over time.

What is the common resource available to us here? The industry's amazing ability to create value through innovation. And yet, lack of expertise in win-win negotiations is undermining the parties' ability to reach optimal or at least superior deals, because they have no way to overcome their differences, fears, and distrust in collaborative and effective ways. Most parties want to provide access to safe and efficacious drugs at a fair price, but disagreements or ignorance about the best process can lead them astray.

Pharma companies are businesses and have to juggle their dual goals of maximizing patient well-being and shareholder value. Similarly, individual governments have to juggle their goals of providing citizens with access to quality treatments, protecting their budgets, and treating businesses fairly. Patients and doctors want the innovations available as quickly as possible, but also want assurances that the new drugs are safer and more effective than previous ones and appropriately prescribed.

All these stakeholders have grievances and suspicions regarding one another, and feel the need to protect themselves based on past misleading and abusive behaviors, which were often not penalized. This adversarial history, plus the current fear and mistrust among the parties, leads to overly protective negotiations. Parties seek to maximize their power, not with an intention to attack each other, but rather in response to the fear of what the counterparty can do to them. Independent of the intention, the resulting effect of this negotiation arms race is value-destroying for the collective.

The problems in healthcare are complicated, and as the population gets older, and more and more new drugs arrive, it is likely to get worse if we do not act to counter the trend. We need to optimize the current system to cope better, and one high-impact avenue to do so is optimizing negotiations.

Here is how the situation currently plays out in its extreme or when the dynamics in a given country start to escalate: Pharma companies strategize and design their clinical trials with great care to validate the efficacy and safety of their drugs and enhance their chances of having them approved at premium prices. In this process, they attempt to avoid additional risks or unnecessary costs to their clinical trials, and thus may choose not to test a product against some useful already available products. Unfortunately, in some instances, these choices can be or come across as opportunistic moves to increase Pharma's informational power in the P&R negotiation. Conversely, governments sometimes create more stringent, yet arguable, standards to entitle new drugs to be reimbursed or for the pharmaceutical companies to be paid a premium, which can be seen as an abuse of their legislative power. This stringency can derail into biased or politically motivated scientific assessment that artificially lowers a drug's clinical value, and increases the government's power to negotiate a lower price for the drug.

Both sides fail to optimize the overall outcome of the negotiation as they are too focused on protecting themselves from one another, escalating adversarial moves and further increasing the desire for protection and the flight to power moves in an accelerated vicious cycle.[1] P&R negotiation stakeholders must appreciate that these power tactics and their adversarial approach are the problem, not the path to a solution. As already mentioned, the current P&R negotiations resemble an arms race, pushing the healthcare system into a downward value spiral where every single stakeholder is bound to lose.

We worry that such poor negotiation dynamics can lead Governments to blow their ever-increasing healthcare budgets or be forced to deny access to innovative drugs at the expense of patients. It may lead to patients overpaying and still forming long lines to wait for less-than-adequate treatments. Hospitals may have no choice but to overwork their staff, cut costs, and see medical errors rise. Pharma may fail to recoup investments, shy away from innovation that does not ensure enough financial returns or shift funds away from R&D toward finding profitable loopholes as opposed to pursuing the best path toward improving societal health. Shareholders may get discouraged from investing in lower-returns and volatile pharmaceutical companies, turn off the money tap for pharmaceutical innovation, and shift to other industries with a smaller societal benefit.

In summary, we make the case that drug pricing and P&R negotiations are not only about price. They are about shaping the incentive system within healthcare, about promoting investment and innovation, but also about controlling budgets and government spending. They are about the resource allocation of almost 1.5 trillion dollars annually in the pharmaceutical market (Mikulic 2023). They are about who captures the profit or value produced and who pays the bill, about the social value of healthcare, the underlying human rights, and the economic benefit of a healthy society. P&R negotiations are about defining the relationship and the power among pharmaceutical companies, shareholders, governments, hospitals, and patients, about giving access to the best healthcare available and our aspirations for our future health. The current state of affairs is in need of fixing.

1.3 What Will you Learn from this Book?

In the spirit of helping to fix this stressed P&R negotiation system and helping to give readers the fullest and most complete understanding of the problems and possible solutions, this book has two parts. First, we offer a broad analysis of the current healthcare and pharmaceutical landscape as it shapes several of the structural challenges that affect P&R negotiations. By better understanding the overall context the broader healthcare history, systems, parties, structural tensions, main negotiation strategies, and how they play out in different countries, and the challenges faced by Governments and Pharma in P&R negotiations—we can diagnose the real problems more accurately and focus on the ones we can change.

[1] Of course, this is not to say that government standards are to blame for the problem. If not for government restrictions, it's very likely that some Pharma companies would be at least tempted, if not forced, by deregulated competitive pressure to increase their prices or engage in misleading advertisements even more.

The second part of this book (Chap. 6) delivers more prescriptive negotiation advice. It aims to provide readers with a new vision of how to conduct improved P&R negotiations that can increase value for all, while avoiding potential mistakes that could lead to the future deterioration of the pharma environment and of healthcare in general. While we often illustrate our approach to the negotiation challenges from the Pharma side, given our direct experience, we provide a guide on how all involved in such negotiations can negotiate more productively, and build from the bottom up a better and more sustainable system for us all.

Specifically, we will explain how healthcare negotiations should move from a power-based model to a value-oriented, non-power-based model. We will analyze the conditions needed for this to work well, and illustrate how to conduct these types of negotiations without the use of power or adversarial moves.

We wrote this book aiming to make a contribution to the healthcare ecosystem overall and the pharmaceutical industry specifically. While the P&R system seems stressed—maybe even stuck—in the presence of so many challenges, we believe we have a useful understanding of why we are trapped in a downward value spiral of the tragedy of the commons. We believe that our ideas can help evolve the system bottom-up, step-by-step, negotiation-by-negotiation, into something new, better for all, and more aligned with all of our present and future healthcare aspirations. We hope this book can help you better understand the problem and become part of the solution so that we can together grow a more sustainable healthcare model. For the sake of society, every negotiation matters.

References

Dawes DE (2020) The political determinants of health. Johns Hopkins University Press

Gallup (2007) Business and industry sector ratings. Gallup. https://news.gallup.com/poll/12748/business-industry-sector-ratings.aspx

Glassman A (2021) Big pharma is not the tobacco industry. www.barrons.com. https://www.barrons.com/articles/big-pharma-is-not-the-tobacco-industry-51620315693

Hiltzik M (2021) That Buffett-Bezos-Dimon healthcare venture goes bust—predictably. Los Angeles Times

Investopedia (2022) Average research & development costs for pharmaceutical companies. https://www.investopedia.com/ask/answers/060115/how-much-drug-companys-spending-allocated-research-and-development-average.asp

Kapur P, Chalil J (2020) Beyond the COVID-19 pandemic. The UNN Corporation

Migliara G (2020) Study finds biopharmaceutical innovation is responsible for 35% of the increase in life expectancy from 1990 to 2015. catalyst.phrma.org. https://catalyst.phrma.org/study-finds-biopharmaceutical-innovation-is-responsible-for-35-of-the-increase-in-life-expectancy-from-1990-to-2015

Mikulic M (2020) Topic: global pharmaceutical industry. www.statista.com. https://www.statista.com/topics/1764/global-pharmaceutical-industry/

Mikulic M (2023) Pharmaceutical market worldwide revenue 2001–2022. Statista. https://www.statista.com/statistics/263102/pharmaceutical-market-worldwide-revenue-since-2001/

National Institute on Drug Abuse (2024) Drug overdose death rates. National Institute on Drug Abuse. https://nida.nih.gov/research-topics/trends-statistics/overdose-death-rates

Ostrom E (2009) The Sveriges Riksbank prize in economic sciences in memory of Alfred Nobel 2009. NobelPrize.org. https://www.nobelprize.org/prizes/economic-sciences/2009/ostrom/lecture/

Valet V (2018) The world's most reputable companies 2018. Forbes

Van Zee A (2009) The promotion and marketing of OxyContin: commercial triumph, public Health tragedy. Am J Public Health 99:221–227. https://doi.org/10.2105/ajph.2007.131714

Wikipedia Contributors (2019) List of largest pharmaceutical settlements. Wikipedia. https://en.wikipedia.org/wiki/List_of_largest_pharmaceutical_settlements

Yaşar Y (2009) It's the prices, stupid: the underlying problems of the US social security system. J Econ Issues 43:843–865

2 Understanding Healthcare Systems and Their Negotiations

In this chapter, we examine the broader healthcare history, systems, parties, structural tensions, main negotiation strategies, and how they play out in different countries. This chapter provides the background for us to best understand and suggest improvements to P&R negotiations later in the book.

2.1 Too Many Stakeholders Perceive an Unfair Split of Resources

Most healthcare stakeholders believe they are getting the short end of the healthcare bargain. Physicians and nurses feel undercompensated when compared to Pharma revenues. Pharma worldwide at times feels their drugs are much less appreciated and rewarded than in the USA. Pharma companies in the USA feel underpaid compared to Pharmacy Benefit Managers (PBMs).[1] Healthcare insurance plans feel they don't get fairly rewarded for what they save their clients. Hospitals feel they are making less than anyone else given the benefit they bring to patients. Finally, patients in the USA or payers in Europe feel that treatment prices are rising to absurd levels. Doctors in Europe feel unfairly compensated compared to their colleagues in the USA. Interestingly, no one seems happy, and yet everyone seems to feel unfairly rewarded when compared to others.

And whose fault is it? Maybe no one, as the grass may just look greener on the other side. Maybe everyone's, as there are, within all parties, bad apples who get more than they deserve. Then every party is always wanting more of everything: profits, efficiency, stability, health, growth, innovation, discounts, life. Once we see someone else having what we perceive to be more, especially if we believe it was

[1] Pharmacy benefit managers or PBMs are companies or intermediaries between insurance companies, pharmacies, and drug manufacturers, who aim to secure lower prices for insurers and insurance companies.

H. Falcão et al., *Pharma, Prices and Power*, Future of Business and Finance,
https://doi.org/10.1007/978-3-031-93933-4_2

undeserved, then we want more as well. Under such conditions, most negotiators get sucked into the **relative success mindset**, where we misguidedly measure our negotiation outcome or success in comparison or relative to the counterparty's outcome or success. Consequently, these parties only feel having done well in a negotiation if their results are bigger or better than those of their counterparties.

The relative success mindset pushes people into believing that negotiations have fixed or limited value (a.k.a. **zero-sum or fixed-pie assumption**). Under this assumption, negotiators believe that there is not enough value on the table to satisfy everyone and thus the only rational negotiation move is to claim as much of that value as one can, often by any means necessary. Such negotiators see themselves as gladiators, and resort to power moves to either proactively beat their counterparties or reactively defend themselves from the counterparties' power moves.

Within the healthcare industry, given it is often a cost center not designed to satisfy every stakeholder's desire, and that its imperfect institutions allocate funds based on power more than value, direct comparisons become inevitable, even if harmful and counterproductive. Our argument is that the relative success mindset should not become the main measure for the success of healthcare negotiations.

Here is a US-based example that helps illustrate this relative success problem. In 1990, the USA witnessed a decade-long drug expenditure growth of 9.6% a year, compared to 4.5% annual growth of other healthcare costs in the country. The US government interpreted the data as drug companies having contributed less than other stakeholders (i.e., patients, hospitals, or doctors) to reducing the federal budget deficit. To correct this imbalance, the USA introduced legislation so drug companies had to give Medicaid[2] the same discounts as they gave to other big customers.

The pharmaceutical industry argued that the 1980s saw a disproportionate rise in R&D costs to justify their higher expenditure growth in the 1990s. And then, rather than lowering prices for Medicaid, they raised them across the board. This way, even after giving the larger mandated discounts, the net amount stayed the same. Infuriated US Senators and Representatives argued that price increases "may meet the letter of the law, but certainly do not meet the spirit of the legislation" and that they were a foolish "attempt to circumvent the new Medicaid law [and] get around the intent of Congress." Conversely, Pharma accused the law of being a violation of free market principles. They even expressed surprise over the government's lack of anticipation of Pharma's resistance given the law's significant reduction of their revenues.

Had Pharma complied with the spirit of the law, what would have prevented the US Congress from increasing the demanded discount the following years? The lack of predictability or assurances by a negotiation counterparty usually pushes the other to distrust them and opt for self-help moves. If Pharma were to passively accept the law, they would be agreeing to the dangerous precedent of allowing the US Government to set their prices in the future without any consultation or negotiation. Pharma likely felt the need to defend their profits and show the US Government

[2] Medicaid is the US government-funded health insurance for low-income citizens.

that unilateral power moves can backfire, so that they would think twice before using their legislative power for unilateral gain in the future.

This example illustrates how the different healthcare stakeholders have been engaged for decades in a value-destroying escalation of power moves that hurts all parties involved. The good news is that it doesn't have to be this way. Let's take another look at this 1990 law example. Both sides had valid points. It seems reasonable to raise prices in line with rising costs when developing new, beneficial drugs. It also seems reasonable to ask Pharma to help reduce the federal healthcare budget deficit, together with other stakeholders. Consistently, each side believed their arguments to be fair, but then mistakenly discounted the validity of their counterparty's arguments and blamed the problem on them. This discounting could just be an intentional dialectic tactic to win an argument and show strength to one's constituents, and yet there is more to it than that.

Believing we are right, and our counterparty is wrong, is a common, well-researched phenomenon to which we're all susceptible. Most of us not only believe we're just, virtuous, and moral, but also that we surpass the average person in these virtues (Tappin and McKay 2016), which cannot be true as by definition half of us have to be below the average. And yet, many of us suffer from this **illusion of moral superiority** (Tappin and McKay 2016) that makes us perceive ourselves as selfless when discussing right and wrong. In contrast, others become egoistic, evil, or just wrong (Peters et al. 2004).

Governments and pharma companies, imbued with this moral superiority illusion, lock themselves in battles, where each genuinely believes the other to be wrong. This belief hampers the openness for amicable solutions. Instead, each side raises their adversarial tone, seeks validation within their own group, and hardly ever sees the other side's point of view or attempts to improve their own. When others claim moral superiority over us, we become defensive and refuse to revisit our moral standing (Täuber and van Zomeren 2012), even if they are right. In many such cases, our moral superiority derails further into **self-righteousness**, making us intolerant of differing opinions and behaviors. To make matters worse, the more we feel self-righteous, the more we tolerate our own or our group's immoral or power moves (Brewer 1999), thus rationalizing our own or our group's negotiation misbehaviors or abuses as necessary or nothing worse than "they" would have done to us.

This moral bias is a major challenge in negotiations, as openness to improve our moral standing is crucial to overcome our limited illusions, comprehend others, or craft superior outcomes. Another challenge is that, as people see negotiation benefits flowing toward those who employ power tactics (e.g., threats, lies, manipulation), their restraints weaken, leading to a cycle of escalating lack of moral behavior and unhappiness.

Ultimately, Governments and Pharma are structurally and systematically locked in P&R negotiations, and many claim to want broader, collaborative solutions. However, powerful psychological forces push them apart into self-righteous corners, granting moral license for less moral behavior while worsening the conflict and subsequently the P&R negotiations. So we're compelled to return to the initial question: Whose fault is it? The unsatisfying answer is that it's everyone's and no one's fault simultaneously; it's the system's fault. A system that allows the wrong incentives or forces to generate value-destroying negotiations. Therefore, we must ask: How can we improve the system? To answer, we must first understand how the system came to be this way.

2.2 How Did Our Healthcare Systems Develop?

> "It's an unbelievably complex subject, nobody knew that health care could be so complicated."—Donald Trump, Former President of the United States of America

Healthcare is incredibly complex and convoluted, especially once you start digging and looking at the reality in different countries. Indeed, we do not attempt to cover it all, but rather focus on the driving forces and negotiations that shape our healthcare. Healthcare systems emerged as negotiated solutions to the health vs. wealth dilemma that potentially forces people, at some point in their lives, to ask: "Do I pay for this treatment and risk financial struggle, or save my money and hope to get better on my own?"[3]

The first healthcare system in the world was the out-of-pocket one, and not being much of a system, it gave rise to the health vs. wealth dilemma. It is, in a way, the default state of affairs in the absence of an organized structure: individuals buy healthcare products or services as in any market. When someone needs a doctor, they simply pay for the treatment fees. The problem arises when patients lack funds. They end up unable to afford a particular treatment, and either unnecessarily endure pain or diseases, or desperately seek lower-cost, but on most occasions, ineffective treatments. These scenarios are also suboptimal for healthcare providers, who lose the revenue from foregone treatments. Society also loses as overall health declines, and funds are misallocated. Patients, providers, and society can benefit from a healthcare system that increases quality and affordable access.

An organized healthcare system needs a high enough concentration of potential patients with enough resources to collectively afford it. For example, low income or remote rural areas often lack resources to finance a system of their own. If other groups do not subsidize their healthcare, these populations stay in the out-of-pocket system, commonly relying on inexpensive traditional healers.[4]

---

[3] While somewhat extensive in our coverage of different healthcare systems, we are not attempting to cover every healthcare system in the world. We have focused our analysis on healthcare systems of developed nations and some representative of large, less developed nations, as that is also our area of professional expertise.

[4] We should note that there is political value in having these populations believe they have access to healthcare through traditional healers. In China, the government goes to great lengths to promote widely available and affordable Traditional Chinese Medicine (TCM) to give patients in rural areas the feeling they are getting quality healthcare. While delivering hope, TCM healers deliver scientifically untested therapies with questionable practical efficacy, despite using the poor's already limited resources.

Until the late nineteenth century, Western medicine was very ineffective. But scientific advances and social changes enabled the replacement of the out-of-pocket system. As medical sciences improved, seeing a doctor finally became safer than not seeing one (Magee 2019). Socially, the ruling classes saw workers' welfare as a tool against the rise of socialism in Europe. In 1883, Otto von Bismarck, the Chancellor of Germany, passed the first Sickness Insurance Law, entitling industrial, and later also agricultural, workers to needed medical treatment, up to 13 weeks of sick leave, and later added a workplace disabilities' pension. The system was and continues to be co-financed by workers' wages and employer contributions.

For almost 140 years, Germany has had a paid healthcare system, managed by not-for-profit bureaus (sick funds), which maintains its overall layout despite adaptations to twentieth- and twenty-first-century events. This resilience may be a testimony to the quality of the system's original design, or a case study in healthcare system's resistance to change.[5]

Around World War II, other European nations created their healthcare systems, as did other industrialized nations by the end of the twentieth century in an explosion of tailored healthcare systems to each country's particular situation (Reid 2010). The systems fit roughly into four categories, mostly defined by the role of the State in financing or providing care:

1. **State as Facilitator (Sick fund systems)**: The State sets up the structure and legislates to clarify the game's roles and rules. The system is then mostly organized and financed via sick funds or similar highly regulated institutions.
2. **State as Provider (Government systems)**: The State finances healthcare through general taxation and centralizes operations in a single public system.
3. **State as Safety net (Market systems):** Healthcare operates in a free market, similar to an organized out-of-pocket system, where private healthcare plans act as sick funds with more freedom and profit orientation, and the State steps in minimally and mostly to support those marginalized by free-market forces.
4. **State as Choice (Mixed systems)**: Similar to a Provider, the State finances and operates a public healthcare system available to everyone but also offers to those who want the choice of a parallel private healthcare system, with similar or competing services (Reinhardt et al. 2019; Roberts et al. 2008).

2.2.1 State as Facilitator: Healthcare Organized and Financed via Sick Funds

As a facilitator, the State legislates to ensure the proper functioning of systems organized and financed through sick funds or similar entities (e.g., Germany, Japan, and

[5] Not being so pessimistic, several countries have changed their healthcare systems in recent years. Among developed nations, Taiwan and Switzerland changed their healthcare to the Sick Fund system in 1995 and 2000.

Switzerland[6]) at a total cost of around 11% of GDP. Originated from the Bismarckian healthcare model, adherence and thus payments to a sick fund is mandatory and enforced, with the State covering the payments for those unable to afford them. They usually work well in countries with high GDPs per capita due to their relatively high absolute cost.

Sick funds operate as non-profit, non-governmental organizations, and cannot compete on plan coverage or demographic segmentation. They must cover every treatment deemed valuable by the government's strict scientific evaluations, made independently from those covering expenses to ensure that all necessary services are available. Procedure prices are typically uniform across providers, either dictated by the State (Germany, France, and Japan) and sometimes further negotiated between the sick funds and the provider (Germany). To ensure coverage in remote areas, the system may provide higher payments to providers in these regions or establish a regional price list instead of a national one.

Patients often can choose just about any doctor or hospital without gatekeepers,[7] promoting competition among providers to enhance patient satisfaction within the fixed fee per service. The government, not the medical association, determines how many doctors are needed and thus how many will be trained.

Universal coverage is the norm, except at times for illegal immigrants, specific services (e.g., dental and eye care), elective surgeries, branded pharmaceuticals when generics are available, or providers charging above stipulated prices. In such cases, the patient covers the price difference over the covered service. For-profit insurers may offer plans to cover these optional or additional expenses. Copays or upfront payments may occur but are generally a small fraction of the cost, mainly to prevent system abuse or excessive utilization.

The government or sick funds negotiate fees with providers (e.g., doctors, hospitals, and pharmaceutical companies) and use a simple and transparent structure to prevent providers from manipulating patients or the State into making opaque decisions. The negotiators attempt to ensure a level playing field among providers, close transparent and straightforward deals, where they leverage data to optimize resource utilization, combat resource wastage (e.g., services not deemed adequate by the State), corruption, or power concentration. Sick funds' negotiation power often secures low prices for its members.[8]

[6] Switzerland is an interesting exception as it substitutes sick funds for private for-profit health insurers, who must by law offer all residents an affordable coverage. Conversely, Swiss residents are legally obligated to purchase health insurance from an approved provider, whose role is purely administrative, which pushes them to compete mostly on efficiency.

[7] General practitioners are in some systems the gatekeepers of specialty doctors, in the sense that a patient needs to first visit a general practitioner that will recommend it to visit the adequate specialty doctor.

[8] A Payer, or sometimes payor, is the entity that pays for an administered medical service. Depending on the system, that can be a Sick fund, an umbrella of Sick funds, the Government, or an insurance company. A payer is responsible for processing patient eligibility, enrollment, claims, and payment.

At the same time, these systems aim for the best possible care, and sick funds cannot limit or delay care that the State deems valuable. Consequently, new clinically valuable drugs or treatments become rapidly and widely accessible. However, sick funds also visibly link the amount they pay to members' contributions. Thus, increases in provider fees means that members must, sooner or later, contribute more. As they normally resist such increases, healthcare providers on average receive relatively low pay and are capped as middle-class earners (Reid 2010).[9] The centralized pricing scheme prevents providers from charging higher prices, thus better providers are not rewarded for their superior value, unless they are a much needed exception in which case they may claim a premium.

Sick-fund-based healthcare systems achieve some of the best outcomes globally, as in Japan, which, as of 2020, boasts a public healthcare system covering every citizen and resident with reasonable fees and high quality care choices from routine doctor visits to emergencies and hospitalizations (Dornhege 2020).

2.2.2 State as Provider: Healthcare Financed and Managed by the Government

Sick fund-based systems achieved universal care gradually by adding members, while government-based systems (e.g., UK, some Nordic countries, and Canada) established universal coverage from the outset, usually post-WWII. These systems were conceived and implemented by visionary politicians,[10] who became national heroes after successfully navigating the intense social and political negotiations that shaped their healthcare systems.[11] They share in common a strong ethos of providing equal care, often free of charge at the point of service, and of being financed by general taxation.

Except for Canada,[12] governments primarily run these systems. Healthcare workers are public servants or service providers paid by the State, with government-set

[9] Some years back, the Japanese government decided they were spending too much on MRI exams. So, they lowered the fee for an MRI to such a level that Medical Doctors engaged Toshiba to create a much cheaper, simpler MRI scanner, which it did. This serves to illustrate that the idea of "cost" in healthcare is very often much more complex than in some other industries, being influenced by the willingness to pay of the Payer, the negotiation power of the provider, the many equations used to calculate prices in healthcare, and some other effects we will detail later in this book.

[10] Examples are Tommy Douglas in Canada, and Beveridge and Bevan in the UK.

[11] Having a (public or private) system funding healthcare impacts different providers differently. The system funds therapies that many people would not be able to pay for out of pocket, hence increasing volume for providers. On the other hand, it negotiates their prices down and commoditizes them. So, in an out-of-pocket system, the doctors with more prestige, lack of competitors or whose therapies are less expensive to perform tend to make much more money than when being paid by a healthcare system. It is not surprising that when implementing the UK system, General Practitioners successfully negotiated not to be public servants as the remaining doctors but falling under a special (better) remuneration system that lasts until today.

[12] The Canadian Healthcare system (called Medicare) is an outlier in this group of systems mostly run by the Government. It is similar to the US Medicare, with the State paying private providers to

prices and budgets to cover them. The government is either the only employer or the only buyer of healthcare services or products, and thus has monopsony power to negotiate prices or opt-out of specific treatments. Some governments centralize planning for hospital construction and care delivery methods, while others opt for decentralization to mitigate the effects of distant and unaccountable administrators.

Its lack of direct connection between taxation revenues and healthcare costs dilutes accountability and gives room to a misallocation of healthcare funds toward other politically urgent priorities. Taxation-financed healthcare can also lead citizens to consider all paid and overindulge, thus efforts are made to educate patients that unnecessary treatments may appear free, but are in fact quite costly. In similar lines, governments may delay or decline treatments or exams to patients less likely to benefit from them.

Given that no one wants to pay more taxes, government-based healthcare becomes cost-centric, which regularly leads to longer waiting times or limited access to services or products. The government cost focus also hinders P&R negotiations, given their cost-effectiveness formula. If a drug costs too much or does not bring much benefits, then the government can opt not to buy/reimburse it or to ration it, that is, provide it to only the patients considered to benefit more from it. This formula becomes problematic for P&R negotiations of innovative, and thus more costly, drugs, because evaluating their benefits is made harder by the lack of long-term data. As a result, the government may only find the new drug cost-effective if the manufacturer gives a steep discount, but given how steep some discounts may need to be to meet the cost-effectiveness demands, some manufacturers may prefer to walk away instead.

This fundamental disconnect between the system's healthcare goals and the price of innovative treatments means that many countries would forego valuable but hard-to-measure healthcare innovations, or drugs with low cost-effectiveness, but considered a priority by the population. Each country addresses this issue in their own way. The UK, for example, established a controversial Cancer Drugs Fund (CDF) in 2011 to bypass its own cost-benefit rules and finance innovative oncological drugs for its citizens. However, this form of CDF was short-lived and closed in July 2016. Ultimately, these systems prioritize providing the most cost-effective quality care available to reach all citizens within limited taxpayer funds, rather than striving to offer the best care for each patient individually. While costing less than sick fund based systems with an average healthcare cost around 10% of GDP[13] (OECD 2022), they do not rank at the top in access or quality.

---

deliver healthcare. Differently from the US, Canadian Healthcare private providers are not allowed to provide care outside of the official Healthcare system paid for by the State, preventing them from competing with the State-sponsored healthcare system, to ensure there is no inequality in health access between Canadians.

[13] 10.3% in the UK, 10.8% in Canada, 10.0% in Denmark.

2.2.3 State as Safety Net: Free-Market Healthcare with Government Support for the Underprivileged

The USA stands out among developed nations by embracing a market-based healthcare system. Even though, certain segments of its population enjoy coverage similar to other systems. For example, US Medicare and Medicaid mirror the Canadian healthcare system, albeit limited to the disabled, elderly, and impoverished. Similarly, the US Veterans' health system offers a government-run healthcare solution akin to the UK but limited to war veterans. The majority of the US population relies on for-profit health insurance plans provided by employers. It's essential to differentiate these plans from sick funds, which operate under strict regulations and mandates, while for-profit health plans compete in a freer market.

Why is the US healthcare system so unique? The USA took a distinct path after World War II, prioritizing scientific research to combat diseases over universal care. When comparing with the rest of the world, US citizens have won more Nobel prizes in Physiology and Medicine, and its National Institutes of Health (NIH) have funded more medical research then everyone else combined (Appropriations (Section 1) 2019; Viergever and Hendriks 2016).[14] This research focus significantly advanced medicine for the past 80 years, and it would probably not be where it is without the US investments.

Having opted to invest in research, the USA left its healthcare industry to the free market with support from most stakeholders at the time. Hospitals and doctors watched their UK and Canadian peers fiercely resist healthcare nationalization and wanted to protect their free-market earnings. Investors and corporations liked the healthcare investment possibilities and stable returns. Even labor unions lauded employer-paid healthcare as their biggest success story.[15] Citizens hoped the high innovation coupled with free-market competition would improve quality and lower prices. Indeed, the free market encouraged the USA to develop some of the world's top centers of excellence, providers, scientists, and products. So yes, citizens who can afford may have access to cutting-edge healthcare technology delivered at the highest quality and efficiency, but they also pay the most (Magee 2019).[16]

To rein in the high costs and expand access to quality healthcare, several former US Presidents pushed for centralized systems. Even John F. Kennedy[17] had

---

[14] Some yearly NIH budgets for research in medicine: 1938: US$400,000; 1948: US$14.5Mi; 1958: US$158Mi; 1968: aprx.US$1Bi; 2000: approx. US$14 Bi; 2019: US$41.7Bi. As a comparison (using 2013 data), the NIH was the largest contributor to scientific research in medicine, with a contribution more than 4 times larger than that of the second one, the European Commission.

[15] During WW2, wages had been frozen, so labor unions instead negotiated the provision of healthcare for employees. Healthcare through a national healthcare system would wipe out the largest advantage a worker had in belonging to a union.

[16] For more details on the history of the US healthcare system, we recommend reading the very informative (and entertaining) book: Magee M. (2019) Code Blue. Atlantic Monthly Press.

[17] Interested readers can watch YouTube videos on the fight between JFK and the American Medical Association regarding a national healthcare system, as well as the latter hiring Ronald Reagan to narrate a very successful LP against Socialized Medicine, claiming that Medicare would lead to a

universal care as one of its two key presidential goals, but it was landing on the moon that proved to be the easier goal, maybe as it required fewer social and political negotiations. In 1965, healthcare stakeholders allowed US President Lyndon Johnson to create the State-sponsored Medicare and Medicaid for the elderly, disabled, and poor, but these patients were not the only ones who benefited. Private healthcare plans now covered only the most profitable clients (e.g., young, healthy, and employed). Hospitals saw more paying patients and reduced their pro-bono or charity treatments. Pharmaceutical companies saw their market grow dramatically.

In 2003, the *Medicare Prescription Drug, Improvement, and Modernization Act* drastically reduced Medicare's negotiation power[18] as it prevents Medicare from importing cheaper drugs,[19] or negotiating discounts with Pharma—despite the success of such negotiations by healthcare plans in the USA or by Payers around the world.

In 2012, the *Affordable Care Act* (ACA) in the USA increased access, but also costs for US taxpayers and premiums for certain households,[20] (Klobucista 2022; Mikulic 2019) although for how much is a matter of a very politically polarized debate (Kurt 2023).

More recently, the *US Inflation Reduction Act*, passed in August 2022, was not targeted exclusively at but greatly impacts healthcare. It included curbs on annual drug price rises above inflation and new compulsory price negotiations for the costliest Medicare drugs.

In market-based systems, the lack of regulation or clear rules of the game translates into the parties investing more in trying to control the healthcare market than in differentiation through superior clinical or customer value. Pharmaceutical companies, health plans, PBMs, and other healthcare-related companies[21] (Makary

socialist dictatorship. This LP that was distributed to the wives of MDs, instructing them to write to their representatives in Congress, thus creating a powerful feminine movement against a national healthcare system.

[18] Most developed countries' healthcare systems have a system that regulates the ways a Payer can exert power, what are appropriate target prices for a drug as a function of its clinical benefit, other therapies available, etc. However, given that many of these topics are complex and subjective, this still leaves a large discretionary power on the side of the Payer.

[19] While the Payer not being able to negotiate lower prices is uncommon, for it not to be able to import from other countries is a common provision in pharmaceutical contracts. If this was allowed, pharmacists, where the drug is more expensive, would buy from countries were the drug is cheaper, creating several problems: key among them would be that national payers would not be able to negotiate prices lower than other countries, as their drugs would be bought from somewhere else, so manufacturers would need to price drugs everywhere at the same price, not allowing for different valuations by different healthcare systems, and not being able to charge less to poorer countries, as is sometimes the case nowadays.

[20] The 300+ million US citizens contribute 33% of worldwide pharma revenue, which is the same amount as all 3.8 billion citizens of China, India, Brazil, Mexico, Argentina, Colombia, Chile, Russia, Japan, Indonesia, and Saudi Arabia combined. The US pharmaceutical spending is 50% higher than the European Union's coverage for over 400 million citizens.

[21] Another very successful business is that of healthcare transportation (ambulances and air ambulances). Given that emergency patients requiring their services are usually unable to shop around

2019; Papanicolas and Smith 2013; Rosato 2017; Jones 2019) invest heavily to capture negotiation leverage at the customers' expense and, in extreme cases, without adding any value. For example, Pharmacy Benefit Managers (PBMs) (Megan Thompson 2018) use their size and negotiation power[22] (Fein 2019; Porter 2019) to acquire drugs in bulk and at a discount from Pharma companies and resell them to health plans. Patients rarely see these savings and, at times, copay amounts are higher than the total drug cost (Van Nuys et al. 2018). PBMs may artificially raise drug prices given their relative success KPI based on the rebates they obtain over the drug's list price. Pharma's incentive is to increase prices yearly to protect their margins while allowing PBMs to obtain increasingly higher relative rebates.

Despite substantial spending, the US healthcare system faces challenges, with higher costs and mortality rates for treatable causes being at the level of much poorer nations (Reinhardt et al. 2019; Wikipedia Contributors 2019).[23] Another particularity of this system is its fascinating extremes and contradictions, typical of any free market. The USA is currently the innovation powerhouse in Pharma worldwide, though such innovation seems at times taken for granted. US Pharma companies operate with relatively few legal restraints in the largest Pharma market in the world on revenues. This combination gives room to a disproportionate share of the Pharma abuses worldwide happening locally. As a global cultural influence center, events in the USA also command relatively more media and attention, thus shaping our perception of Pharma even outside of the USA. Together, these extremes contribute to Pharma's negative reputation worldwide, despite the stricter regulatory and pricing environment everywhere else. Finding a balance between innovation, quality, compliance, and affordable access remains a pressing issue for the market-based healthcare system.

2.2.4 State as Choice: Healthcare Financed and Managed in Competing Public and Private Systems

The mixed healthcare system category combines government-provided universal access with private sector competition, mainly targeting individuals with disposable income seeking premium-quality care, better access, or shorter waiting times (e.g., Australia and Brazil). People will often purchase health insurance for private sector access, while some may sporadically use private providers on an out-of-pocket

---

for different providers, these businesses have plenty of negotiation power over their customers. That's probably why private equity investors have acquired air ambulance companies and now use this power to maximize fees: the largest operator in the USA increased its average fee 400% between 2007 and 2016. The average bill for air ambulances was US$32,895 in 2014. For comparison, a helicopter ride in the USA does not cost more than US$500 in most cities.

[22] Two PBMs are among the top 10 companies in the Fortune 500 list.

[23] Here we consider mortality from amenable causes, which excludes homicides and other violent causes such as car accidents, and thus makes for a good measure of outcomes in healthcare.

basis, and still benefit from reasonable prices kept in check by the competition from the public system.

This system fosters competition, expanding choices for healthcare providers and patients, promoting innovation, and enhancing quality at lower costs.[24] High earners choosing private healthcare can ease demand, waiting times, and costs in the public system, sometimes offset by tax deductions or direct public payments to the private system (Glover and Woods 2020).

However, mixing public and private healthcare structures poses challenges. It weakens the public system's bargaining power against healthcare providers, potentially affecting wages and doctor availability, especially in remote areas.[25] Doctors may focus on their private practice, prolonging public waiting times or redirecting patients to avoid the wait, leading some countries to prohibit dual practice. As such, some countries prevent parallel private systems (e.g., Canada),[26] others offer private sector conveniences (e.g., private rooms, shorter waiting for non-urgent treatments) but not better clinical care (e.g., Sweden), and others (e.g., Italy) do not allow doctors to work in both public and private hospitals.[27]

Other challenges include the ethical yet pragmatic concerns from the disparities and incentives against public healthcare. Wealthy elites, content with private care, may neglect public system support, stalling its progress, funding, or political prioritization (Roberts et al. 2008). Private healthcare plans may cherry-pick patients, pushing less profitable cases back to the public system, who cannot deny them care and thus see worsening success rates and costs.[28]

Poorly managed, the mixed system could see the market take over and push the government to the fringes or the other way around. Despite these challenges, mixed systems combine market and single-payer advantages, less driven by ideology in an attempt to strike a pragmatic balance and seek the best of both worlds. In reality, it is a difficult balance to keep.

---

[24] There is a much higher pressure to lower costs in these private systems that compete with the public system than if there would be no public option for patients. This sometimes can be quite intense, as the entity that manages the public system is often very influential toward the regulator of the private system. For example, in Brazil, the regulator sometimes forces the private system to provide treatments that the public system does not provide itself, at the same time that caps yearly increases on healthcare plans.

[25] The competition for doctors between the systems can be ameliorated by increasing the often artificially scarce number of medical school openings imposed in several countries by the local Medical Associations.

[26] That caters for the same patients providing the same procedures. There are private options for services the public insurance does not cover and for (the few) people not eligible for the public service. Furthermore, not all provinces support and then fully respect this federal guideline.

[27] Italy actually allows public doctors to see patients privately in public hospitals (albeit a limited number), as long as they pass on a share of their earnings to the public hospital.

[28] This can be problematic in "very mixed systems," where public funds are also used to also pay for private care. For example, in the case where, to alleviate the waiting times in the public system, the State decides to pay private hospitals to treat public patients. This can be done on a per patient basis, and the estimates of cost per patient become important negotiation arguments.

2.2.5 Conclusion to the Discussion of Healthcare Systems

There is no single correct healthcare system, given that each country's historical events, political forces, and value choices must be considered. Besides, when comparing healthcare outcomes such as life expectancy or per-patient cost, given that each system invests in different priorities, no one can claim clear superiority across the board. Most well-functioning countries have tinkered with their healthcare system for decades, seeking continuous improvement and mitigating its drawbacks. At the end, the different systems have in common that they have all been shaped by the healthcare negotiation among its many stakeholders, who we look at next.

2.2.6 The Players in Healthcare

In any negotiation, it is important to understand its context as it influences how power is allocated, what the parties want, what is possible, what is fair or feasible, and how they interact. Above, we examined the four main healthcare systems within which P&R negotiations take place. Here we examine their relevant parties and stakeholders, even if not all sit at the P&R negotiation table directly, as they all influence its processes and outcomes.

2.2.7 The State or the Government

In all organized healthcare systems, the State or the government is a major player, given how important healthcare is to running any country. Most governments are expected to ensure the proper functioning of its healthcare industry, either by full or partial direct participation, or by establishing clear rules of the game and policing it for the benefit of all. Democratic governments are expected to represent the interests of all citizens, and work unbiasedly toward maintaining a healthy population.

Ideally, the State acts mostly as a facilitator or a custodian of healthcare negotiations, and ensures the proper implementation of negotiated outcomes. It should be less concerned about the direction of the outcomes in favor of fair and balanced negotiation processes leading to desirable outcomes to its citizens. Take the example of a Ministry of Health wanting to maximize quality of care across the country. The Ministry of Finance may prefer to keep health costs sustainable and within budget. Both have valid goals, and must negotiate fairly to define the line between the desirable and affordable levels of care that is deemed the best possible outcome to its population.

However, the government in most healthcare systems takes on multiple roles, which may at times be in conflict with the best interests of its people. In fact, the State often negotiates with private companies, healthcare professionals, or its own citizens. When acting as a provider or being more engaged, the State may end up deviating from its neutral status to become a biased stakeholder and thus being more invested, for better or worse, in shaping our healthcare.

2.2.8 Healthcare Users

Organized healthcare means users paying a subscription to an institution, whether fees to a company or NGO, or taxes to a government, in exchange for access to quality health services. Due to this subscription-based system, all healthcare users must remember that we not only use the system but also finance it.

In any healthcare system, users can be categorized into two subgroups: **net contributors**, who pay more than they benefit, and **net beneficiaries**, who use more healthcare services than they pay for. This categorization is not static or a stereotype, but rather a means to distinguish individuals at different stages of their health care contribution and usage. For instance, most people are net contributors until they get to a certain age, when their healthcare needs increase, turning them into net beneficiaries.

Net contributors are crucial as they disproportionately finance healthcare for everyone. From wealthy citizens who pay high taxes/fees while being average users of healthcare, or citizens who opt out of the public system but still contribute without depleting resources. Net contributors may also include the young and healthy, who may not contribute more than the average person but may spend less on health than the nation's average per capita. Even when they do not use or minimally use the public healthcare system, net contributors gain peace of mind knowing it is there when needed and can take pride in living in a country that takes care of its citizens' health.

Net beneficiaries consume more than they contribute and are in many ways the reason why public healthcare systems exist. These include the chronically ill, the sickness-prone, the elderly, the poor, and people living in remote or sparse areas.

2.2.9 Healthcare Providers

Providers can be categorized as value-positive or value-negative, and most providers can be split into both. **Value-positive providers** are those who deliver clinically valuable products or services and charge a fair compensation for the value they provide to society. This group includes most medical doctors, nurses, health technicians, hospitals, and clinics when delivering evidence-based care. It can also include their administrative staff or governments, when they increase efficiency, access, and quality care or reduce its costs and waste. Pharmaceutical and medical device companies fall under this category when delivering clinically valuable products at reasonable costs. Medical associations acting in a value-positive way can negotiate with users for a reasonable fee schedule to protect doctor income, increase the attractiveness of the profession, bring more talent in the medium-term, and benefit users through price predictability and reasonable affordability. When they act as value-positive providers, we refer to their services as value-positive as well.

The **value-negative providers** include the same players, but when they deliver unnecessary or harmful services or products, or abuse their power to maximize profits. This category includes doctors performing not-recommended or unnecessary procedures or prescribing avoidable addictive medication to enjoy recurring revenue. Non-evidence-based healthcare providers like traditional healers (e.g., homeopathy) or those disseminating harmful information (e.g., anti-vaxxers) also belong here as they lure patients away from value-positive services until it is either too late or much more expensive to treat them. Pharmaceutical or distribution companies are value-negative when selling harmful products or abusing their pricing power.

The categories above are fluid and value-laden, and they help us understand more nuanced healthcare negotiation dynamics. For example, if value-negative services grow within a country through win-lose, illegal, or unethical moves, they negatively affect its population's health and wealth. Users pay more for worse products and services. Value-positive providers are underutilized or underpaid. Understanding the composition of the major healthcare players (State, users, and providers) clarifies the negotiation processes between them and how they shape different healthcare systems and outcomes.

2.3 The Main Healthcare Negotiation Tensions

Changes to healthcare systems are quite often much-debated and controversial. We all want healthcare improvements, but improvement for one does not necessarily mean improvement for all. Because healthcare systems are complex, it is not immediately apparent who will benefit from a proposed change. That uncertainty contributes to making individuals and groups risk-averse and suspicious, who in doubt may prefer to play it safe and negotiate to keep the status quo. After all, change usually means losing something today in hopes of a potential, though uncertain, gain tomorrow. The more complex a system is, the harder it is to anticipate if the gains will materialize as anticipated.

Another obstacle to change stems from our differing ethical and moral perspectives being activated by the dramatic life-and-death decisions surrounding healthcare and its massive unequal financing. Healthcare can quickly trigger our emotionally driven ethical perspectives, and we already examined how it can lead us to the illusion of moral superiority where we see others' opinions as cruel, immoral, or just wrong, which in turn prevent us from having a constructive negotiation with someone outside our worldview. The book *Getting Health Reform Right: A Guide to Improving Performance and Equity* (Roberts et al. 2008) categorizes the main ethical perspectives in healthcare as:

1. **Utilitarianism** judges a policy by its *consequences or pragmatic results.*
2. **Liberalism** judges a policy less by its consequences, and instead focuses on the *rights* inherent to human beings.
3. **Communitarianism** judges a policy less by its consequences or the rights involved, and instead focuses on how it incentivizes or rewards desired *values and behaviors.*

These ethical perspectives rest in the background of different healthcare systems as they guide the valuation of negotiated outcomes. Cost-effectiveness may be seen as a successful utilitarian outcome, while sick funds may feel a liberalism kind of pride when offering every citizen the best treatment available even if not cost-effective. The resulting values will also influence how the three primary negotiation tensions inherent in healthcare evolve:

1. Negotiation tension #1: **What is the right price?** (Providers vs. Users)
   - This tension is between providers and users. Users want the best healthcare at the cheapest possible price, while providers want the highest compensation or profit.
2. Negotiation tension #2: **Who pays for it?** (Users vs. Users)
   - This tension is between the different users. Net contributors may not want to fully finance every healthcare desire of others, but must finance some in order for the system to function.
3. Negotiation tension #3: **Who gets paid?** (Providers vs. Providers)
   - This tension is among different providers of healthcare as they negotiate who gets paid for its delivery. Service providers have an incentive to jostle for a higher share of the limited healthcare budget (Fig. 2.1).

These three negotiations are the pillars behind P&R negotiations: **Who pays how much to whom?** They influence how services operate on a daily basis, including how much innovation is promoted and how much is paid in taxes and by whom. Below we further elaborate on each of them.

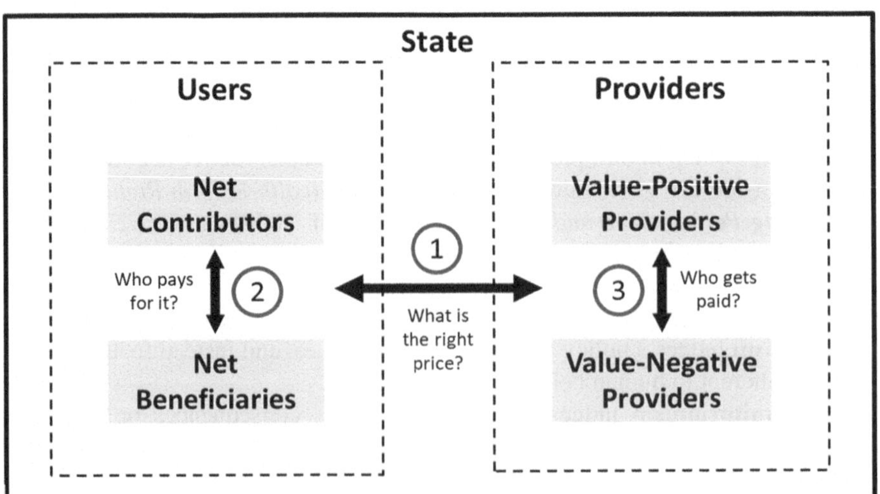

Fig. 2.1 The healthcare negotiation parties and the three negotiation tensions

2.3.1 Negotiation Tension #1: Providers vs Users

The first negotiation tension involves a balancing act between prices and access, and thus between healthcare providers and users. Healthcare providers want low costs and high fees for the highest possible profit, but fear that if their prices are too high, demand will decrease, and revenue will drop. As such, providers seek the optimal point on the supply/demand curve to maximize profit. Conversely, users want to negotiate the lowest possible prices, as long as they still get high healthcare access and quality in return.

In most countries, governments, health plans, or not-for-profit healthcare organizations represent users in these negotiations, but bring their own set of institutional interests, be they profits or politics. For example, governments may not raise doctors salaries to manage their budget, or raise them during election year to gain votes. In both cases, the State is using the negotiation mandate from users for its own benefit and not the users´. Such principal–agent conflict of interest distorts the negotiation tension #1, especially given the broad subjectivity of a "right" price or "fair" profit allowing deals to fall just anywhere.

Provider and user negotiators can generate tremendous value if they manage to negotiate prices at a point where the system operates both fairly and efficiently to all. Success in setting the right incentives and rewards can support a constantly innovative smooth-running high quality healthcare system at affordable prices to all users. Failure will inevitably result in sicker and impoverished patients, either now or in the future, if prices are too high; if prices are too low, quality, innovation, and access to care will plummet sooner or later.

2.3.2 Negotiation Tension #2: Net Contributors vs Net Beneficiaries

The second negotiation tension is about who pays for the healthcare system. It involves a balancing act between net contributors and net beneficiaries. Users always pay for their healthcare, either via general taxation, specific contributions collected by the State, or an individual or corporate health insurance policy. But this negotiation revolves around how much of a premium the net contributors are willing to pay (either by higher contribution or lower usage) over and above the amount paid by the net beneficiaries.

While net contributors often accept a certain imbalance of pay and usage, their ongoing negotiation deals with how much imbalance is fair, desirable, or tolerable. For example, net contributors in most systems agree to finance emergency procedures to the net beneficiaries, but are more resistant to paying for elective surgeries. If the net contributors believe they are being asked to pay too much of a premium over what the net beneficiaries pay, or see net beneficiaries free-riding or abusing the system, they may challenge that split and ask net beneficiaries to pay more, or walk away from the system when possible, or vote for a political party that best defends their interests.

2.3.3 Negotiation Tension #3: Value-Positive Providers vs Value-Negative Providers

The third tension is about which services get paid for. Fortunately, in organized healthcare systems value-positive providers capture most of it. However, value-negative providers inevitably capture a share of the limited healthcare resources, despite attempts to optimize resource allocation, identify value-negative providers, and reduce wastage financing their useless or improper services.

One view is that healthcare systems will spend whatever money we inject into them, and grow as much as we feed them, so limits must be placed. Many users accept or tolerate paying for some non-evidence-based, innocuous, value-negative providers such as practitioners of alternative medicine. But how much are users willing to siphon away from value-positive services to pay for value-negative ones?

The negotiation becomes clearer, albeit not easier, when value-negative services are harmful or have been approved, prescribed, or delivered using deceitful or unethical means. The value-negative services steal our money, prevent investment in value-positive services, and damage our health. They need to be eradicated from our healthcare systems. So even if the negotiation tension #3 is represented as a tension between value positive and negative providers, everyone should have the responsibility to remove harmful providers from healthcare systems, as it otherwise erodes the health and wealth of a nation.

2.3.4 Negotiation Tensions: Conclusion

These three interconnected negotiation tensions shape our healthcare system through thousands or millions of daily interactions. **Negotiation Tension #1: *"What is the right price?"*** is the most frequent of the three, which involves Governments and Pharma in P&R negotiations as the main focus of this book. **Negotiation Tension #2: *"Who pays for it?"*** is commonly a political negotiation at the nation level on the scope of universal care and how to finance it. In less centralized systems, this negotiation happens when health plans or sick funds demand price or scope changes. In such cases, net contributors and net beneficiaries debate fiercely to avoid being worse off by undesirable changes. Finally, **Negotiation Tension #3: *"Who gets paid?"*** is also a large negotiation over what is a value-added healthcare contribution, and it impacts P&R negotiations when a pharma company fools the government into overpaying beyond the value of their products, and thus reducing the budget to properly pay for better value drugs.

2.4 Strategies: Different Negotiation Choices

Healthcare negotiations are often so arcane and opaque that even experts fail to fully understand them, let alone the average citizen. That is why we are covering the context and the players, as well as the tensions among the players. Now that we have the structural elements in place, we look briefly at the two main negotiation strategic choices the parties can make, and how they have been playing out in P&R negotiations.

The common understanding of win-win and win-lose is that they qualify outcomes or situations where either both win (win-win) or one loses (win-lose). Under the Value Negotiation system, we believe one does not control the outcome or the situation, and thus we invite the reader to look at them differently. For us, win-win or win-lose are choices, primarily of strategy. They are the two main ways which negotiators can pursue their objectives, based on their choice over the role of power in how they will negotiate.

1. When negotiators choose, consciously or not, to use whatever power they have to get what they want from the counterparty in a negotiation, they are opting for a **win-lose strategy**. This choice translates into negotiators using aggressive or manipulative moves (lies, threats, etc.) to force or fool the counterparty into doing whatever they want. We say that someone has power in a negotiation when they can change the behavior of others even against their will or preference.
2. Conversely, a **win-win strategy** happens when negotiators choose ***not*** to use whatever power they have to get what they want from the counterparty in a negotiation. Win-win strategies often translate into creating a safe environment to share information so the parties can collaborate to enhance the odds of increasing the value of the deal and of reaching one, even if their counterparty chooses a different strategy. Win-win strategies attempt to make power moves unnecessary throughout the negotiation.
3. Many mistakenly see win-win strategies as weak, which give up value in return for conflict avoidance or a nice relationship. This is a mistaken view of win-win and we call it **naïve win-win strategy**. In this distorted and ineffective naïve win-win, the negotiator blindly trusts the other, gives up value to please the other, compromises to avoid conflict, and naïvely expects reciprocation, which often times does not happen. We find the naïve win-win strategy to be a poor negotiation choice overall, and definitely not what effective collaboration or win-win really mean. Avoiding conflict or making the other side happy are appropriate negotiation moves in some situations, but they should not be dominant or blind go-to negotiation strategies.

Both negotiation strategies are valid and work well in different instances; however, the research literature is clear in that true (not naïve) win-win negotiation strategies deliver more and better deals on average compared to win-lose strategies. Given the simplicity of win-lose compared to win-win strategies, most people, even well-intended ones, resort to win-lose much more often than win-win.

Unfortunately, win-lose is the predominant strategy in P&R negotiations. It starts with most healthcare negotiators developing unrealistic assumptions about a fixed pie (more for me must mean less for you and vice-versa) and a relative success mindset (my win has to be bigger than their win). As a result, most negotiators choose to negotiate win-lose as it mistakenly appears to be the only rational way to negotiate.

In countries with a developed Health Technology Assessment (HTA) system, their negotiation process, in general, goes like this: Pharmas open with high prices and a submission dossier where the positives of their drug are mentioned often and where shortcomings of their data are not usually given enough attention, if not omitted; an Expert body affiliated to the Government evaluates that dossier, determining the clinical value of the drug and sometimes its expected usage. In theory, this evaluation is unbiased. In practice, it is not. However, it is not more biased than the manufacturer's submission was.

On top of these divergences, there is also uncertainty on a series of parameters about clinical value and expected usage. Governments then demand price discounts to, in theory, match the drug price to its clinical value and reduce the uncertainty for themselves. In practice, they demand more than that. Pharma counters by disputing the evaluation and the requests for discounts with biased arguments of their own. At this point, both sides mistrust each other and their moves. Underneath a technically complex discussion, both sides are resorting to bargaining and power moves to try to secure what they want.

In countries without developed HTA systems, the negotiation process is simpler. In fact, it follows a usual bargaining process: Pharmas open with high prices, be they legitimate or not, and governments demand large price discounts, again legitimate or not, from Pharmas. Both mistrust each other and their moves, and thus resort to bargaining and power moves to secure what they want. Many Pharma companies then start to inflate prices to give fake discounts, while most governments start to use tricks and threats to push prices down.

In both systems, P&R negotiators on both sides often opt for win-lose strategies. They become players in a cat-and-mouse game to see who can outsmart the other in an escalation cycle that destroys value, time, creativity, and effort for all. Instead, these wasted assets could be invested in a win-win collaborative negotiation to increase value for all.

We know from experience that instead of having to negotiate win-lose, anyone can choose to negotiate win-win to improve everyone's satisfaction by increasing the pie (more for me does not need to mean less for you), and having an absolute success mindset (my win is independent of your win). It is also the case for P&R negotiations, but of course there are obstacles to be overcome.

2.5 Healthcare Is Sick with the Win-Lose Virus

The reason for a lack of win-win in P&R negotiations can be traced back to how healthcare systems developed. Unfortunately, healthcare systems did not evolve with the different stakeholders sitting down and deciding how to collaborate. Instead, the many healthcare stakeholders have been shaping healthcare through numerous intense, power-based struggles for dominance over the three main negotiation tensions. Below we see how the resulting power structures keep defining the three negotiation tensions and forging the four main plus the out-of-pocket healthcare systems.

2.5.1 Out-of-Pocket System

In an out-of-pocket system, users are not organized or at least not enough, and the negotiation power often lies with the providers, given the often limited competition or no economies of scale. Indeed, there is little negotiation power in the hands of a patient (user) that is suffering or dying compared to someone who can heal them (providers) and has a line of other patients willing to pay for their services.

As such, the **negotiation tension #1 (What is the right price?)** favors value-negative and value-positive providers who have the power to set prices at the user's highest willingness to pay. Given the value of life or the desire to get rid of pain, willingness to pay is very high. The **negotiation tension #2 (Who pays for it?)** also means that each user is on their own. These two negotiations often combine to exclude a large section of poorer users from quality treatment and to help value-negative services to prosper. For example, non-evidence-based healers become the only affordable recourse for the many users who can't afford value-positive services. Finally, the **negotiation tension #3 (Who gets paid?)** is the easiest in out-of-pocket system, as the power advantage of providers over users allows them to capture enough value that there is enough value for every provider and no need for value-positive or value-negative providers to fight over the total healthcare spend.

To sustain this system, providers work hard to resist any user effort to organize healthcare, since organization would reduce the providers' power, earnings, and freedom. Given the downsides to patients, out-of-pocket systems nowadays tend to happen in poor countries/regions or those with weak public institutions.

2.5.2 Centralized Healthcare Systems

Within the centralized healthcare category, we included the three different systems where the State adopts a significant role (as a Facilitator, Provider, or Choice) to reduce the user's negotiation power disadvantage. The user centralization effort organizes them behind the State, who negotiates with providers on their behalf or becomes the provider itself. This superior organization creates a significant power shift from providers to users, though the advantages for users vary depending on the role of the State.

When it comes to the **negotiation tension #1 (What is the right price?)**, the State steps in as a facilitator, a provider, or a choice, which turns the State into an intermediary and splits the negotiation tension #1 into two separate processes: State with providers, which reflects its more espoused mission, but also the internal negotiation between State and users.

When negotiating with providers, the State centralizes and leverages its collective power from representing most or all users within a country. It becomes the single (i.e., a monopsony) or largest buyer of healthcare services on behalf of all users, which gives the State significant power to negotiate lower prices or compensation with Pharma companies or healthcare workers, for example.

When the State serves solely as a healthcare facilitator, it may contribute to lower pharmaceutical prices but may be less effective in reducing the compensation of healthcare workers since it lacks oversight over service delivery. However, when the State acts as a healthcare provider or largest choice, healthcare worker compensation also tends to be lower as a result of the State negotiation power from being the only or main healthcare employer or fee setter in the country. Doctors, for example, may have few counters against low compensation offers from the State. They may resort to very unpopular strikes, move to private practice, if allowed, or to another country. However, these all seem fairly high cost and low power alternatives, that are unlikely to be used collectively, successfully, or frequently against negotiation abuses from the State. Such lower prices or compensations may not reflect the true value of healthcare services or products, but rather the result of the negotiation dynamics between the State and the providers.

The internal negotiation with users has the State in organized systems be responsible and thus accountable for both healthcare costs and the delivery of quality care. And while the State is only the agent, its institutional concentration gives it negotiation power over the users on both responsibilities. It has the power to raise taxes when healthcare costs increase, and users can often say little about it. This is a lesser problem for the State as Facilitator as sick-funds focus on cost management and have relatively less pricing power over users.

On the delivery side, the State as a Provider or as Choice commits to providing affordable, quality healthcare, but some take shortcuts, and users again may have little negotiation say. For example, it can ration care, either directly (not providing it) or indirectly (allowing waiting lines to grow so it ends up providing less care). Another example is the lack of tracking or sharing of doctor performance statistics in many countries, which prevents users from making informed decisions about their healthcare and commoditizes providers. Actually, in some of these systems, patients can't really choose Doctors. The State can claim quality care delivery without truly measuring or proving it. It also allows the State to keep doctors salaries artificially low, as undifferentiated doctors have no legitimacy to claim higher pay. In the medium to long run, unreasonably depressed salaries can discourage the best brains in a country from becoming doctors or investing in becoming better doctors. So are users paying "the right price" for healthcare? After all, the State ensures lower prices from providers, but it may charge too much as it incurs unnecessary costs or offers inferior quality relative to the price paid.

The **negotiation tension #2 (Who pays for it?)** in organized systems is still about users, but the State responsibility to collect taxes to pay the healthcare bill on behalf of users adds a twist. Given that it is unlawful for citizens not to pay their taxes, the move to organized systems transfers negotiation power to net beneficiaries at the expense of net contributors. This negotiation often takes the form of a broader ethical debate with large social and political implications that includes how much healthcare coverage should our taxes finance. Another negotiation forum is the political arena where each user establishes their preferences by voting left- or right-wing. Despite the multitude of issues in any political platform, right wing politicians are less likely to expand healthcare coverage that favors net beneficiaries, while left wing politicians are more likely to do so. As it is politically hard to reduce coverage, net beneficiaries in time eventually accumulate wins to gain expanded coverage.

On the **negotiation tension #3 (Who gets paid?),** the ideal return on healthcare investment is to exclusively fund value-positive providers, while excluding value-negative providers from the healthcare ecosystem altogether. Indeed, organized healthcare systems have more power to negotiate against value-negative providers, but excluding them is challenging.

Value-negative providers use extreme win-lose tactics to disguise their actions and remain profitable. They include government officials negotiating against the best interest of users, MDs getting paid to work in the public service but channeling patients to their private practices or performing unneeded procedures, value-negative pharma practices swaying doctors to push their drugs, non-evidence-based practitioners lobbying for government reimbursement of their ineffective treatments, or healthcare organizations capturing money without delivering value. In addition, they draw resources from society in several ways:

1. They are mostly ineffective.
2. They can cause harm, as with medical malpractice, serious side effects of drugs, surgeries or procedures with a negative risk-benefit, or delay the user from seeking value positive providers until it is too late, needs fixing, or becomes much more expensive to treat.
3. They divert funds away from improvements or increased access to value-positive providers.
4. They often use deceptive or unethical means to disguise, survive, and profit, thus forcing users, value-positive providers, and the State to invest in identifying, preventing, or curtailing them.

Value-negative providers abuse their deceptive power to capture their share of the negotiation tension #3, as they selfishly raise costs at subpar or negative results for society. They probably are the largest waste of healthcare resources. As such, the broader negotiation effort of monitoring and correcting value-negative providers is a necessary evil within the negotiation tension #3 for organized healthcare systems. Unfortunately, it usually takes one to catch one; that is, people from the same group are the ones who can better assess their colleagues' performance. Given the highly adversarial Us vs. Them environment in healthcare, individuals tend to protect those in their group. Difficulties aside, a system that chooses not to engage in such policing efforts risks enabling a multiplication of value-negative providers and experiencing decaying healthcare results.

2.5.3 Market-Based Systems

In market-based systems, the State operates only as a safety net with a much lighter responsibility over healthcare matters compared to centralized systems. As such, States mostly limit themselves to helping the weakest parties. This partial vacuum created by the State's absence in the negotiations pushed users to organize themselves behind health insurance companies (health plans), for a fee, to negotiate with providers on their behalf. As expected, these differences, small as they may seem at first, impact the three negotiation tensions enough that they shift the healthcare landscape dramatically.

When it comes to the **negotiation tension #1 ("What is the right price?)**, market-based systems are not necessarily better as they may fail to fully address market imperfections or imbalances. For example, providers enjoy superior power and definitely more knowledge over users in the absence of a more organized user approach, as we saw in the out-of-pocket systems. Similarly, in a market-based system (e.g., the USA), users do not rely on the State power to negotiate value-positive provider prices down and thus often end up paying, on average, more than in centralized healthcare systems (e.g., the EU).

So why do users represented by health plans in market-based healthcare systems pay more for their value-positive providers (drugs or medical services) than users represented by the State in centralized systems? Shouldn't both users get a similar deal given they both centralized their power within larger negotiation bodies, be it the State or health plans? After all, the health plans organize massive amounts of users and accumulate enough bargaining power to successfully push provider prices down. So what is the difference?

Health plans do not represent all users within a country, so they never become a true monopsony. Not being a monopsony means that the counterpart, in this case the value-positive providers, will always have the alternative (BATNA) to walk away and make a better deal with someone else, normally another health plan. This dynamic limits the power a health plan has to squeeze lower prices from providers to the same extent as a State can in a centralized healthcare system. If a State leaves the negotiation, the provider loses all potential revenues negotiated in that country. Hence, the dissatisfied provider has no good BATNA but to leave the country. Wishing to avoid losing all sales in that country, they regularly give in and accept prices that they would have rejected otherwise.

Given the lower negotiation power from health plans in the negotiation tension #1, insurance companies in a market-based system have an incentive to do whatever it takes to accumulate power and improve their negotiation standing. For example, in the last decades, US health plans aggressively merged with or acquired competitors to represent more users, reduce the number of competitors as negotiation alternatives to providers, thus gaining more leverage to secure superior outcomes in this negotiation tension. However, providers did not watch that happen passively. Hospital networks and Pharma companies also engaged in aggressive M&A activities in an arms race for bargaining power.

Another reason for the lower negotiation power of health plans in the negotiation tension #1 is their lack of legislative power to define the rules of the negotiations, as the States have in centralized systems. Legislative power allows States to force providers to negotiate by their rules, improve their information power advantage, and unilaterally set quality standards or impose limits, even on pay. Thus, providers enter healthcare negotiations with the State already at a disadvantage as if playing an away game. As the State legislates the negotiation process, it unilaterally decides on its favor, and may go as far as demanding concessions before the "actual" negotiation starts.

Of course, the legislation of negotiation rules is already part of the broader negotiation process, it just happens to be one where the provider has little to no say. Here, providers are in a similar position as individuals wanting to use Internet services. Most websites often ask us to agree to an enormous list of legal terms and conditions before allowing us to use their services. The catch is that we have no room to negotiate a clause or two if we dislike the terms, so we usually just give up, agree to all terms without even reading them (what is the point if I can't change them anyway!) and go on hoping for the best.

Given its negotiation impact, health plans and healthcare providers do whatever they can to influence such legislative power. They engage in an arms race of lobbying the US government to ensure that they get legislations that favors them. As an illustration, healthcare providers in the USA have been lobbying consistently to keep the free market-based pricing of medical services or pharma products, so that they can set prices up to the users willingness to pay. Given the relative importance of health, willingness to pay for these providers is extremely high, and thus this legislation increases their leverage within the negotiation tension #1.

In time, the larger organizations with stronger lobbying capacity will likely gain better deals and a competitive advantage, which they can use to fund new power accumulation moves. This search for more power is likely to keep feeding this arms race even if antitrust laws would never allow any one party to become a single player like the State. As the different parties grow and accumulate power, we envision a market-based system with only two or few massive players on each side of the table (e.g., two health plans and two hospital networks) endlessly negotiating with one another, where prices will be defined by their win-lose moves much more than the value of their products and services.

Another undesirable effect of this power accumulation may rest in the internal negotiation that both health plans and other value-positive providers will have with users. We will discuss that during the negotiation tension #3. For now, let's quickly examine the **negotiation tension #2 (Who pays for it?)**, where it is never enough to remind the readers that the answer is always the users. Here there are similarities with the out-of-pocket systems as users are left to their own luck for the most part. The difference in market-based healthcare systems is that the State does have a role as a safety net.

In that role, the State (e.g., the USA) will pay for part of the healthcare bill in two main capacities. First, it may regulate and provide basic services to ensure the well-functioning of the healthcare market, including for example, investment in fundamental research at public universities or even co-funding research from private institutions, creating and running a patent office, controlling the quality of products (e.g., the Food and Drug Administration, FDA) or certification of healthcare professionals, etc. These services benefit all users, and thus do not create much debate internally.

The second way in which States pay for part of the healthcare bill in market-based systems is to fulfill its safety net role. The US government pays for almost 50% of the total nation's enormous health spend (Centers for Medicare and Medicaid Services 2020). While it still spends a lot, it does interfere little to none in the dealings between net contributors, health plans, and providers, under the assumption that they can fend for themselves in a free market. However, the State does attempt to provide a safety net for the net beneficiaries (e.g., the chronically ill, elderly, or poor), who are dropped by health plans for being unprofitable, cannot afford their own health bills, or have insufficient power to negotiate for meaningful discounts. In these cases, the State steps in to subsidize health insurance services such as Medicare or Medicaid in the USA, operate a share of public hospital services at a cheaper rate than private providers (Public vs Private Hospitals–Your Options in the U.S 2021), or, in some extreme cases, legislate so providers must deliver free or reduced services to low-income patients (Fontinelle 2020), etc. Despite all the State help, with rare exceptions, net beneficiaries in market-based systems still need to pay for at least part of their healthcare bills.

The debate between net contributors and net beneficiaries on how tax revenues should be spent on healthcare should be less relevant than in centralized systems, given the relatively smaller subsidy taking place in market-based systems. However, as they evolved from liberal values, the negotiation tension #2 seems more vocal, aggressive, and adversarial than in centralized ones, as some net contributors oppose the very idea of subsidies for net beneficiaries, and not just the amount.

Finally, when it comes to the **negotiation tension #3 (Who gets paid?)**, the broader negotiation between value-positive and value-negative providers mimics the centralized systems. However, the largest difference lies with the increased role and power of health plans in market-based systems. Market-based systems are expected to improve health outcomes for users through increased competition on innovation, meritocracy, and efficiency. Indeed, value-positive health plans leverage such assets or at least their bargaining power with providers and increase savings and quality care to users through cheaper plans, lower co-pay, or better care standards and practices.

However, many health plans dominated by profit motives leverage their intermediary position to selfishly capture an inordinate share of the national healthcare spend from both ends. They leverage their power against providers but also against users, as they overpromise benefits, are opaque about provider outcome quality, use vague and confusing language, hide plan weaknesses, push net beneficiaries away, and create obstacles to access, claims, or reimbursements (Makary 2019). These value-negative practices lead to users on average paying more and receiving lower quality care than in centralized systems to no advantage of other value-positive providers.

In essence, market-based systems have seen the industry move away from competition based on offering superior value to users toward a more aggressive pursuit of bargaining power as the means to secure higher profits. This environment suggests a dynamic of power accumulation and an escalating survival of the biggest scenario, currently dominated by a few powerful entities—governments, large healthcare plans, hospital conglomerates, and pharmaceutical companies—further diminishing the focus on delivering value to users. This is not surprising, as negotiation power is often seen as a positive asset in business competition, according to business analysts and scholars. However, when this power accumulates excessively, as it may be happening here, it hurts consumers or users, who then welcome government regulation, such as antitrust laws.

The healthcare industry here may be plagued by two challenges. First, the healthcare industry should limit the waste and abuses that happen in the name of competition and shareholder value, to refocus the industry toward the end user. Second, the governments are players in the healthcare industry, but have tended to prioritize the accumulation of power for their own purposes rather than regulating and curbing its use in healthcare negotiations.

Should we promote a power balance among all? Could healthcare negotiations be solved by giving more power to the weaker parties so they can initiate or reciprocate attacks on the other side? You would not be alone in thinking that. Indeed, parties in a stalemate fear escalation and become more keen to pursue a collaborative outcome, but there is no guarantee they will.

In fact, balancing power between parties to prevent abuse doesn't work frequently, as negotiators bring different power sources to the table (e.g., I'm stronger, but you are faster) and often are overconfident. For example, if you make two parties very powerful, they are more likely to misjudge their power advantage, fail to appreciate the full power and determination of the counterparty, and mistakenly believe that using their power will lead to a win. Think of labor-management negotiations, where giving more power to management over its workers doesn't help management counter the union's strike power. Instead, this power transfer misleads management into believing in the effectiveness of power moves to control its workforce. However, under pressure, the workforce feels increasingly unfairly treated and calls for more strikes. The reverse is also true: giving more strike power to unions, which could be dissuasive to management, probably will end up not diminishing the number of strikes but increasing it. In the end, resources are wasted in this win-lose fight, people, even those not party to the negotiation, are unhappy, and no one truly wins.

Healthcare's no different; giving one stakeholder more power to negotiate harshly doesn't lead to collaboration or value-enhancing negotiations, but rather a permanent escalation of conflicts and waste of resources that hurt everyone involved, especially users. Instead of boosting weaker players' power, it's better to set up a negotiation environment that discourages power accumulation, struggles, and abuse altogether, and facilitates the adoption of win-win strategies. Given the essential and social nature of the healthcare industry to all of us, we can learn from labor-management negotiations and consider improved regulations against value-negative practices, and penalties for infringements even in market-based systems. Learning how to negotiate win-win and craft collaborative processes can also help.

In the upcoming chapters, our journey continues as we zoom in on the government and the pharmaceutical industry P&R negotiation challenges, followed by a deeper dive into our recommended negotiation strategies and tactics for a bottom-up change, one negotiation at a time.

References

Appropriations (Section 1) (2019) National Institutes of Health (NIH). https://www.nih.gov/about-nih/what-we-do/nih-almanac/appropriations-section-1

Brewer MB (1999) The psychology of prejudice: Ingroup love and outgroup hate? J Soc Issues 55:429–444

Centers for Medicare and Medicaid Services (2020) NHE fact sheet. Cms.gov. https://www.cms.gov/research-statistics-data-and-systems/statistics-trends-and-reports/nationalhealthexpenddata/nhe-fact-sheet

Dornhege M (2020) Japan Healthcare system: everything you need to know | Tokyo cheapo. https://tokyocheapo.com/. https://tokyocheapo.com/living/japan-healthcare-system/

Fein AJ (2019) Profits in the 2019 fortune 500: manufacturers vs. managed care vs. pharmacies, PBMs, and wholesalers. Drug Channels. https://www.drugchannels.net/2019/06/profits-in-2019-fortune-500.html

Fontinelle A (2020) What to do when you can't pay your medical debts. Investopedia. https://www.investopedia.com/personal-finance/medical-debt-what-do-when-you-cant-pay/

Glover L, Woods M (2020) Australia | commonwealth fund. The Commonwealth Fund. https://www.commonwealthfund.org/international-health-policy-center/countries/australia

Jones O (2019) Let's all take a helicopter ride. Forbes

Klobucista C (2022) U.S. life expectancy is in decline. Why Aren't other countries suffering the same problem? Council on Foreign Relations. https://www.cfr.org/in-brief/us-life-expectancy-decline-why-arent-other-countries-suffering-same-problem

Kurt D (2023) Did Obamacare make premiums go up? Investopedia. https://www.investopedia.com/articles/personal-finance/071415/did-obamacare-make-premiums-go.asp

Magee M (2019) Code Blue. Atlantic Monthly Press

Makary M (2019) The Price we pay. Bloomsbury Publishing

Megan Thompson (2018) Why a patient paid a $285 copay for a $40 drug. PBS NewsHour. https://www.pbs.org/newshour/health/why-a-patient-paid-a-285-copay-for-a-40-drug

Mikulic M (2019) Pharma revenue: worldwide share by country 2017. Statista. https://www.statista.com/statistics/784420/share-of-worldwide-pharma-revenue-by-country/

OECD (2022) Health resources–health spending–OECD data. Organisation for Economic Co-operation and Development. https://data.oecd.org/healthres/health-spending.htm

Papanicolas I, Smith P (2013) Health system performance comparison an agenda for policy, information and research European Observatory on Health Systems and Policies Series edited by

Peters SL, van den Bos K, Bobocel DR (2004) The moral superiority effect: self versus other differences in satisfaction with being overpaid. Soc Justice Res 17:257–273. https://doi.org/10.1023/b:sore.0000041293.24615.f7

Porter S (2019) Trump's war on middlemen might reach well beyond PBM rebates. Healthleadersmedia.com. https://www.healthleadersmedia.com/strategy/trumps-war-middlemen-might-reach-well-beyond-pbm-rebates. Accessed 1 Jan 2024

Public vs Private Hospitals–Your Options in the U.S (2021) Immihelp. https://www.immihelp.com/public-vs-private-hospitals-your-options-in-the-us/

Reid TR (2010) The healing of America: a global quest for better, cheaper, and fairer Health care. Penguin Books

Reinhardt UE, Krugman PR, Frist WH (2019) Priced out: the economic and ethical costs of American health care. Princeton University Press
Roberts M, Hsiao W, Berman P, Reich M (2008) Getting health reform right. Oxford University Press
Rosato D (2017) Air ambulances: taking patients for a ride. Consumer Reports. https://www.consumerreports.org/medical-transportation/air-ambulances-taking-patients-for-a-ride/
Tappin BM, McKay RT (2016) The illusion of moral superiority. Soc Psychol Personal Sci 8:623–631. https://doi.org/10.1177/1948550616673878
Täuber S, van Zomeren M (2012) Refusing intergroup help from the morally superior: how one group's moral superiority leads to another group's reluctance to seek their help. J Exp Soc Psychol 48:420–423. https://doi.org/10.1016/j.jesp.2011.08.014
Van Nuys K, Joyce G, Ribero R, Goldman DP (2018) Frequency and magnitude of co-payments exceeding prescription drug costs. JAMA 319:1045. https://doi.org/10.1001/jama.2018.0102
Viergever RF, Hendriks TCC (2016) The 10 largest public and philanthropic funders of health research in the world: what they fund and how they distribute their funds. Health Res Policy Syst 14:12. https://doi.org/10.1186/s12961-015-0074-z
Wikipedia Contributors (2019) List of countries by total health expenditure per capita. Wikipedia. https://en.wikipedia.org/wiki/List_of_countries_by_total_health_expenditure_per_capita

The Government (Payer) Challenge 3

Having closely examined the building blocks of our healthcare systems and negotiations, we now shift our focus to P&R negotiations and zoom in on the two main parties, their interests, and their challenges. We start with Governments in this chapter, and then move to Pharma in Chap. 4.

Governments everywhere face structural and institutional challenges that make their P&R negotiations harder than they would otherwise be. Their structural challenges come from health-related trends where health problems and expectations are growing and evolving. Governments cannot hope that health needs and demands will become smaller, easier, or solve themselves. In fact, we need to prepare to face larger health challenges, as evidenced by the COVID-19 pandemic.

The second set of challenges, institutional in nature, stems from governments having a larger societal role beyond healthcare. This larger institutional responsibility creates a vast set of needs and concerns that demand a never-ending balancing act involving multiple dilemmas, competing priorities, limited resources, and conflicting interests. Together, these two sets of challenges put significant pressure on Governments and shape how they approach P&R negotiations.

3.1 The Government Structural Challenges

In the past two decades, healthcare spending across OECD countries has consistently risen (OECD 2022).[1] Notably, the USA spent over 17% of its GDP on healthcare in 2019 vs. 14% in 2002 (Vanka 2024), with other developed nations averaging around 8% to 12% (Health OECD 2015). Developing countries such as the BRICS (Brazil, Russia, India, China, and South Africa) have also witnessed similar increases in their healthcare costs, even as they allocate lower percentages of their

[1] Note that health expenditures are the same as healthcare industry growth; the two terms are merely looking at the numbers from a different perspective.

H. Falcão et al., *Pharma, Prices and Power*, Future of Business and Finance,
https://doi.org/10.1007/978-3-031-93933-4_3

GDP to healthcare. For instance Brazil healthcare spent on GDP rose from 8% in 2002 to 10% in 2020. While the absolute figures matter, it's the growth trend that raises concerns.

On the positive side: the rising healthcare costs reflect improved health outcomes, evidenced by higher life expectancy, lower child mortality, and enhanced access to various healthcare resources, including infrastructure and treatments from drugs to malaria bed nets (Matthews 2014). But putting the positive aside for now, the growth in healthcare expenditures has surpassed GDP growth rates, resulting in a higher proportion of national resources allocated to financing healthcare. In 2000, global healthcare spending accounted for 8.6% of GDP; by 2020, it had climbed to 10.9% (World Health Organization Global Health Expenditure database 2024). Governments have started a wave of initiatives and reforms to address and contain this unsustainable trend.

The escalation in healthcare costs is often attributed to a few key factors: population growth, particularly in the aging segment; an increased prevalence of specific diseases; higher resource utilization per patient; a rise in patient expectations worldwide; and rising prices.

3.1.1 Population Growth

Population growth contributes to healthcare cost growth due to the increase in potential patients, leading to the need for more healthcare facilities, professionals, and treatments. Advancements in sanitation, medicine, and nutrition have reduced death rates, particularly among the under-5 age group (Institute for Health Metrics and Evaluation 2017), and increased life expectancies globally, driving population growth, which seems to be on the rise, as the EU's population expanded by 4% (17.6 million people) from 2003 to 2023 (Eurostat Demography of Europe 2024). Projections suggest ongoing growth due to increased migration and fertility, while death rates are lowering. Between 1950 and 2017, the world's population grew from 2.6 to 7.6 billion (Institute for Health Metrics and Evaluation 2017), with an annual peak growth rate of 2.1% in 1962 (Ritchie et al. 2024).

However, the population growth rate has been declining since 1962 down to 1.07% annually in 2018–2019 (Worldometer World Population Clock n.d.). As societies develop, their birth rates drop as more and more people choose and have the means to have fewer babies. Demographic models imply that the population boom of the twentieth century may have been temporary, and future growth will likely be more controlled, even if the projections of total population may still be quite high at over 11 billion people by 2100 (Ritchie et al. 2024). The good news is that if population growth rates drop below GDP growth rates, then population growth ceases to be a factor in a potential unsustainable rise of healthcare costs against GDP.

3.1.2 Aging Growth

While population growth may not turn out to be much of a threat to our healthcare systems, the growth of the elderly population may still be. Declining fertility rates over the past decades have led to an aging trend worldwide. In 1962, the proportion of older people stood at 5.1% (PopulationPyramid.net 2024a), but by 2019, it grew to represent 9.1% of the global population (PopulationPyramid.net 2024b). Some projections suggest that the elderly may represent 11.4% of the global population (PopulationPyramid.net 2024c) and grow as high as 22.7% in Europe by 2029 (PopulationPyramid.net 2024d). Even if the projections are inaccurate, they do seem to point in the direction of a growing older population.

Older individuals (>65 years old) bring two challenges to the healthcare system: they consume more and they contribute less. In sum, they are often net beneficiaries. The elderly tend to consume more healthcare resources due to increased susceptibility to severe conditions like cancer, heart disease, and dementia. They also tend to contribute less to the healthcare budget because most, though not all, are retired. As such, aging is likely a key driver of healthcare costs growth, and addressing its implications is crucial for healthcare system financing and resource management.

3.1.3 We May Be Getting Sick More Often: And a Different Kind of Sick

While we are living longer lives, we also seem to be getting sick more often (Institute for Health Metrics and Evaluation 2017). Conditions like Alzheimer's disease, cancer, cardiovascular diseases, diabetes, and asthma are becoming more prevalent, not solely due to improved diagnostics (Institute for Health Metrics and Evaluation 2017), though it could be due to longer lives as described in the previous section. The research challenges whether people are experiencing better health than their parents did at the same ages (Crimmins and Beltran-Sanchez 2010), thus hinting that it is not just a matter of adding more old but sick years at the end of life. In 2017, while the average life expectancy worldwide was 73 years, healthy life was only expected until age 63, indicating an average of 10 years spent in less-than-good health (Institute for Health Metrics and Evaluation 2017). Americans in their late 50s suffer up to 50% more physical and mental health problems and limitations than those of the same age did just 15 years ago (Choi and Schoeni 2017). Younger populations are also facing more injuries and illnesses (Institute of Medicine and National Research Council 2013; Henig 2013), and disability is increasing by around 52% across all age groups since 1990 (Institute for Health Metrics and Evaluation 2017).

Another reason why our healthcare costs may be growing faster than our GDP is due to a relative increase in chronic diseases.[2] Historically, infectious or acute

[2] Such as autoimmune diseases, diabetes, cancer, chronic obstructive pulmonary disease (COPD), rheumatoid arthritis, Alzheimer's disease, chronic kidney disease, hypertension, and asthma.

diseases were our main healthcare challenge,[3] and medical science tackled them with great success. The medical frontier moved to tackling chronic diseases, which last much longer than infectious or acute ones. Current treatments have already succeeded in managing several chronic diseases but not yet in curing most of them. As such, chronic disease patients stay on medication for months or years, and these prolonged treatment cycles cost more than a single intervention for an infectious or acute ailment.

In addition, chronic diseases are more common in an aging population, and they can be interconnected, as one chronic disease may lead to another, and many such patients end up carrying several chronic diseases concurrently. That aside, there is no medical consensus on the reasons why we are possibly getting sicker and suffering from more chronic diseases. There is converging evidence to blame factors including sedentary lifestyles, unhealthy diets and sugar, alcohol, stress, pollution (in the form of chronic exposure over decades to micro-doses of chemicals from our daily environment, e.g., fire-retardant chemical treatment of the fabric of our sofas), and also climate change (Institute for Health Metrics and Evaluation 2017; Mokdad et al. 2019; Barrett et al. 2015; President's Cancer Panel 2008; McMichael 2013; Grandjean and Landrigan 2014).

The complexity of chronic diseases demands a multifaceted approach that may require a paradigm shift in healthcare, and a potential combination of new medical interventions and lifestyle changes. The problem goes beyond higher healthcare costs or consumption to include reduced healthcare revenues (as getting sick more often can cause early retirement, reduced workforce or earning capacity, and lower healthcare contributions) (Chang et al. 2019). Ultimately, the aim of our healthcare systems is not just extending life expectancy but ensuring that our additional years are healthy ones. However, it seems that we are doing a better job of staying alive than staying healthy (Preidt 2015), which unfortunately increases healthcare costs.

3.1.4 We Have More Treatments and Expectations

The landscape of medical treatments has transformed in the last couple of decades. Fifteen years ago, there was only a single treatment approved for metastatic melanoma; now, more than 30 possible treatments exist (National Cancer Institute Drugs Approved for Melanoma n.d.). This treatment innovation wave has covered ailments from asthma to zygomycosis,[4] and patients now have an array of options. Previously, if a treatment failed, patients had no alternatives. Today, several drugs can be administered in combination or sequentially for improved odds of success. This is great news, but which comes at a significant cost increase in the form of more treatments—and more expensive treatments—per patient.

[3] Infectious diseases include malaria, hepatitis, measles, dengue fever, pneumonia, tuberculosis, influenza, and HIV/AIDS, caused by pathogens such as bacteria, viruses, or parasites.

[4] A serious but rare fungal infection caused by a group of molds called mucormycetes.

In addition, patients around the world are demonstrating increasing consumer standards and demands. Much like we came to expect more from our smartphones or other consumer products, we increasingly want better and faster healthcare products and services without compromising on any other factor. Especially when suffering or at risk, patients and their families can become quite demanding and impatient. However, demands for higher quality usually have the provider incurring higher costs, which could explain another lever causing healthcare costs to grow faster than GDP.

3.1.5 And Don't Forget Prices of Branded, Patented Drugs

Many people assume that the increase in healthcare costs derives mainly from an increase in prices. There are indeed some data points hinting in that direction. Before examining them, let's understand healthcare costs in more detail. Given that price increases have been different across services, we must break them down per type of service to grasp their real and separate impact.

The OECD average healthcare cost breakdown is: 60% for inpatient (28%) and outpatient care (32%), 18% for medical goods (mostly, but not only pharmaceuticals), 13% for long-term care, and 9% for preventive care, governance, and administration costs (OECD 2023). Before the COVID-19 pandemic (2015–2019), pharmaceuticals had the smallest average yearly increase in spending at 1.2%, followed by inpatient care at 2.2%, whereas the other categories stood between 3.0% and 3.5%. During the pandemic (2019–2021), all healthcare categories increased their yearly costs, and pharmaceuticals had the lowest yearly increase at 2.6% (OECD 2023).

Despite the widely shared idea that pharmaceuticals are the main culprit behind the rapidly increasing costs of healthcare, that does not seem to be the case. Not only are pharmaceuticals a small share of the total cost (18%), but it has been rising much less than other categories according to OECD official data.

Prices in different categories increase at different rates, some are more labor-intensive, others benefit more from digitalization or technology advancements, and so on. As more drugs go off patent, generic manufacturers compete on the same molecules with more efficient manufacturing and distribution processes. In addition, drug prices in most OECD countries are negotiated so that they cannot be raised after launch. Hence, prices for post-launch treatments tend to drop, and average pharmaceutical prices often only rise as enough new medications enter the market with significant benefits to command higher prices.

Pharmaceuticals average 18% of healthcare expenditure in the OECD, but this number varies from 10% in Nordic countries to 30% in Greece and other poorer countries. The relative burden of pharmaceuticals is higher in poorer countries, because drug prices, set internationally, are somewhat similar across countries. Meanwhile, the remaining healthcare categories are much cheaper due to lower local salaries, in line with local living standards.

Finally, the global prevalence of the US media may export the perception of US-specific problems as being worldwide problems. In the USA, given their market system, Pharma launch prices are freely set and have been rising steadily above inflation, which increases patient out-of-pocket costs, financial pressures in the system, and negative consequences to healthcare (Shrank et al. 2006; Yang et al. 2020).

Note that estimating discounts and rebates, and thus how much lower net prices at launch or post-launch are from their list prices, is extremely hard to do given their confidential nature. One study attempted to estimate US net drug prices from publicly listed pharmaceutical companies by dividing their net revenues over the number of units sold (Hernandez et al. 2020). That study found that these branded drug net prices at launch[5] (Hernandez et al. 2020; Feldman et al. 2021) increased 11% per year, and their post-launch net prices at an average rate of 4.5% over the inflation rate per year from 2007 until 2018 (Hernandez et al. 2020; Rome et al. 2022). Note that the same study found that net prices stabilized after 2015 and that the Inflation Reduction Act in the USA caps drug price increases at the level of inflation.

A common Pharma's explanation for new drug launch prices outpacing inflation is that innovation is becoming increasingly harder as low-hanging fruits are a thing of the past. Indeed, the drugs that most contributed to the recent high rate of price increases are new ones such as cancer drugs, potentially curative gene therapies that can be worth US$1–two million per treatment, drugs for rare diseases that have small populations to divvy up their development costs and ensure continuous investment among the number of patients, or other objectively more costly drugs to research or produce (Rome et al. 2022). Another argument used in the USA is that these increases happen in list prices and do not account for or underestimate the confidential discounts and rebates, and that more accurate estimates of net prices at launch or post-launch offset 62% of the list price increases between 2007 and 2018 and greatly reduce the final price paid (Hernandez et al. 2020; Janssen Pharmaceutical Companies of Johnson and Johnson 2019; Heather Bresch 2016; Tirrell 2017).

But, if R&D is the explanation for launching more expensive drugs, what justifies increasing prices above inflation year-on-year after their launch? Why were some post-launch drug prices in the USA raised by US$20,000 or 500% in 2022 alone? (Bosworth et al. 2022) One explanation is that a few pharma companies are indeed abusing the free-pricing system in the USA to raise prices even after a drug's launch and maximize profits whenever they can (Kesselheim et al. 2016). However, most companies are just trying to protects their margins as they negotiate prices with PBMs, as we will see in detail in the next chapter.

Importantly, the outlook reverses when we consider the expenditure for all Pharma products and not only newly launched branded drugs as above. Contrary to popular perception, even in the less-regulated free-pricing US market, overall cost of drugs has remained relatively stable at around 15% of the US healthcare budget since 2002 (OECD 2017a; 340B Health 340B Drug Pricing Program n.d.),[6] given

---

[5] The rebates and discounts are estimated as they are not publicly available data.

[6] Anecdotally, a relatively new market trend in the USA has been for large hospitals to buy a small Medicaid covered practice. This acquisition enables the large hospital to register for the 340B drug

the counterbalancing effect of generics lowering overall drug prices, for example. This stability does not mean, however, that patients have not suffered more with drug prices, as there has been an increase of high deductible plans in the USA, exposing patients to drug prices more through higher co-pays.

Meanwhile, in major pharmaceutical markets outside the USA, both patent-protected drugs and generics are subject to highly regulated P&R negotiations and other price-reduction mechanisms.[7] As a result, Pharma costs in these countries have been increasing very lightly and decreasing as a percentage of healthcare spend (Reinaud 2022).

Despite the US pharmaceutical price increase, year on year, being less impactful than most think, the freely set US drug prices are significantly higher than the heavily negotiated prices in the rest of the world. It is therefore not surprising that more and more Americans advocate for the USA to drop its free launch pricing system and start negotiating HTA launch prices (Rand and Kesselheim 2020).

3.1.6 The Trend Is Up, Up, and Away

While some factors above are less extreme than common perception would suggest (e.g., population growth or total pharma spend), the overall trend still seems to show costs growing faster than most countries' GDP or inflation, suggesting continued pressure on healthcare costs, unless a healthcare breakthrough takes place soon. These factors present complex and uncharted territory for healthcare, where old solutions are insufficient and new ones are elusive. We find ourselves in a state of transition, knowing change is necessary but uncertain about its direction. Governments are left scrambling and feeling the responsibility as their people look to them for solutions.

However, governments cannot claim there is a single right direction without oversimplifying the problem. Healthcare and P&R challenges are not one-dimensional mathematical puzzles; governments will not solve them with a few technical reforms. Attempts at doing so are likely to have governments experiencing breakdowns, resorting to win-lose strategies, fear-based behaviors, backlash, resistance, and even sabotage in the path for suboptimal or unsustainable solutions. Governments have consistently tried to control overall healthcare costs with mixed results. For example, if you decrease the number of physicians to save on salaries, soon you will have long waiting times, a rise in burnouts and medical error, and the associated backlash.

---

pricing program and extend the Medicaid drug rebate program to all their drug purchases, not just to drugs for Medicaid patients. Such a maneuver yields significant and mandatory net drug price reductions. While the free market allows for free pricing, the different actors also try to find their own ways, sometimes against the spirit of the law, to reduce their drug expenditures.

[7] In addition to P&R negotiations, most EU states apply additional price reduction measures, including price freezes, strict price regulations, budget cuts, lowest-price tender rules clawback measures, mandatory rebates, rebate contracts, automatic price reduction measures known as reference pricing, and non-negotiable price reductions.

Governments will always face significant trade-offs and ever-evolving institutional challenges. Instead of the current P&R strategies, governments are much more likely to craft sustainable and superior solutions if they facilitate win-win negotiations, experimentation, and collaboration among stakeholders to test and refine various options.

3.2 The Government Institutional Challenges

When it comes to healthcare, most Governments are expected to reconcile very disparate interests into workable solutions with limited resources in a constantly shifting landscape. Besides the structural challenges, governments face many institutional challenges while managing healthcare, such as:

1. **Social–political (Who gets covered?)**
   - Provide quality health coverage to their citizens in accordance with local value paradigms.
   - Decide which is our collective healthcare target: wellbeing, health, disease/pain-free, quality of life, age-adjusted mortality (death), budget, being economically active, or some other measure?
2. **Financial (How do we pay for it?)**
   - Continually find resources to keep up with growing healthcare demands, while remaining competitive and not choking the economy.
3. **Legal–economic (What is the best institutional arrangement?)**
   - Provide a safe and rewarding commercial and research environment for pharmaceutical companies to keep improving treatments.
   - Follow the rule of law and resist the temptation to abuse their power.
   - Ensure a level playing field for different pharmaceutical competitors.
   - Support local companies, scientific advancements, and job creation.

These issues create difficult and pragmatic queries that move our healthcare systems away from utopian answers. For example, do we want comprehensive healthcare access? Can we afford the healthcare choices we make as a nation? Are there institutional hurdles hindering our healthcare goals or are there better models?

Rather than providing definitive answers, this section's goal is to frame governmental challenges and stimulate broader discussion for improved global healthcare solutions. We will examine broader political considerations and some well-known minority or alternative views on several healthcare aspects, even if we personally disagree with them. By scrutinizing such questions, we can understand better the backdrop for the Government's interests, possibilities, and limitations against which P&R negotiations occur. In this way, we can ultimately suggest targeted and feasible ideas for improvement.

3.2.1 The Social–Political Challenge (Who Gets Covered?)

While the desire to offer comprehensive healthcare for all might seem obvious to most, our experience and research suggest a variety of scenarios where this isn't always the case. The social–political question of "who gets how much coverage and when?" is fundamental because it forms the basis for government's healthcare mandate and objectives.

Values, history, and aspirations generate social–political preferences that define a country's healthcare coverage. For example, the more social–democrat EU nations align with universal care ideals, while the more politically liberal USA sees healthcare mostly as a private responsibility. Different healthcare political choices do not indicate a better or worse system, but rather that, political as they are, these choices generate a different set of winners and losers in each country. And once a healthcare strategy is chosen, changing it becomes difficult due to vested interests, aversion to loss, and resistance to new systems.

Despite differing political stances, the goal of accessible, affordable, high-quality healthcare for all is often the shared preference. The debate then shifts not to the what, but rather to the how or how much or who pays, as many debate their preferred strategic path toward this goal.

3.2.1.1 Who Should Be Responsible for Our Healthcare?

All governments seem to be involved in healthcare management to some extent (Provider, Facilitator, Choice, or Safety net), and have been taking on the responsibility for its success (Himmelstein and Woolhandler 2016; Leonard 2016).[8] As seen above, structural challenges have been creating new healthcare cost pressures and pushing some to reopen questions that were until recently considered settled over the appropriateness of the government's centralizing role or around personal freedom and responsibility.

During the COVID-19 pandemic, most countries found themselves not knowing how much they could do and how much was up to the individual. Some were comfortable with experiencing a higher degree of government intervention (e.g., China), while others were not (e.g., Sweden). We even saw huge conflicts within some countries where large segments of the population were on opposite ends of the spectrum (e.g., UK & US).

Another example is the new wave of chronic diseases often linked to individual lifestyle choices. In this case, people disagree over whether governments are or are not mandated or responsible to do whatever it takes to improve our collective healthcare, and whether action would be beneficial or detrimental. Others question whether net beneficiaries should be contributing more or having more limitations put on their coverage.

Governments already regulate smoking and alcohol consumption, but should they ban them altogether? How about poor sleep patterns, sedentarism, sugar, junk

[8] Even in the USA, the government was responsible for 64% of overall health spending in 2013 through a combination of publicly funded health coverage and subsidies to the private sector.

food/beverage consumption, or other unhealthy habits which more recent research has suggested may lead to poor health? China recently limited the amount of video game their youth can play in a single week (Pruitt-young 2021) to promote healthier habits.

Is it appropriate for governments to establish health regulations or guidelines that penalize individuals living unhealthy lifestyles, even if research demonstrates the impact of lifestyle choices on health? Should they limit themselves to promoting healthcare best-practices education? (Mozaffarian and Stampfer 2010) Should those not adhering to health guidelines pay higher taxes (e.g., sin taxes)? Several US cities have enacted a soda tax to reduce consumption or create a fund to pay for community programs or the harmful health consequences of the consumption of sugary drinks (Urban Institute 2019; Smith 2022). If some products are clearly unhealthy, shouldn't governments just make them illegal even if it massively disrupts the industry that produces them?

Should those who adopt unhealthy habits lose healthcare coverage over the researched consequences of such habits? (Stender et al. 2006; Mozaffarian et al. 2006; Morris et al. 2006; Ascherio et al. 1999) How much research consensus is needed for the government to decide which unhealthy behaviors are to be punished? And what if the research supported by the government in the past is now proven wrong? Will those who followed its advice but suffered negative health consequences be penalized or compensated? (Mozaffarian and Stampfer 2010) What if unhealthy habits are proven to be much less relevant than genetic or environmental factors in causing ailments? Shall we then ignore people's choices and let them be?

Do we then also punish those who work too much as overworking leads to several health ailments as well, but then risk seeing national productivity drop? Can the government then mandate or reward healthy behaviors as opposed to punishing unhealthy ones? In sum, how should decisions be made (if ever) about healthcare exclusion or penalties based on lifestyle choices? Notice how even a single challenge like this, regarding unhealthy habits potentially increasing the odds of chronic diseases, can raise a slew of ethical and political questions that potentially re-pivot a government's responsibility within healthcare.

Different countries are bound to have different political preferences related to the questions above and many more, thus making different healthcare choices. Much of this debate revolves around how to define who is a net beneficiary, and then if and how a government should either reduce their growth or impact on the system. Behind it all, the responsibility debate remains: is healthcare an individual or government responsibility, and if shared by both, where are the boundaries between them? Ultimately, governments around the world are having to rethink who is responsible for healthcare's future.

3.2.1.2 Who Should Be the Recipient of Our Healthcare?

In market-based systems, healthcare is an individual issue, where individuals are responsible for themselves or their families, and thus they will be healthcare recipients to the extent that they can pay. Still, the pursuit of universal health coverage remains a priority to most countries, but governments are increasingly facing access, quality, and value trade-offs. In centralized healthcare systems, net contributors finance net beneficiaries, but the rising costs and shifting political preferences are inviting a reevaluation over whether to reform, reengineer society, or exclude some from healthcare to ensure sustainability. As the promise of universal healthcare seems threatened by its affordability, are we ready to revisit the promise itself?

As many governments carry the enormous institutional responsibility of trying to offer the best care for everyone at any time for "free" (i.e., no payment at the point of service), some see themselves forced to compromise or cut corners to face their political or financial realities. In the process, governments are asking themselves tough questions such as:

1. **What if we do not offer it to everyone?** Many countries discuss the possibility of excluding or in fact do exclude specific population groups from healthcare coverage (e.g., illegal immigrants, national citizens residing abroad) or are concerned with the moral hazard and financial costs of those who adopt unhealthy habits (as seen in the previous section). Some even argue to exclude the wealthy, as they can afford their own healthcare and should not burden the national system. Many wealthy citizens already resort to private health insurance or seek treatments abroad in any case (Amadeo 2020). And yet, defining wealth levels for exclusion could be tricky, alienate net contributors, and have broader negative impacts on the public healthcare system (Donohoe 2004; Australian Institute of Health and Welfare 2017; Papanicolas et al. 2018; Bell 2019; Dixit and Sambasivan 2018; Lee 2018).[9] In sum, if deciding not to treat everyone, should it be a decision based on funds, accountability, tribalism, or other values? And what happens with compassion and human rights for those disenfranchised?
2. **What if we do not offer the best healthcare at all times?** Many countries (e.g., UK & Australia) prioritize cost-effective treatments over the absolute best, adopting the Quality-adjusted life years (QALY) framework[10] (Annemans 2019) to quantify how a new treatment benefits a patient's quality of life. Unfortunately, QALY measures drugs and does not focus on patients, which can create distortions, discrimination, and potential ethical considerations (Neumann and Cohen 2018). For example, say the cost-effectiveness upper limit is £100 per QALY and one patient with 100 diseases has the State pay for its 100 drugs as each

[9] Competition for private healthcare money can lead medical resources to pivot toward wealthy patients, leading to treatments supported by little scientific evidence, an erosion of professional ethics, and increased social inequities and injustice as these centers divert their intellectual and financial resources away from programs designed to promote individual, community, and global health.

[10] QALY measures a person's ability to carry out the activities of daily life free from pain or mental disturbance. It is calculated as Years of Life x Utility Value derived from Quality of life = #QALYs. For example, if the drug extends lives by 1 year in perfect health that will equal one QALY. If the drug extends lives for 1 year with only half of perfect health, then it provides only 0.5 QALYs (1 Year of Life x 0.5 Utility Value). In sum, if a new drug is truly improving health, it should have a higher QALY than the existing drugs in the market. If it does not, then it should not be approved by the government, who then offers the already existing treatments to its citizens.

charge £99 per QALY. Then compare that with another patient with a single rare disease in need of a single medication which has its cost-effectiveness at £101 per QALY and thus is denied treatment. The cost for the State of the first patient is £9900 British pounds, while the second is denied a treatment of £101 pounds. On top of this, if you consider that most patients have multiple pathologies (especially as they grow older), one treatment in such a patient will not deliver the full quality of life used for its cost-effectiveness calculation, as this patient still has its quality of life impacted by other pathologies. As an alternative to QALY and yet similar in its cost benefits, there are discussions around the Value-based health care (VBHC) model, which takes a more patient-centered perspective (Tsevat and Moriates 2018) but which has not yet become the standard in any country at the time we are writing this book. Note as well that the base cost-effectiveness threshold used by The National Institute for Health and Care Excellence (NICE) in the UK was set at 20,000GBP/QALY in the year 2000 and since then has remained unchanged, while the Bank of England reports that the purchasing power of 20,000GBP in 2000 would be equal to 29,992GBP in 2020. We will come back to these tactics to control costs later in the chapter.

3. **What if we do not offer lower value healthcare?** Most lower-value drugs or treatments, as defined by treating common non-life threatening conditions (e.g., aspirin) are cheap but as they are widely used and thus consumed in high volumes, they can end up costing a lot to governments. Thus, if governments were to think about where they could cut and save, one place with potential low pain to the average citizen would be here. Not reimbursing lower-value treatments would allow governments to allocate the savings toward more expensive higher-value treatments, which are harder for patients to bear financially. Lower-value treatments would be paid directly by patients, thus reducing the governments' healthcare bill and potentially reducing the overconsumption of certain medications as well. On the negative side, this choice discriminates against the poor or net beneficiaries in general, who may still be unable to afford the non-covered drugs and treatments (Amadeo 2014a). Operationally, it can be extremely difficult and political to draw the line on what constitutes lower-value as it will define which drugs or treatments to exclude from healthcare coverage. For example, cost as a criterion could exclude essential preventive treatments and lead to increased healthcare costs in the long run, as individuals may delay care until their ailments become more serious or expensive to treat (Office of Policy, Performance and Evaluation Early Childhood Education. CDC Archive n.d.; Amadeo 2014b).
4. **What if we do not offer it every time they need it?** This question usually revolves around governments acting against overprescription or elective treatments, and demanding prehabilitation (Macmillan Cancer Support 2019).[11] Most

[11] Prehabilitation in healthcare is a proactive, multidisciplinary approach that focuses on optimizing a patient's physical and psychological condition before or in spite of medical treatments or surgeries to improve outcomes and recovery. It can take the form of physiotherapy, guidance, and assistance to adopt healthier habits (e.g., healthy eating, limited alcohol consumption, weight man-

agree that elective treatments take valuable resources away from more basic or needed care (Labonte 2015), and argue that such treatments should be charged separately or denied. And yet, many cultural and historical factors come into play here, making this a less-than-obvious decision. For example, the French healthcare system covers homeopathy, which many see as a value-negative treatment (Fulgham 2018; Becker-Witt et al. 2003; Maddox et al. 1988); while Switzerland does not cover dental care, which most believe essential. Many countries are spending billions due to drug overprescription (Bates et al. 2011; He 2014; Nicastri et al. 2009; Wang et al. 1999; Li et al. 2012; Oxford and Kozlov 2013), as it increases drug toxicity (Campion et al. 1987) and the development of super bacteria (Spellberg 2011; Llor and Bjerrum 2014).[12] Overprescription is also blamed as contributing to the US opioid epidemic (Makary et al. 2017), and suspicions hang over its role in cardiovascular drugs (e.g., statins) (Yebyo et al. 2018), and psychotropic medications like antidepressants and ADHD drugs (Safer 2000; Smith 2012). As such, in many developed countries, value-positive providers are reserving antibiotics for more serious cases only. Many studies and reports are validating the benefits and promoting the adoption of prehabilitation (Silver and Baima 2013; West et al. 2017; Wynter-Blyth and Moorthy 2017; Minnella and Carli 2018; Bertram et al. 2010), not only as preventive (Warburton et al. 2006) but as able to treat certain conditions better than medication (Knowler et al. 2002). In such cases, the claim goes that patients who reject prescribed prehabilitation should not have their treatment covered. But what about those who tried and failed? How about the Hippocratic Oath? (Torrey 2010)[13] Could refusing a treatment now result in the automatic denial of future treatment options if a patient's condition worsens, potentially limiting their freedom to choose?

5. **What if we stop providing healthcare to patients after they do not want it anymore?** Like the other questions above, the goal here is to save costs, but here we also consider the growing international consensus that patients have a fundamental right to consent to receiving treatment (World Health Organization 2024). Despite universal care, many people still face obstacles to treatment (e.g., lack of funds, time, or perceived need) (Taber et al. 2015), while others may not want medical care due to not believing in it or for religious reasons. To implement such exclusions, it would be imperative to distinguish between those who actively refuse treatment from those who avoid it due to obstacles. Even if we

---

agement, quit smoking, regular exercising) and other activities proven to improve a patient's physical and mental health as soon as possible after a diagnosis.

[12] Antimicrobial resistance (AMR) is a growing global public health challenge. In the USA, a new drug resistant bacteria, MRSA (Methicillin-Resistant *Staphylococcus aureus*), kills more Americans than emphysema, HIV, Parkinson's, and homicide combined. The current antituberculosis agents (isoniazid and rifampicin) have been insufficient against new resistant tuberculosis strains in 84 countries.

[13] The argument to deny other forms of treatment after failed prehabilitation being in sync with the Hippocratic Oath says that doctors will have complied with their oath by offering care in the form of prehabilitation, but their care was consciously rejected by the patient.

could distinguish them well, what would countries that value life over choice do? Is the more paternalistic patient–physician relationship model, where the physician's judgment is in the best interests of the patient and above the patient's choice, appropriate nowadays beyond emergency situations or incapacitated patients? (Emanuel and Emanuel 1992) How about when parents are denying treatment to their children? The line of responsibility when it comes to life versus personal choice is again based on values, and may differ from country to country.

In sum, trying to solve healthcare challenges by reducing coverage, choice, frequency, quality, or availability ends up with highly sensitive, nuanced, and complex sociopolitical choices. Indeed, many healthcare experts, interest groups, corporations, think tanks, politicians, and academics have been discussing these issues for years without reaching any consensus. Some of the suggestions above may save healthcare costs, but would draw new lines between healthcare winners and losers in society. They may also go fundamentally against the principle of universal care: that is, that we should offer healthcare to everyone and protect anyone against financial distress due to healthcare costs. And yet, these questions and their polarized arguments percolate the broader social–political healthcare debate, influencing governments' mindsets and mandates during P&R negotiations.

3.2.2 The Financial Challenge (How Do We Afford It?)

The option of reducing healthcare costs by reducing treatment scope is limited by several social–political challenges. Reducing healthcare costs through negotiation is part of what we cover later in this book. Now we focus on the financial challenge of how to foot the bill if costs continue growing. We see three main ways to do so: increase public debt, increase taxes, or reallocate funds from other public budgets (e.g., reducing other costs). When it comes to market-based systems, employers and health plans will find themselves in similar shoes, by either raising fees, co-pays, or reallocating funds from other budgets.

Some may wonder why the potential solution of lowering drug prices is not included here. In OECD countries, drug costs typically constitute 7% to 15% of total healthcare expenses, and, for most countries, hospitals and long-term facilities represent 50% of such expenses while physicians account for approximately 20%. Given pharma's relatively smaller size, we believe that this measure alone would be a drop in the bucket, when we are trying to examine broader financial solutions. A discussion on medication pricing will follow later in the book.

In sum, none of the possible options are politically easy, sufficient, or sustainable (Sarnak et al. 2017; Kertscher 2019; Barlas 2019). Projections suggest 19 million fewer tax-paying working adults in the EU by 2060 (European Economy Series 2015). The reduced taxpayer pool plus the growing healthcare demands from an aging population will generate a fiscal squeeze for most governments.

3.2.2.1 Increasing Public Debt

In 2019, the average debt of most of the world's major economies surpassed 70% of GDP, hitting its highest levels since WWII (Stubbington 2019; Cox 2019; Trading Economics 2019). Many economists believe that such high and rising debt levels are linked with slow growth, reduced funds for public priorities, increased risk of a fiscal crisis,[14] and lower ability to handle future financial emergencies (Committee for a Responsible Federal Budget 2019). These consequences are ever so real as experienced by the over 3 billion people who live in countries forced to spend more on interest payments to service their national debt than on education or health (UN Global Crisis Response Group 2023).

While the jury is still out on the best economic approach to handling high public debt, no one seems to be arguing that a country should recklessly throw away caution. Even if what qualifies as high debt could be higher than a 70% debt to GDP ratio for developed countries, governments still have limits on the amount of debt they can handle (Barrett 2018; Coppola 2018), making this an unsustainable solution for long-term healthcare financing.

3.2.2.2 Increasing Taxes

Raising taxes in line with and to cover healthcare cost increases may be an unsustainable source of financing, unsavory to many as no one likes to pay more taxes, and thus a contentious political issue. Many countries already have a relatively high tax rate with little room to move upwards. Opponents of tax increases point toward several studies showing that high taxes deter work, saving, investment, innovation (Tax Policy Center 2020), and economic growth (McBride 2012). However, studies vary and some show limited to no negative tax effect on economic growth (Huang and Frentz 2014; McGuire 2019), while others demonstrate positive growth when taxes fund deficit reduction and education (Miller and Russek 1997). The many complex variables and lack of consensus on the impact of raising taxes on growth (Huang and Frentz 2014) make this a thorny solution for governments given its immediate political costs with no certain or clear benefits.

The debate over economic growth aside, if a government were to raise taxes to fund healthcare, a few options present themselves:

- **Raise everyone's taxes?** While seemingly fair, this risks hitting low-income individuals harder (regressive taxation), as increasing taxes proportionally to income (progressive taxation) is often viewed as fairer. Considering the financial strain on the middle class in developed countries and the prevalence of low-income populations in developing nations (Roser and Ortiz-Ospina 2013; Mühlau 2021; Whelan et al. 2016; Wolff 2010; Tett 2014), raising taxes is almost always an unpopular move, detrimental to a politician's career, and thus unlikely to happen without raising awareness and a sense of urgency.

[14] A fiscal crisis happens when government expenditures become higher than the tax revenues, and the government is unable to make ends meet.

- **Raise taxes on the rich only?** This option is often considered more acceptable due to rising wealth inequality worldwide. Wealth taxes[15] were once common (Kaeding and Pomerleau 2019; Vaird 2019) but dwindled (Greenberg 2019) because they generated minimal additional revenue, failed to meet their redistributive goals, and faced operational concerns (OECD 2018). Indeed, valuing wealth is hard and can unintentionally hit the middle class, while these taxes may increase tax avoidance and cheating (Greenberg 2019). Renewed interest in wealth taxes exists (Greenberg 2019) based on recent innovations in valuation methods, tax design options, and legal frameworks (Gamage 2019). Meanwhile, the rich leverage their lobbying power or wealth mobility against such initiatives. Experts suggest a global financial registry to curb tax evasion (Zucman 2014). In sum, a new wealth tax awaits concrete proposals and successful experiments to avoid past failures and becomes a reliable source to fund healthcare or for other purposes.
- **Raise only corporate taxes?** Modern corporations benefit from publicly funded services like education, infrastructure, and security (McGuire 2019; Shaxson 2011; Mofffatt 2019), but these services particularly benefit the larger ones, who may have been paying minimal or decreasing taxes over the years (Carrillo et al. 2017; Duhigg and Kocieniewski 2012; Citizens for Tax Justice 2012; OECD 2024; Jahnsen and Pomerleau 2017; Pomerlau and Potosky 2016; Streif 2015; U.S. Office of Management and Budget (OMB) President's Budget: Historical Tables, 1934–2029 (Table 2.2) n.d.).[16] Given that since the 2007 financial crisis, most stock markets have seen amazing growth beyond that of individual wages (Li 2019), it may be fair to ask corporations to pay higher taxes to help finance our healthcare. Opponents of corporate tax hikes argue about tax competition and stifling growth, even if, as we saw above, higher taxes, when well invested, can promote growth. This leaves the challenge of countries lowering corporate taxes to compete for talent and investment globally, and every country fearing being the first to try to reverse the trend and then seeing corporations flee. However, recent studies suggest that higher income tax rates don't harm local economies (McGuire 2019) if they provide a good overall business environment with efficient, stable, and fair taxes that support public investments (McGuire 2019). While debates are ongoing, raising corporate taxes may be a source to help finance healthcare costs.
- **Raise corporate taxes of companies that produce unhealthy commodities?** The rationale is that much research suggests that products such as tobacco, alcohol, or processed foods contribute to directly increasing healthcare costs

[15] A tax that incurs over the total value of someone's assets, which was designed to increase the tax contribution by the rich.

[16] In the USA, corporate tax revenues went from representing 32.1% of the total federal tax revenue in 1952 to just 9.9% in 2012, while the OECD average was 2.9% in 2016. Between 2003 and 2017, the worldwide average corporate tax rate fell from 30% to 22.96%, while Europe, a region usually known for high income taxes, has the lowest corporate rates at 18.88%. Between 2000 and 2018, corporate tax rates fell in 76 countries and only went up in six.

(Gualano et al. 2014; Gallus et al. 2011; Associazione Italiana di Oncologia Medica 2015; Islami et al. 2015; Passiglia et al. 2019; Russo and Scafato 2006; Goodchild et al. 2017; Organisation Mondiale De La Sante 2015). While many may find taxing them higher to be a straightforward decision (Islami et al. 2015; Britton 2017; Sandoval et al. 2016; Ekpu and Brown 2015; Murray 2013), implementation has proven challenging. For instance, in Switzerland, the estimated health and societal cost of tobacco far exceeded cigarette tax revenues in 2017 and yet the legislature prevented a tax increase on cigarettes (Le News 2017).[17] Even a modest tax increase, e.g., 10 cents per pack, could raise about CHF 50 million/year, and a more aggressive 75% price raise per packet could pay for the problem's full social and health costs (Le News 2017). The Swiss parliament also rejected a proposed ban on tobacco advertising, despite public support and a WHO recommendation, citing lack of evidence that it reduces tobacco consumption (Le News 2016). The aim is not to single out Switzerland or the tobacco industry, but to highlight the influence and interests of unhealthy commodities companies when considering such tax hikes, even in strong democracies and well-regulated nations.
- **Raise out-of-pocket expenditure for patients?** The appeal of this suggestion is its simplicity and apparent fairness—pay more per use and spare those who don't. Health insurers globally employ co-pay models arguably to lower premiums, overall costs, and unnecessary medical visits, though as already seen, some do so to increase profits. So why do governments not do the same? Co-payments, no matter how small, risk disproportionately burdening net beneficiaries, if they fail to consider economic circumstances, thus de facto excluding them from essential care, leading to financial hardship and diminished quality of life (Kirzinger et al. 2019; Detollenaere et al. 2018; OECD 2019; Bor et al. 2017).[18] A suggestion to enhance fairness is to tie co-payments proportionately to one's income. However, operational questions arise such as who classifies as wealthy, how much more a wealthy person should fairly pay, and if the poor co-pay nothing how much they may overburden the system seeking unnecessary treatments. Plus, this suggestion may not move the needle for healthcare funding in countries with a sizable low-income population. Overcomplicating the system might raise administrative costs and lead to classification issues, affecting access and affordability. While not insurmountable obstacles, these are variables to consider if a country wants to implement this new tax well and fairly.

In summary, raising taxes has merits and challenges, with varying opinions, political preferences, and disparate studies complicating the landscape. Nevertheless,

[17] Of the CHF 5.6 billion, CHF 1.7 billion goes for medical treatments and CHF 3.9 billion for compensation for work absenteeism and invalidity.

[18] About one-third of low-income earners on prescription drugs costing them US$100 or more per month reported stopping treatment due to cost concerns. Similarly, low-income populations even in OECD countries suffer shorter life expectancy, poorer health, and higher rates of mental illness and of HIV infection than middle and high-income populations.

it's an idea with several angles and possibilities worth exploring for countries grappling with healthcare funding issues.

3.2.2.3 Tapping into Other Public Budgets

Tapping into other public budgets is a controversial idea, as it involves cutting government costs, which sparks political debates about necessary services versus non-essential ones, with some advocating for limited government involvement in healthcare (Mofffatt 2019). This dilemma arises because government resources are finite, and increasing healthcare budgets often requires reallocating funds from sectors like education, security, and pensions, which are currently facing their own sets of financial challenges (Conseil d'orientation des retraites (COR) 2020).

While governments occasionally adjust budgets for emergencies, a significant, permanent shift toward healthcare funding could jeopardize essential services and create conflicts among government responsibilities. In essence, it's not a viable or sustainable solution as it risks causing tensions with and gaps in other areas of government responsibility.

The financial challenge facing governments is complex, multifaceted, and requires careful consideration and implementation. Options like raising debt, taxes, or reallocating existing revenues can provide short-term relief and potentially address long-term deficits, but are neither straightforward nor guaranteed to be effective. In sum, it's crucial for stakeholders to collaborate and explore sustainable financing avenues for universal healthcare.

3.2.3 The Legal and Institutional Challenges (How Do We Deliver It?)

Beyond figuring out how to pay for healthcare, Governments must figure out how to deliver it within their legal frameworks and institutional priorities. Many well-intended, though not necessarily pragmatic, suggestions to help governments negotiate lower pharmaceutical prices are made harder to implement due to such legal and institutional constraints. Some of the suggestions to give governments more control over drug prices made harder by legal and institutional challenges include:

1. Set drug prices unilaterally through legislation.[19]
2. Nationalize pharmaceutical companies.
3. Break patents and replicate necessary or very expensive medication.
4. Make pharmaceutical prices or costs transparent.

[19] Here we are not referring to price regulation, as most countries have a vast body of laws or rules on how to price or negotiate the price of medications, including the demand for certain discounts or other price reductions. However, Pharma still has the right to bring forward their preferred price to submit to the regulated conditions or P&R negotiations and can still decide to walk away if they do not like the proposed outcome. As such, when we refer to legislating prices, we are referring specifically to a government using its legislative power to unilaterally set and thus impose drug prices without consultation or input from the drug's producer.

5. Substitute patents with delinkage.
6. Curb pharmaceutical advertisement.

These ideas are based on the benevolent goal of keeping healthcare costs low and affordable to all. However, from a negotiation perspective, most are win-lose moves as they invite governments to use their power in P&R negotiations to achieve said goal.

3.2.3.1 What If Governments Could Unilaterally Define Drug Prices Through Legislation?

Each country could decide on its maximum healthcare budget, then legislate individual drug prices to fit into it. Governments could multiply each medication's yearly volume with its government-legislated price based on desirable criteria (i.e., efficacy), and define its total cost while making all drugs fit into its budget. While technically doable with a certain margin of error, it would be a complex option to implement in most free countries as Pharma companies would probably disagree or some would walk away.

Governments everywhere heavily regulate P&R negotiation processes and, more recently, realized they can do so to raise their bargaining power. They have not legislated individual drug prices yet, even if they have been threading quite close to that line in the angst to control or influence prices. For example, some Payers (e.g., France, Italy, and the UK) have, for many years, set the budget for the total drug market or sometimes just a category (e.g., treatments for one particular condition). Revenues exceeding the budget envelope are paid back in the form of claw-backs annually. With these tactics, a drug, no matter how successful, will never cost more to the government than its budgeted amount.

When it comes to individual categories, however, governments have not legislated caps, but rather negotiated them with Pharma companies, even if often through win-lose moves. As expected, Pharma strongly sees caps as arbitrary power moves that devalue their products, set bad precedent, and unfairly transfer all uncertainty onto them.

In 2014, France saw itself at the center of an unprecedented legislative move over drug prices in response to a new wave of hepatitis C[20] treatments (Mullaney 2014; McCorvey 2015). Treating the estimated patient population of 200,000–367,000 people (Brouard et al. 2015; Huet 2014) with the new drugs would have cost up to 20% of the country's total 2014 medication budget. In response, France made several moves to avoid blowing up its healthcare finances. France created a progressive contribution scheme (a.k.a. W-rate) to fund the new drugs for all patients (Huet 2014; Brennan and Shrank 2014; Jeantet and Lopez 2014; Traynor 2014; Mouterde et al. 2016), and a committee to prioritize reimbursement to those with chronic conditions (e.g., patients simultaneously infected with HIV) (Mouterde et al. 2016).

[20] Hepatitis C is a viral disease that ravages the liver and is a leading cause of cirrhosis, liver cancer, and transplants in many countries. An estimated 70 to 130 million people around the world suffer from HepC and the disease used to kill between 400,000 and 700,000 people per year.

The W-rate taxed different pharma companies proportionately to their HepC revenue after the total cost exceeded France's 2014 or 2015 HepC-specific budgets (Huet 2014; Mouterde et al. 2016).

The Pharma companies, led by Gilead, the producer of the leading new HepC drug (Sovaldi), argued that their high prices reflected a new cure rate at or above 95%, in as little as 8 weeks, with milder side effects, and a lower likelihood of expensive hospitalization and liver transplants compared to existing medications (Mullaney 2014; McCorvey 2015; Huet 2014).[21] Despite all these benefits, the high price tag of €56,000 in France and $84,000 in the United States may have thrown governments into a relative success trap especially when projections had Sovaldi generating $12 billion in revenue for Gilead in 2014 (Huet 2014).

Despite being a legislative move, France allocated a generous budget to the new HepC drugs for 2014–2015 (450 and 700 million euros, respectively), and a limit to its own W-rate, and the tax only went into force after a signed agreement between the HepC drugmakers and the French Economic Committee of Health Products (Mouterde et al. 2016). These conditions suggest that the French response resulted more from a negotiation with Pharma companies than from an isolated legislative exercise. Given that France is one of the biggest pharmaceutical markets in the world, it has significant bargaining power over pharmaceutical companies, who would hate to or be unable to walk away from its market. The France example helps us appreciate how difficult legislating pharma prices of breakthrough therapies without alternatives can be in a free market economy, even in a country with a relatively high degree of government intervention and bargaining power (A French Habit is Spreading 2019).

Besides not being a straightforward option, one complication with legislating drug prices is that governments would be resorting to their *imperium* power to facilitate their commercial role. A government's *imperium* power is its executive power to legislate over matters of state including the use of force or coercive power. In parallel, many governments also have *dominium* power over the use of their material resources to act as commercial players and facilitate services to its population, such as when they negotiate drug prices with pharma.

In most countries, governments act as the sole significant buyer (i.e., monopsony) of medications, holding substantial negotiation power that allows them to potentially render a new medication unprofitable in their nation if the pharmaceutical company refuses to meet their price demands. If, on top of such considerable *dominium* power, the government adds its *imperium* power, it may represent power abuse, independent of its potentially benevolent intentions (Meletiadis 2018). Tempting as it may be, governments that respect the rule of law have to resist wanting to (ab)use their *imperium* power to gain advantages when behaving as commercial players (Turpin and Tomkins 2007).

---

[21] Indeed, interferon-based treatments offered cure rates between 45% and 80%, lasted for up to 48 weeks, and had several side effects—nausea, stomach pain, personality disorder—often considered as bad as the disease. Indeed, several patients refused the interferon-based HepC treatments to avoid their side effects.

Even if governments could legally mandate pharmaceutical companies to accept fixed prices, significant challenges remain. Price fixing can distort markets, lead to unintended consequences, or provoke resistance from pharmaceutical companies, who, as independent actors, may prefer to walk away than sell under a legislated price scheme. At each price setting, governments would risk pushing a provider away and making a desirable medication unavailable to its citizens. This risk is substantially higher for poorer countries as pharmaceutical companies would be more willing to withdraw from negotiations. Even countries with prominent local pharmaceutical companies rely on foreign medications, and their foreign manufacturers can walk away in refusal of legislated prices due to their extraterritorial status.

The power to legislate drug prices can tempt governments down a slippery slope of price reductions over time until, at the extreme, they find themselves legislating that a particularly important medication should be free. Pharmaceutical companies, anticipating such trends, will likely do whatever it takes to resist legislated prices. In sum, legislating drug prices is more likely to escalate the power exchange and problems in P&R negotiations than solve them.

3.2.3.2 What If the Governments Nationalized and Fully Owned the Pharmaceuticals?

Nationalized pharmaceutical companies would be compelled to accept legislated prices under government control, but to do so potentially requires a reversal of privatization efforts in many countries. Nationalizing the pharmaceutical industry presents challenges, especially in nations without local pharmaceutical companies, where seizing local subsidiaries of foreign firms could provoke international conflicts and disrupt supply and innovation. Even in countries with a strong pharmaceutical industry, nationalization would pose complex decisions, such as whether to maintain separate entities or consolidate some or all firms into national champions.

Some economists argue that government planning and intervention in the economy can support growth even within a capitalist regime (Chang 2012). Examples include the South Korean government nudging LG away from textiles and into electronics, or the US government's significant role in launching the Internet, and how it supported the development of the biotechnology and aircraft industries (Chang 2012). But these examples usually do not include full nationalization as even those in favor of more government intervention argue that the old Soviet Union failed because they were trying to control too much (Chang 2012). Nowadays, even communist China has non-state-owned local pharmaceutical companies competing alongside government-owned ones (Top 10 Pharmaceutical Companies in China 2017).

The complexity of nationalizing the pharmaceutical industry is compounded by ongoing R&D challenges. The average cost and time for developing a new drug have been rising. A 2022 estimate found R&D costs per drug above \$2 billion and 7.1 years from starting clinical trials to approval (Deloitte 2023). The annual global Pharma R&D investment in 2022 reached US\$ 244 billion up from US\$ 137 billion dollars ten years earlier (Mikulic 2024). And for all these costs, pharmaceutical profitability is falling from 20% in 2005 to around 15% in 2020, behind tobacco, mining, financial services, software, and computer services, more or less at par with beverages (Shaw et al. 2023). This declining trend was temporarily reversed by the event of COVID-19 in 2020–2021 (Why pharmaceutical companies are on a shopping binge 2019; Pategou 2019). As such, nationalizing pharmaceuticals would potentially mean decreased investments in R&D or funding it with additional taxes, given that the purpose of nationalizing would be to reduce prices and thus the income that would otherwise finance such innovation.

As the industry has struggled to discover new drugs profitably for the past decade or so, large pharmaceutical firms have increased their M&A activity in the hopes of buying innovation from smaller players (Teitelman 2019). Unfortunately, this M&A strategy has not yet proven to raise innovation industry-wide as opposed to just capturing its benefits for the larger players (Haucap and Stiebale 2016; Comanor and Scherer 2013; Shepherd 2018; Bonaime and Wang 2024).

Even if a country were to nationalize its pharmaceutical sector, the choice between keeping companies separate or merging them carries R&D risks. Merging may reduce innovation, and finding innovative smaller biotech and pharma companies after nationalization could prove challenging. Alternatively, maintaining several separate entities could encourage competition and diversity, but also introduce operational complexity and the risk of failure.

3.2.3.3 What If Governments Broke Patents and Replicated Branded Drugs into Generics?

Patents Are a Successful Driver of Innovation

Originated in ancient Greece, patents were designed to stimulate and protect our innovative efforts, while also promoting the broader good (Pearl 2017). They grant the inventor a short-term monopoly-like pricing power over its invention, which expires after a pre-determined time to deliver public gains in perpetuity (Pearl 2017). Despite only 3% of patented inventions being profitable enough to recoup their patent filing cost (Key 2017), many consider patents as critical for the functioning of some industries, as they promote innovation, encourage investment, economic growth, knowledge sharing, and the efficient use of resources (Economic Benefits of the Patent System 2010).

Patents have been essential to Pharma's profitability and high level of investment in innovation (Avery 2008; Blit 2017). Breaking patents reduces revenues and discourages investment and future innovation (Kennedy 2019). Indeed, pharmaceutical innovation suffers from high R&D costs and failure rates,[22] (Mahdavi 2017) ease of imitation, and the need for a high level of commercial success to recoup investments. Without the superior profitability odds from patent protection, many investment decisions on new drugs would have otherwise been rejected and we would likely have 60% fewer drugs in the market today (Avery 2008). Patents help pharmaceutical companies increase their odds of recouping their R&D costs (WIPO

[22] In 2014, the Tufts Center for the Study of Drug Development reached an estimate of $2.6 billion within 10 years to develop and license a new prescription drug.

Reasons for Patenting Your Inventions n.d.), increasing their appetite to invest and endure the high failure rates and costs involved.

In sum, patents and their temporary price premium based on improved clinical value are two pillars of the pharma highly productive innovation engine. For pharmaceutical patents to work well and deliver on societal benefits, two main conditions must be satisfied. First, patents associated with low to no clinical value (fake) innovations must not be rewarded with price premiums. In Europe, health technology assessment (HTA) systems prevent the innovation premium from being misallocated to those who do not demonstrate real benefit. Second, for the patent-innovation engine to deliver worldwide benefits in perpetuity, especially for the poor, once patents expire, cheaper-priced biosimilars and generics must be available. Furthermore, to ensure that Payer resources are channeled to reward new innovation, they should rapidly obtain a very large share of the market.

3.2.4 Patent Expiration Could Be More Beneficial than It Is

In India, generics make up as much as 97% of local prescriptions (Hargreaves 2019; International Generic and Biosimilar Medicines Association 2019), one of if not the leading country in generics' penetration worldwide. In the USA, generics represent 90% of all prescriptions and saved the US payers US$408 billion in 2022 (Association for Accessible Medicines 2023). Despite its 90% penetration and large savings, the US system discriminates against biosimilars not specified as interchangeable, and thus reduces their market benefit. PBMs prefer to obtain larger percentage-based rebates from patent-expired and yet still high-priced branded drugs over the much smaller rebates from cheaper biosimilars in their formularies (Cohen 2023). As an example, Humira, the best-selling pharmaceutical of all time, still commands 97% of the US market despite its much higher price and years after patent expiration and biosimilars being available (Cohen 2023).

Even if rewarding innovation justifies paying high prices for new drugs, healthcare systems have failed to and yet must avoid paying high prices for drugs after patent expiration. The share of generic prescriptions in OECD countries is extremely varied (e.g., 90% in Chile vs. 18% in Luxembourg) and has an average of 54% (OECD 2023). Low generic penetration can result from doctor's or pharmacist's commissions or lack of concern with cost savings, brand recognition, patient and physician right of choice, and other institutional obstacles that we examine below. In some markets, there are compulsory price drops of branded drugs after patent expiration and similar mechanisms that make the generic switch less relevant.

Besides low generic penetration, many OECD countries also experience a lack of generic competition, whereby having generics does not lead to a drastic drop in prices. The low generics penetration and competition equate to payers leaving large sums of money on the table. It is hard to understand such waste of resources and of expired patent advantages, even for wealthy countries.

In any case, it seems many Governments could do more to reward innovation, increase access, while reducing costs. The fact that they continue paying more for branded drugs after patent expiration, because of patient or physician preferences, suggests that among the many Governmental challenges, maximizing the public benefits of the patent system is not a top priority.

3.2.5 Patent Criticisms

Like any modern institution, patents are not without their flaws or critics, and at times they fail to deliver on their societal goals. There are many who claim that the patent system is an outdated, if not perverse, mechanism that favors private interests over public needs, at least for pharmaceutical products (Public Eye 2017). They argue that innovation in pharma should be public and free, particularly when it relates to knowledge and ideas (Blit 2017), as when universities publish their findings to make them accessible to all. After all, health is a public good and a right in many countries, and probably the most fundamental part of anyone's quality of life. Public universities often conduct basic pharmaceutical research, which sometimes contributes significantly to private drug innovation (Toole 2012), to the point that pharmaceutical firms can be seen going from the prime locus of drug discovery to becoming 'network integrators' of external and internal research (Rafols et al. 2014). Under such views, some believe that breaking patents to help governments negotiate lower drug prices can be reasonable.

Another argument in favor of breaking patents relies on the fake innovations and patent abuse (e.g., evergreening or patent thickets) (Boldrin and Levine 2013) by pharmaceutical companies done to block competition, create artificial monopolies, and inflate prices (The Campaign for Sustainable Rx Pricing The Truth About Big Pharma's Patent Abuse n.d.; Johnson and Brough 2019). Evergreening involves several tactics to extend the exclusivity of a drug beyond its initial patent expiration[23] (Nawrat 2019; Faunce and Lexchin 2007; Faunce et al. 2008; McDermott 2019) often through multiple patent applications based on slight drug modifications (e.g., modes of administration, new dosages, new combinations or variations, or even color) (Nawrat 2019) with no increase in patient safety, adherence to treatment, or reducing adverse effects (Saez 2019). As discussed above, these approaches are usually ineffective in many countries outside of the USA, where prices are set after a careful evaluation of the incremental clinical benefit versus standard of care by HTA agencies.

Patent thickets use a complex set of patent rights to force competitors to worry about lawsuits or obtaining licenses from multiple patentees (Shapiro 2000; Wu and Cheng 2020). In sum, patents are meant to give Pharma a temporary price premium based on the improved clinical value of a new drug, and not to be extended several times into a semi-permanent state of price protection based on a series of little to no-value added modifications.

[23] Evergreening often involves multiple patent applications for the same drug, launching a second-generation version of the drug, misleading advertisement against generics, threats of patent lawsuits, and reluctance to share clinical data or samples to block the entry of generics.

These abuses operate within the rules, but undermine patent systems' good intentions (Abbas 2019) and take advantage of lenient patent approval standards (Gleeson and Moir 2014). For example, nearly 80% of recent patent applications were for patent extension, and 50% were for drugs with multiple extensions (The Campaign for Sustainable Rx Pricing The Truth About Big Pharma's Patent Abuse n.d.; Feldman 2018; I-MAK 2018a; Komendant 2019). These extensions have been used to increase average prices in the USA by 68% (2012–2017), and delay the competition from generics (The Campaign for Sustainable Rx Pricing The Truth About Big Pharma's Patent Abuse n.d.; I-MAK 2018a). That said, not all patent abuses are necessarily evergreening or patent thickets, as they may include the exploitation of patents' monopoly pricing power or other mechanisms. Examples of patent abuses happen mostly, but not exclusively, in the USA and include:

1. AbbVie's Humira, the world's top-selling brand drug in 2020, accumulating 247 new patent applications (Nawrat 2019; I-MAK 2018a; Komendant 2019; Sagonowsky 2017).[24]
2. Purdue Pharma using its OxyContin patent to delay several new entrants (Roth 2005; Mack 2006) and earn US$ billions even though it was eventually found to have a "clear pattern of intentional misrepresentation" when applying for patents (Roth 2005; Brazil 2005; Harrison 2008).[25]
3. Martin Shkreli exploiting his patent-protected AIDS-medication Daraprim to raise its price from $13.50 to $750 per pill in 2015 (Mahdavi 2017).
4. Allergan's transfer of its eye drug Restasis patents to a Native American tribe to benefit from its sovereign immunity against intellectual property lawsuits in the USA (Nawrat 2019).
5. In Europe, the EU Commission issued a fine of €60 million to AstraZeneca in Sweden and the UK due to their patent abuses in 2005 (Fagerlund and Rasmussen 2005).
6. More recently, several European countries (e.g., Belgium, Czechia, Germany, Italy, the Netherlands, Poland, Spain, and Switzerland) have started to open investigations against pharmaceutical companies who hold dominant positions and have been allegedly engaging in patent abuses or unwarranted patent litigation to block or delay generic competitors from entering the market (Garcia et al. 2022).

Given the widespread, little-regulated, and endemic legal and institutional vulnerabilities of patent systems (Feldman 2018), it is no surprise that there are advocates for breaking patents, especially abusive ones. But while Europe (Fagerlund and Rasmussen 2005; I-MAK 2018b) and the USA (Johnson and Brough 2019; McDermott 2019; Luthi and Owermohle 2019; DeArment 2018) have been pushing new laws, lawsuits, and fines against patent abuses, they have also been increasing

[24] Humira is responsible for two-thirds of AbbVie's total revenue and $100bn in sales since its launch in 2002.

[25] A later ruling stated that the misrepresentation never happened.

intellectual property protection, and lobbying against processes for canceling bad or invalid (poorly granted) patents (Johnson and Brough 2019). This seemingly contradictory behavior suggests lobbying and rent-seeking (Boldrin and Levine 2013) practices as developed countries push developing ones for stronger intellectual property protection to ensure the profitability of their local pharmaceutical companies (Baker 2020; Cox 2013).

Meanwhile, developing nations watch millions suffer from treatable diseases they can't afford to buy drugs for because of patent-protected prices. Note that although some vivid cases are particularly newsworthy and reported, patents or patent-protected prices are not solely to blame for the health plight of some developing nations. Indeed, diseases such as malaria and even AIDS remain leading causes of death in some countries despite the wide availability of effective low-cost generic treatments, which unfortunately do not reach patients given lack of infrastructure to ensure diagnosis, treatment, supply, and follow-up of the patients.

Regardless, many poorer nations have started an access-to-medicines movement where they break patents based on the basic right to health. India initially ignored HIV drug patents that reduced the treatment price from $10,000 down to $100/year, and saved countless lives (Boseley 2018) before the WTO forced it to align its legislation with the international framework (Lowe 2021). Brazil also challenged international patents (Day 2007), breaking one on an HIV/AIDS drug to provide free treatment (Massarani 2024; Bowe and Colitt 2005), which reduced HIV rates down to developed nation levels and saved the country hundreds of millions if not billions in costs (Massarani 2024). The WTO endorses patent breakages, as well as compulsory licenses and parallel importation, during health emergencies, which has benefited many countries, including developed ones like Canada, Taiwan, and Italy (WHO 2015; Cherian 2016).[26]

Some pharmaceutical companies have started to empathize with the underlying access vs. patent tension in low-income countries (LaMattina 2013). Many have started to relax patent protections and increase partnerships for drug access in the world's least developed nations (Bloomberg 2016). While there are many regulatory, funding, and capacity obstacles in getting the right drugs, even free ones, to the right people, these access initiatives are growing (Medicines Patent Pool 2020; Keown 2018; Frick and McKenna 2019).

An obstacle for access initiatives is that many pharmaceutical companies have learned to fear that developed nations may want to copy developing ones and start breaking patents or demanding similarly low prices (Phelan and Cook 2014). Their fears are justified as the US and many European governments got mad at and demanded lower prices from Gilead after it sold its HepC drug significantly cheaper to Egypt (Campos and Gomes 2014; Kelland 2015), even though Egypt had a severe HepC epidemic and is a much poorer country (Alcorn 2018; Waked et al. 2020).

[26] Compulsory licensing gives a country the right to license a patented invention to another producer without the consent of the patent holder. Parallel importation happens when a country imports, without the consent of the patent holder, a patented product from another country, usually to profit from the lower prices in this other country.

Luckily for Gilead, this indignation did not result in much (Kelland 2015), but it raised the fears of the entire industry (I-MAK 2015).[27] This nightmare scenario for pharmaceutical companies could wipe out their profits, given that 89% of drug sales launched during 2013–2018 came from only seven developed economies (US, UK, Germany, France, Italy, Spain, and Japan) (EFPIA 2019). Understandably, many companies will fight as hard as they can against these patent violations on principle or to avoid bad precedents to developed nations, even when they have little financial stake in the poorer countries (I-MAK 2018b; Boseley 2018; Campos Mello 2019).

Another reason that pharma companies oppose breaking patents is their fear of having their drugs copied and turned into generics against intellectual property laws and before a patent expires, again risking their profits and ability to finance innovation in the medium to long run. Some countries, often developing ones, may disregard a patent (equivalent to breaking it), and authorize a local generic company to copy it. Once that is done, not only can the generic copy be sold in the home market, but it also risks being exported to other markets that are equally open to disregarding patents in exchange for lower prices.

Generics represent a wide category of drugs, often produced and sold by a different manufacturer than its original inventor after the patent ends (EFPIA 2019). In the USA, generics capture, on average, 80–90% of the market, and reduce prices by 50 to 95% within 1–5 years (IMS Institute 2016). A positive example happened when Prozac generics took 65% of Prozac's market in the first month, and almost 90% in 1 year (Druss et al. 2004). If generic penetration were this effective all around, there would be strong savings to be made.

Without fully tapping into the savings that generics of out-of-patent drugs can bring, high-income countries have started to complain that drug prices have become a painful cost to their universal coverage systems and a threat to access and healthcare sustainability (Saez 2019; Hoen 2017; Plüss 2019a; Moon 2019).[28] Governments have to balance curtailing abuses, responding to demands to revisit the patent system, while wanting to help their pharmaceutical industries thrive and continue innovating for the benefit of healthcare in general. On the other side, some pharmaceutical companies' abuse of patent extensions' lax requirements (e.g., evergreening) are perceived very negatively. A more populist Government trying to avoid looking Pharma-friendly could eventually be tempted to break patents for short-term support from its voters if drug prices continue to rise and no better solutions are brought to the table.

As seen earlier, total Pharma expenditures have either remained stable or decreased as a share of healthcare costs in the past two decades. These trends are evidence of how patents, despite all the problems mentioned in this section, have

[27] In these lawsuits, local organizations or governments argued that Sovaldi was based on previously published information and an existing compound. Because it could not be deemed novel, non-obvious, and useful, the argument was that Sovaldi was unworthy of a patent.

[28] Even rich countries have problems when treatment costs of hundreds of thousands to millions of dollars are becoming the new normal, such as the US$D4 million price tag for a spinal muscular atrophy treatment.

been working on balance to encourage innovation, pay innovators a temporary premium, and eventually revert their benefits to society affordably. As such, patent breakage can be an overreaction to the few bad apples, unfair to the law-abiding Pharma, and risk disrupting or reducing innovation in the medium to long term. Such negative consequences disqualify patent breakage in our view as a significant or sustainable way to reduce drug prices.

Ultimately, most agree on the need for change to reduce prices while maintaining innovation incentives (Hoen 2017). For now, the majority seem to accept patents as the best available institutional way to promote innovation. Instead of breaking patents, the more sustainable solutions seem to be to enhance patent protection, fight against patent abuses, or rewarding fake innovation as done by HTA systems in Europe, limit patent breakages to specific cases, promote cheaper access to generics once patents expire, and assist with access initiatives and infrastructure in poorer countries.

However, some still believe we should overhaul the patent system from the ground up in the search for a superior incentive system for innovation (Blit 2017), which we explore after examining the more mainstream discussion around increasing drug development cost transparency.

3.2.6 What If We Make Drug Prices Visible, Transparent, and Public?

Another large challenge for Governments is price transparency, namely, that pharmaceutical prices are transparently available to all stakeholders. While every country has a published list price, most pay only a net price after confidential rebates or discounts. This disparity raises media accusations and suspicion of lack of transparency, wrongdoings by public officials, and even corruption by Pharma. Indeed, why do Governments hide these rebates?

Confidential rebates result from an initiative by the World Health Assembly (WHA) to reduce Pharmaceutical prices. The WHA created the International Reference Pricing (IRP) system, where countries publish how much they pay to provide other countries with legitimacy to negotiate lower prices for themselves. This IRP system helps countries without developed HTA capabilities to benchmark their prices with those with highly sophisticated HTA systems (e.g., the UK), instead of relying exclusively on the manufacturer's price. Each country chooses which countries' prices to benchmark, and most often choose economically or geographically similar countries or those with more sophisticated HTA systems.

Despite the benefits listed above, IRP reduces rebates for the referenced countries (i.e., whose prices others benchmark), as Pharma knows that any discount to them will be seen and thus demanded by other countries as well. As such, IRP increases the Pharma cost of giving a rebate to a referenced country, as it becomes economically better not to offer the discount or even not sell in the referenced country than to lose money in multiple markets with one negotiation move.

To bypass this hurdle, Governments hungry for discounts started to publish their (fake) list price for IRP purposes, while hiding confidential, and at times significantly large, discounts provided by a Pharma now less concerned with discounts triggering an IRP domino effect. So when discussing drug prices, we always need to consider the visible list price, and the real yet hidden net price.

This is a multifaceted governmental challenge. If Governments publish their real prices, they receive fewer rebates and pay more for medication, which goes against the best interest of their taxpayers. However, by not publishing real prices, Payers mislead poorer countries into negotiating with inflated information and securing worse deals. Despite its questionable ethics, it is understandable why Payers engage in this two-price system. Highly referenced countries have highly developed HTA systems and large markets, which serve as bargaining chips to obtain large discounts from Pharma. These countries (e.g., the UK) entered the IRP system to help others, but in doing so they saw their discounts dwindle.

With time, Payers across the globe learned about the two-price system and focused less on list prices, except for the German List price. Why so? Since 2011, Germany's list and net prices are transparent by law (Henschke et al. 2013; Paris and Docteur 2008; Kupferschmidt 2010), as an attempt to lead other countries into a more transparent world. The result? Few followed, and Germany is considering ending its transparent pricing and adopting confidential discounts (Koyuncu and Aretz 2024).

Confidential prices present another challenge as internal stakeholders only see list prices and thus believe these are the prices paid, instead of the much lower net prices. Government officials work hard preparing for P&R negotiations. They scrutinize every detail in the pharmaceutical product's submission dossier, and model its clinical value and expected costs to secure large discounts in these intensive, and sometimes aggressive, negotiations. After all this effort, their visible end-product is a frustratingly high list price. Confidential prices fuel rumors of secret or shady deals that lead citizens to believe that Payers are cozy to Pharma for personal gain while wasting tax-payers' money. For healthcare workers, these high-list prices are the visible proof that their Governments do not negotiate with Pharma as hard as it negotiates their salaries.

IRP also changes Pharma's access strategies who want to avoid an IRP domino effect. Manufacturers sequence their new product launches, starting with countries more agreeable to high list prices to avoid establishing low prices for IRP. Thus, transparent pricing countries are double-penalized as they receive fewer discounts, as seen above, and are pushed to the end of the launch queue. Until 2023, Germany's launches were not delayed as it paid the drug's launch price (freely set pre-negotiated price) for 12 months before negotiating a lower price and making it visible. However, recent laws (e.g., GKV-FinStG and ALBVVG) shortened the free-pricing period to 6 months and extended the retroactive rebate of the launch premium over the negotiated price (Koyuncu and Aretz 2024; Koyuncu 2023). Their impact is still unknown.

Another unwanted consequence of the German price transparency happens when a product's visible price is assigned significantly below other countries' prices due to a worse HTA analysis. In such cases, manufacturers may prefer to walk away from the German market to avoid the IRP domino effect. If even Germany, as the largest and best paying market in Europe, faces these risks, imagine if smaller countries adopted transparent pricing.

The biggest challenge of IRP is how it made international drug prices visible in the USA. The USA pays, on average, 3.4 times the list price of brand-name prescription medications compared to the remaining OECD member nations, while US prices for unbranded generic drugs are slightly lower on average (Parasrampuria and Murphy 2022). This price difference became a hot topic in US politics, where many resent that Europeans are free-riding on US higher prices funding the lion's share of pharmaceutical innovation.

If the USA starts referencing Europe, Pharma will likely raise European prices or walk away from some EU markets. First, to avoid dropping their prices and thus their revenues in their biggest market, the USA. After all, 52.3% of the world's pharmaceutical sales in 2022 happened in the USA and Canada compared with only 22.4% in Europe (EFPIA 2023). The other reason is that Pharma have been agreeable to sell at low prices and margins in Europe because the bulk of their revenue comes from the US market. If US revenues were to drop to European levels, it would likely choke Pharma's current revenue model. Pharma would need to make changes to maintain their current level of innovation, probably including an increase in overseas prices and revenue.

3.2.6.1 What If We Make Drug Costs Transparent?

In most Healthcare systems in developed countries that support innovation, the negotiated price of a new drug is a function of the clinical value they bring to patients. The higher the benefits to patients, the higher the price the healthcare system is willing to pay. However, when important stakeholders outside of P&R negotiations, such as journalists, politicians, laymen, or healthcare workers discuss drug prices, they usually ignore their value.

Instead, mainstream public debates often sound like: *"Look at Pharma high profits, their prices must be too high. People can't afford their medication, this means that drug prices are too high. The cost of producing drugs is residual, thus their prices are unfairly high and mostly profit."* Indeed, when considering the median gross profit margin, manufacturers seem to have extraordinary profits: 76.5% on 35 large pharmaceutical manufacturers vs. 39.1% of 357 S&P 500 companies (Ledley et al. 2020). Pharmaceutical products are indeed much cheaper to manufacture than products in most other industries. However, after we discount R&D and administrative expenditures, and control for company size, their difference in real profits (net income) is much smaller at 3.6%. This is significantly less than the amount of price reductions that critics of Pharma profits expect to see.

Nevertheless, profit critics reject the current system used by HTA agencies and advocate that prices should not be based on value (clinical or economic) but instead based on a "fair" profit over R&D spend. That is, the more a manufacturer invests in developing a drug, the more it would receive for it. This formula discourages efforts to increase efficiencies or save R&D costs, and allows dishonest companies to fudge costs to increase prices. Conversely, it risks being either too generous or too stingy.

For example, it costs more to develop a drug 10% better than the standard of care than one 50% better, as the first needs more patients to show statistical superiority. The 10%-better drug would receive a higher price (higher R&D costs), which could improperly reward the inferior product.

The R&D cost plus fair profit formula requires the Payer estimating or knowing a drug's R&D cost, and knowledge over the real costs of developing a drug can become a win-lose negotiation tool, if Payers leverage it to unilaterally cap Pharma earnings. Studies on R&D cost estimates vary from as low as US$164 million to as high as US$2.87 billion (Austin and Hayford 2021; Prasad and Mailankody 2017), mainly due to subjective research choices, limited data (Harris 2017), assumptions, and extrapolations (Public Eye 2017; Prasad and Mailankody 2017; DiMasi et al. 1991a, b, 2003, 2016; Avorn 2015).

Formulas based on R&D costs ignore the role of profits or other expenses. If an industry fails to return enough profit, investors eventually migrate somewhere safer or more profitable, reducing Pharma's funds to invest in innovation and lessening its overall benefit to society. Critics of Pharma profits argue that innovation will continue even if profits fall as an improved equilibrium emerges between acceptable innovation losses and a much-needed increase in drug access. Many healthcare stakeholders (Government, healthcare workers, or voters) carry this critical view of Pharma profits, which hardens P&R negotiations.

3.2.6.2 Cost Transparency Would Be Too Risky Under Current Monopsonist Tactics

In the search for a negotiation upper hand, many Payers are pursuing pure price reduction tactics. Governments have been creating several win-lose tactics to reduce prices, including affordability thresholds (through a cost-effectiveness approach used by NICE in the UK for which the threshold has not been increased for 20 years), sales caps (France, Italy, and Spain), special budgets (France), price moratoriums (Germany), drug expenditure fixed envelope with payback (Italy, France, UK), entry agreements (Italy, Belgium), pooled procurement processes (Benelux, Nordic countries, Southern countries), targeted taxes or legislation, mandatory discounts (Germany, Italy, Spain), fast-track approval of competitors (generics or biosimilar drugs), delayed reimbursement (most EU countries), prior authorization (Spain, Italy, Austria), preferred drug lists, compulsory licensing, and even new transparency legislation to gain leverage toward drug affordability (Saez 2019; Dana et al. 2017; Flume et al. 2018; Ryan and Sood 2019).

While some are common business or governmental purchasing practices to gain acceptable levels of bargaining leverage, many of the above moves rely on the government's monopsony power and would be considered abusive commercial tactics if they took place among two private entities (e.g., mandatory discounts or sales caps) (UNCTAD 2023).[29] For example, a monopsony buyer who can force a seller

[29] Monopsony power is an area of competition law enforcement that has not received commensurate enforcement attention compared with cases of monopoly power. Enforcement in cases of market concentration and anticompetitive agreements has increased exponentially over the years,

to provide an unlimited quantity of free products after reaching the buyer's budget ceiling is deploying an unfair and unethical power move. And yet, governments have been imposing such win-lose tactics in P&R negotiations increasingly. While governments have anti-competition laws against monopolies, they have done little against monopsonies so far (UNCTAD 2023).

Instead, Payers have been giving in to the temptation of benefiting from this legal vacuum over monopsonies to leverage their own monopsony power for lower prices in P&R negotiations. As a result, it becomes harder for Pharma to agree to increased price transparency when they can justifiably expect that Payers will likely use said information against them.

Governments are supposed to promote a level-playing field among competitors, uphold the rule of law, curb abuses of power, promote or at least exemplify legal and ethical behaviors whenever possible, and promote a fair, equitable, and predictable negotiation environment. And yet, in their desperation to stick to their budgets and inebriated by their newfound power levers, Payers have been sacrificing these other mandates at the altar of lower drug prices. These win-lose moves not only raise the cost of compliance with extended regulation, they also raise Pharma risks dramatically, and raise massive obstacles against collaborative negotiations, namely, risk and loss aversions.

However, what if governments invite Pharma representatives to collaborate in an open conversation about fair drug prices and price transparency common principles, with research to be done on diverging points, how to create superior value, and craft mutual gain solutions? (Roediger 2019; Plüss 2019b) Given Pharma's calls for careful consideration of the long-term implications of increased transparency (Shaw and Mestre-Ferrandiz 2020), agreeing to jointly examine and create options to mitigate undesirable risks or liabilities could be a productive exercise.

Pharma would feel that they are coming to a negotiation *with* the governments and not against them. These risk or loss-reduction or inclusion moves can transform parties from adversaries into genuine and willing negotiation partners, and lead to Pharma agreeing to increased price transparency, and fairer prices and profits.

3.2.7 Delinkage: The Future, or Multiple Dead-Ends?

Dating back to the eighteenth century, delinkage describes different innovation incentive models that attempt to price a new drug without linkage to its R&D costs (Knowledge Ecology International 2015). Delinkage models aim to reward,

---

but enforcement in cases of monopsony power has not increased at the same pace. However, research indicates that the abuse of monopsony power can be as damaging as any other anticompetitive conduct. Monopsonies raise concerns in labor markets regarding wage suppression, as workers are unable to negotiate higher wages when there is a single employer. Buyer power in the retail sector has also come into the debate, regarding small producers and suppliers that face unbalanced and abusive transaction terms and conditions. Competition authorities are increasingly monitoring anticompetitive practices in monopsonistic markets and discussions are taking place in various forums as to how competition issues in such markets can be addressed.

optimize, and focus R&D fund allocation on innovations that add clinical value, eliminate the need for large marketing expenditures, target neglected diseases,[30] (Hoen 2017) and increase price affordability, and drug access (UNITAID 2016). These models may even try to reduce the high costs of appropriately introducing and scaling up a new drug in a new market (Frick and McKenna 2019).

There are several delinkage schemes in discussion among politicians, academics, and other interested parties (Hoen 2017; Årdal et al. 2020; Outterson and McDonnell 2016; Hoen 2020).[31] One of the most common examples of delinkage is pull-financing, where governments pay the innovating Pharma firm a prize (S.2210–110th Congress (2007–2008), 2007), conditional lump-sum, or fixed sum over a number of years to cover the R&D costs plus a "fair profit." In exchange, the Pharma company makes the new formula public. Anyone can copy it and enter the market, thus increasing access and competition, and eventually pushing prices down. The innovative Pharma company, already financially rewarded, can choose to compete or not in the open market (UNITAID 2016). Another such scheme, transferrable exclusivity vouchers (TEV), pairs delinkage with patents to promote innovation of financially uninteresting drugs such as antibiotics. TEV rewards Pharma by granting additional patent time on another of a company's more profitable drugs. While rejected in the USA in 2018, the EU signaled openness to the idea (Årdal et al. 2020).

Delinkage promises superior incentives for new drugs against neglected diseases, which mostly affect low-income or small markets. Despite their limited commercial potential, Pharma still needs to comply with the increasingly expensive safety, quality, compliance, and regulatory requirements. In the patent system, the high cost and low upside makes for an unsustainable and unprofitable eq. (Frick and McKenna 2019), which discourages R&D investments. Over 35% of the most-invested, often small companies in neglected diseases in 2018, despite growing public R&D financing (OECD 2017b), failed to cover operational costs and ended up either going bankrupt, abandoning, or drastically reducing that specific line of R&D by 2020 (Årdal et al. 2020). Unfortunately, this drop-out phenomenon reduces access to antibiotics and other much-needed medications (Årdal et al. 2020).

The UK and Sweden recently announced pull-financing pilots to delink antibiotics prices away from sales volume or market value, and toward their value to the local health system (Marschang 2019). While not expected to stimulate innovation, these payments sought to cover national access needs. South Africa tried delinkage by allowing a sped-up development timeline and thus reduced costs for a new

[30] Many low- to middle-income country diseases afflict either a small or a poor population that renders R&D into them unprofitable under the patent system. Delinkage suggests public–private collaborations that may reduce the costs of developing drugs for such diseases by co-investing, reducing administrative and approval costs, or guaranteeing a return on the investment.

[31] Others include diagnosis-related groups (DRG) carve-outs, stewardship taxes, "pay or play" fees, auction of patent-extending vouchers, public financing of private R&D in exchange for products priced at marginal production cost or at pre-agreed proportionate discounts, patent buyouts, direct financing, not-for-profit drug development, pooled funds for global health R&D, prize funds, targeted research partnerships, advance market agreements, and licensing of related patents.

neglected disease drug. The USA has offered priority review vouchers to lower the review and approval time for drugs with high potential for strong positive results.

Experimenting may help us evolve into a better, even if potentially more complex, innovation system. In the process, we avoid the possibility of a radical revolution where we risk losing all of the proven benefits of the current patent system. Besides, by piloting delinkage models, Pharma can observe how the innovation landscape evolves and prepare to operate within different reward systems to keep on innovating (Frick and McKenna 2019). However, countries are not embracing delinkage as most models require large upfront payments with uncertain delivery or results (Årdal et al. 2020; Stevens and Ezell 2020).[32] For example, the US$1 billion/drug pull-financing negotiable estimate for antibiotics R&D was rejected by many countries (Årdal et al. 2018, 2020), even if it seems relatively low compared to the overall healthcare bill. Transferrable exclusivity vouchers (TEV) were criticized as being many times more costly than the US$1 billion pull-financing estimate (Årdal et al. 2020; Outterson and McDonnell 2016; Rome and Kesselheim 2020).

As delinkage challenges reveal a deeper need for coordination, many argue that global cooperation toward a global R&D policy framework reform is needed to improve our pharmaceutical innovation system (Hoen 2017). Should we have a global fund to co-invest with Pharma companies in new R&D? Who will invest in this fund? How much for each country? Who benefits and by how much? A hypothetical global drug innovation council, which decides which drugs or companies to fund, would suffer significant lobbying pressure as every country would want to earn that money to finance high-paying jobs and a vibrant Pharma industry. The recent bribery scandals around the selection of World Cup and Olympic host cities is a cautionary tale here.

Alternatively, countries could bid for the right to perform the R&D, but would the financing go to the place with the highest odds for successful drug development or just the highest bidder for the opportunity? And what if no one bids? Will the prizes rise in value? If they do, Pharma will eventually learn not to bid at the first opportunity.

To further illustrate the coordination challenges of such models, we can imagine a global fund of nations to co-invest in R&D. Should it exclusively invest in neglected diseases? Should Denmark invest more in the fund than India given that its GDP per capita is 30 times larger? Or should it invest less given that its total GDP is seven times lower? (Countryeconomy 2024) Or should Denmark have the right to reject contributing to particular R&D projects which are aimed at diseases with zero occurrences in its territory? Could Denmark vote on co-funding R&D for Danish-based companies only? What if the fund decides not to invest in a Danish-based Pharma R&D project, because they believe it is for a non-neglected disease? Can Denmark then do it alone?

Imagine now that Denmark is allowed and chooses to be the only country to co-finance the home-based Novo Nordisk R&D for a new diabetes drug. Should it

[32] For example, what if a pharmaceutical company, after receiving the delinked payment, goes bankrupt or the drug needs to be removed from the market for safety reasons?

agree to a pre-determined discount for Danish citizens, or for the whole world? Should it ask for a price discount or a share of the profits? If Denmark is trying to optimize the return of its healthcare R&D funds, it will claim benefits for its citizens but allow Novo Nordisk to charge whatever it wants anywhere else. And, in this case, will Denmark be comfortable disclosing its R&D costs transparently, which will likely reduce Novo Nordisk's potential revenues elsewhere, and thus its tax contributions to the Danish government?

Let's add a couple of additional mechanisms in our next example. Imagine that the US government co-finances a local Pharma's R&D for a new drug and then awards a prize to the Pharma in exchange for its formula. Will the USA open the new drug to the world? Allow for generic producers to copy it? If it does, it not only financed cheap prices for the rest of the world, but it also potentially transferred innovation profits to foreign companies and countries. The US Pharma will have earned a reasonable profit through the prize and may now choose to compete against generics, many from India and China, but its US base will eliminate any cost advantage to compete against foreign generic producers.

The end result is that the US company and US government will have taken all the innovation risk, but the company will have earned a limited upside and the government will have earned less in taxes. Pretty quickly, the USA or any other country that hosts Pharma HQs will create national boundaries to their new innovation models and limit many of their potential benefits. Or if a large market such as the USA implements prizes, Pharma may leverage patents abroad to increase prices and profits, thus exporting the problem from one country to another. The above delinkage models may end up resembling the compulsory licensing currently used by some developing nations, where several countries, at the expense of the prize-paying country, guarantee access to the new drug for free or at a price far below market value.

If not well-coordinated, delinkage can perpetuate the access divide between rich and poor, since rich countries host most Pharma companies, have the most money to invest in new R&D projects, and have the most profitable markets to leverage in negotiations. Conversely, delinkage may promote free-riding by poorer nations, as rich nations finance most of the innovation but then make them available for poorer ones for little to no financial gain. Eventually, richer countries will resist distribution to countries that do not contribute, or the world will risk longer-term underinvestment in drug innovation.

Delinkage proponents suggest solving this problem with a worldwide mandatory Medical R&D Treaty, where every country would have a proportional financial obligation to a new centrally controlled R&D body with significant discretionary power toward the funding of diseases considered as priorities (Stevens and Ezell 2020). Unfortunately, such intergovernmental organizations have limited power over bigger nations, and end up being quite ineffective when it matters most. So this solution may not work well until intergovernmental organizations become more respected.

The patent system works by rewarding greed, and greed can seem ugly, especially when linked to matters of life and death such as healthcare. Besides, a patent's monopolistic protection reduces access artificially, instead of by natural limits (e.g., insufficient raw material, limited production capacity, etc.), giving us something to point fingers at. And yet, isn't the current system rich on innovation and one where expensive medications, after patent expiration, become significantly more accessible? What other system delivers on innovation, price, and access as well as or better than patents? Maybe delinkage models will increase access, but they also risk increasing costs and reducing innovation. Will the net benefit for society be larger? Maybe, but maybe not. We truly do not have the answer in this debate. At least in the short term, delinkage models still lack the patent system's decades of evolution and tweaking to overcome its weaknesses and be seen as a reliable institutional substitute or complement model for encouraging innovation.

3.2.7.1 Can We at Least Regulate or Forbid Advertisement?

Pharmaceutical advertising promotes prescription drugs to patients or healthcare professionals. Direct-to-consumer advertising (DTCA) seems to be allowed only in the United States and New Zealand (Khokhar et al. 2022). The US$ 8.1 billion spent in DTCA in 2022 (Adams 2023) in the USA, up from US$ 3.2 billion in 2012 (Harvard Health Publishing 2017), attests for this segment's fast growth and relevance.

On the upside, DTCA raises awareness of new or existing treatment options, encourages patients to discuss them with their doctors, and may help lead to better decisions and outcomes. On the downside, it can be misleading or encourage excessive use or misuse of the drugs being advertised. That is why it requires strict regulations to ensure the ads are accurate and fair. Other countries chose not to allow DTCA probably because they do see many downsides and not enough upsides to the practice. A few other countries, such as Brazil, South Korea, and Japan, try to mitigate the downside by only allowing specific DTCA such as ads that raise awareness about medical conditions without promoting a specific drug.

The other much more common type of pharmaceutical promotion happens with salespeople visiting doctors, known as "detailing." (Larkin et al. 2017) While potentially useful to educate healthcare professionals about new treatments and promote better patient care, it can be unethical and increase healthcare costs, when tactics mislead healthcare professionals to over-prescribe expensive brand-name drugs in place of cheaper generic ones (Roughead et al. 1998). Many countries have introduced rules to increase transparency in pharmaceutical sales to doctors, but issues remain over knowing and thus policing what happens or is said within the confines of a doctor's office.

From a negotiation standpoint, broad education on the burden of the disease, direct pharmaceutical advertising (USA and New Zealand only), or detailing once the drug is on the market can strengthen drug companies' positions, often increasing the perceived need for and thus the perceived value of their drugs. This can make it harder for Pharma counterparties to negotiate lower prices or walk away from deals, as there may be more pressure from patients or doctors to make the drug available.

In this chapter, we have examined several social–political, financial, and legal and institutional challenges that constrain governments or payers in general, shape their negotiation mandates, and put significant pressure on P&R negotiations. We explored the ramifications of several different voices and ideas to help governments lower drug prices, and how they can create health, economic, and negotiation consequences to improve or worsen our healthcare. For now, one thing is clear: negotiating through win-lose methods can succeed in lowering prices, especially given Government's power advantage over Pharma companies and reliance on the USA to pay most of the bill. However, while such victories bring short-term benefits to Governments and their healthcare budgets, they also invite great resistance from Pharma, and may come with the unintended consequences of worsening drug access, innovation, quality, and the sustainability of the pharmaceutical industry. Or, one day, a reaction from the US Government.

Unfortunately, the access vs. innovation debate is complex, the pricing problem and patent shortcomings are real, and solutions are far from simple or obvious. The challenge for the Government or Payer in P&R negotiations is that the current system has distortions, biases, and abuses that need correction, but on balance no other system has yet proven more efficacious.

References

340B Health 340B Drug Pricing Program (n.d.). https://www.340bhealth.org/members/340b-program/overview/#:~:text=The%20340B%20law%20prohibits%20the,notice%20available%20on%20OPA's%20website

A French Habit is Spreading (2019). The Economist. https://www.economist.com/leaders/2019/03/07/a-french-habit-is-spreading

Abbas MZ (2019) Evergreening of pharmaceutical patents: a blithe disregard for the rationale of the patent system. J Generic Med: Bus J Generic Med Sector 15:53–60. https://doi.org/10.1177/1741134319848797

Adams B (2023) The top 10 pharma drug ad spenders for 2022. Fierce Pharma. https://www.fiercepharma.com/special-reports/top-10-pharma-drug-brand-ad-spenders-2022

Alcorn T (2018) Why Egypt is at the forefront of hepatitis C treatment. The Atlantic. https://www.theatlantic.com/health/archive/2018/05/why-egypt-is-at-the-forefront-of-hepatitis-c-treatment/561305/

Amadeo K (2014a) Health care costs facts. The Balance, In. https://www.thebalance.com/healthcare-costs-3306068

Amadeo K (2014b) Why preventive care lowers Health care costs. The Balance. https://www.thebalance.com/preventive-care-how-it-lowers-aca-costs-3306074

Amadeo K (2020) Universal health care in different countries, pros and cons of each. The Balance. https://www.thebalance.com/universal-health-care-4156211

Annemans L (2019) Do you know what a QALY is, and how to calculate it? C.E.L.forpharma. https://www.celforpharma.com/insight/do-you-know-what-qaly-and-how-calculate-it

Årdal C, Findlay D, Savic M, et al (2018) Revitalizing the antibiotic pipeline stimulating innovation while driving sustainable use and global access. DRIVE-AB REPORT

Årdal C, Lacotte Y, Ploy M-C (2020) Financing pull mechanisms for antibiotic-related innovation: opportunities for Europe. Clin Infect Dis 71:1994. https://doi.org/10.1093/cid/ciaa153

Ascherio A, Katan MB, Zock PL et al (1999) Trans fatty acids and coronary heart disease. N Engl J Med 340:1994–1998. https://doi.org/10.1056/nejm199906243402511

Association for Accessible Medicines (2023) 2023 U.S. Generic and Biosimilar Medicines Savings Report

Associazione Italiana di Oncologia Medica (2015) I Numeri del Cancro in Italia 2015. Intermedia Meditore

Austin D, Hayford T (2021) Research and Development in the pharmaceutical industry. Congressional Budget Office. https://www.cbo.gov/publication/57126
Australian Institute of Health and Welfare (2017) Australia's hospitals 2015–16 at a glance
Avery M (2008) Continuing abuse of the hatch-Waxman act by pharmaceutical patent holders and the failure of the 2003 amendments. Hastings Law J 60:171
Avorn J (2015) The $2.6 billion pill–methodologic and policy considerations. N Engl J Med 372:1877. https://doi.org/10.1056/NEJMp1500848
Baker BK (2020) Access to medicines activism: collaboration, conflicts, and complementarities. Intellectual property law and the right to Health: a history of TRIPs and access to medicine (Srividhya Ragavan & Amaka Vanni eds., 2020 Forthcoming); Northeastern University School of law research paper no. 369-2020. SSRN. https://ssrn.com/abstract=3538270. Accessed 1 Jan 2024
Barlas S (2019) Are hospital prices a bigger problem than drug prices?: congress doesn't know, doesn't care. PubMed 44:259–299
Barrett P (2018) Interest-growth differentials and debt limits in advanced economies. IMF Working Papers 18(1):1. https://doi.org/10.5089/9781484350980.001
Barrett B, Charles JW, Temte JL (2015) Climate change, human health, and epidemiological transition. Prev Med 70:69–75. https://doi.org/10.1016/j.ypmed.2014.11.013
Bates C, Laciak R, Southwick A, Bishoff J (2011) Overprescription of postoperative narcotics: a look at postoperative pain medication delivery, consumption and disposal in urological practice. J Urol 185:551–555. https://doi.org/10.1016/j.juro.2010.09.088
Becker-Witt C, Weißhuhn TER, Lüdtke R, Willich SN (2003) Quality assessment of physical research in homeopathy. J Altern Complement Med 9:113–132. https://doi.org/10.1089/107555303321222991
Bell RS (2019) Does hybrid health care improve public health services? Lessons learned from Australia. drbobbell.com. https://drbobbell.com/does-hybrid-health-care-improve-public-health-services-lessons-learned-from-australia/
Bertram LAC, Stefanick ML, Saquib N et al (2010) Physical activity, additional breast cancer events, and mortality among early-stage breast cancer survivors: findings from the WHEL study. Cancer Causes Control 22:427–435. https://doi.org/10.1007/s10552-010-9714-3
Blit J (2017) Are patents really necessary? Centre for international governance innovation. https://www.cigionline.org/articles/are-patents-really-necessary. Accessed 1 Jan 2024
Bloomberg (2016) How to sell a $1000 pill for $10 without losing money. The Irish Times
Boldrin M, Levine DK (2013) The case against patents. J Econ Perspect 27:3–22. https://doi.org/10.1257/jep.27.1.3
Bonaime AA, Wang Y (2024) Mergers, product prices, and innovation: evidence from the pharmaceutical industry. J Financ 79:2195. https://doi.org/10.1111/jofi.13321
Bor J, Cohen GH, Galea S (2017) Population health in an era of rising income inequality: USA, 1980–2015. Lancet 389:1475–1490. https://doi.org/10.1016/s0140-6736(17)30571-8
Boseley S (2018) Why do new medicines cost so much, and what can we do about it? The Guardian. https://www.theguardian.com/news/2018/apr/09/why-do-new-medicines-cost-so-much-and-what-can-we-do-about-it
Bosworth A, Sheingold S, Finegold K et al (2022) Price increases for prescription drugs, 2016–2022. ASPE. https://aspe.hhs.gov/reports/prescription-drug-price-increases
Bowe C, Colitt R (2005) Brazil to break patent on Abbott AIDS drug. @FinancialTimes. https://www.ft.com/content/816699fe-e50a-11d9-95f3-00000e2511c8. Accessed 1 Jan 2024
Brazil M (2005) Purdue pharma loses OxyContin patent appeal. Nat Rev Drug Discov 4:620–620. https://doi.org/10.1038/nrd1820
Brennan T, Shrank W (2014) New expensive treatments for hepatitis C infection. JAMA 312:593. https://doi.org/10.1001/jama.2014.8897
Britton J (2017) Death, disease, and tobacco. Lancet 389:1861–1862. https://doi.org/10.1016/S0140-6736(17)30867-X

Brouard C, Le Strat Y, Larsen C et al (2015) The undiagnosed chronically-infected HCV population in France. Implications for expanded testing recommendations in 2014. PLoS One 10:e0126920. https://doi.org/10.1371/journal.pone.0126920
Campion EW, Avorn J, Reder VA, Olins NJ (1987) Overmedication of the low-weight elderly. Arch Intern Med 147:945. https://doi.org/10.1001/archinte.1987.00370050137023
Campos A, Gomes C (2014) Portugal joins other countries to lower price of hepatitis C medicine. Público. https://www.publico.pt/2014/06/14/sociedade/noticia/laboratorio-que-produz-medicamento-inovador-ara-hepatite-c-apoia-associacao-de-doentes-1639662. Accessed 1 Jan 2024
Campos Mello P (2019) Cost of Hepatitis C drug price skyrockets 1,422% after patent approval. Folha de S.Paulo. https://www1.folha.uol.com.br/internacional/en/scienceandhealth/2019/10/cost-of-hepatitis-c-drug-price-skyrockets-1422-after-patent-approval.shtml. Accessed 1 Jan 2024
Carrillo P, Pomeranz D, Singhal M (2017) Dodging the taxman: firm misreporting and limits to tax enforcement. Am Econ J Appl Econ 9:144–164. https://doi.org/10.1257/app.20140495
Chang H-J (2012) 23 things they Don't tell you about capitalism. Bloomsbury Press
Chang AY, Skirbekk VF, Tyrovolas S et al (2019) Measuring population ageing: an analysis of the global burden of disease study 2017. Lancet Public Health 4:e159–e167. https://doi.org/10.1016/s2468-2667(19)30019-2
Cherian NG (2016) Using compulsory licenses to access pharmaceuticals: a cross case analysis on outcomes. https://www.researchgate.net/publication/350904332_Using_Compulsory_Licenses_to_access_pharmaceuticals_A_Cross_Case_Analysis_on_Outcomes
Choi H, Schoeni RF (2017) Health of Americans who must work longer to reach social security retirement age. Health Aff 36:1815–1819. https://doi.org/10.1377/hlthaff.2017.0217
Citizens for Tax Justice (2012) Big no-tax corps just keep on dodging. Citizens for Tax Justice (CTJ)
Cohen JP (2023) Humira Biosimilars not gaining traction epitomizes dysfunctional U.S. System. Forbes
Comanor WS, Scherer FM (2013) Mergers and innovation in the pharmaceutical industry. J Health Econ 32:106–113. https://doi.org/10.1016/j.jhealeco.2012.09.006
Committee for a Responsible Federal Budget (2019) Why should we worry about the National Debt? Committee for a Responsible Federal Budget. http://www.crfb.org/papers/why-should-we-worry-about-national-debt
Conseil d'orientation des retraites (COR) (2020) Rapport du COR mars 2006–Retraites: perspectives 2020 et 2050. https://www.cor-retraites.fr/rapports-du-cor/rapport-cor-mars-2006-retraites-perspectives-2020-2050. Accessed 1 Jan 2024
Coppola F (2018) Everything you've been told about government debt is wrong. Forbes
Countryeconomy (2024) Country comparison Denmark vs India 2024. countryeconomy.com. https://countryeconomy.com/countries/compare/denmark/india. Accessed 1 Jan 2024
Cox J (2013) Surprise! Big pharma Don't want developing countries having access to cheap medicine. VICE. https://www.vice.com/en/article/american-lobbyists-are-fighting-to-halt-the-availability-of-affordable-medicine-to-the-3rd-world/. Accessed 1 Jan 2024
Cox J (2019) Government debt hits record $66 trillion, 80% of global GDP, Fitch says. CNBC. https://www.cnbc.com/2019/01/23/government-debt-tab-hits-66-trillion-80percent-of-global-gdp-fitch-says.html. Accessed 1 Jan 2024
Crimmins EM, Beltran-Sanchez H (2010) Mortality and morbidity trends: is there compression of morbidity? J Gerontol Ser B Psychol Sci Soc Sci 66B:75–86. https://doi.org/10.1093/geronb/gbq088
Dana KN, Hertig JB, Weber RJ (2017) Drug pricing transparency: the new retail revolution. Hosp Pharm 52:155–159. https://doi.org/10.1310/hpj5202-155
Day M (2007) Threat to break patents saves Brazil $1bn in cost of HIV treatment. BMJ 335:1065. https://doi.org/10.1136/bmj.39402.515706.db
DeArment A (2018) Report blames gaming of patent system for high drug prices. MedCity News. https://medcitynews.com/2018/08/report-blames-gaming-of-patent-system-for-high-drug-prices/?rf=1. Accessed 1 Jan 2024

Deloitte (2023) Pharma R&D return on investment falls in post-pandemic market | Deloitte UK. www.deloitte.com. https://www.deloitte.com/uk/en/about/press-room/pharma-r-d-return-on-investment-falls-in-post-pandemic-market.html

Detollenaere J, Desmarest A-S, Boeckxstaens P, Willems S (2018) The link between income inequality and health in Europe, adding strength dimensions of primary care to the equation. Soc Sci Med 201:103–110. https://doi.org/10.1016/j.socscimed.2018.01.041

DiMasi JA, Bryant NR, Lasagna L (1991a) New drug development in the United States from 1963 to 1990. Clin Pharmacol Ther 50:471–486. https://doi.org/10.1038/clpt.1991.172

DiMasi JA, Hansen RW, Grabowski HG, Lasagna L (1991b) Cost of innovation in the pharmaceutical industry. J Health Econ 10:107–142. https://doi.org/10.1016/0167-6296(91)90001-4

DiMasi JA, Hansen RW, Grabowski HG (2003) The price of innovation: new estimates of drug development costs. J Health Econ 22:151–185. https://doi.org/10.1016/S0167-6296(02)00126-1

DiMasi JA, Grabowski HG, Hansen RW (2016) Innovation in the pharmaceutical industry: new estimates of R&D costs. J Health Econ 47:20–33. https://doi.org/10.1016/j.jhealeco.2016.01.012

Dixit SK, Sambasivan M (2018) A review of the Australian healthcare system: a policy perspective. SAGE Open Med 6:1–14. https://doi.org/10.1177/2050312118769211

Donohoe M (2004) Luxury primary care, academic medical centers, and the erosion of science and professional ethics. J Gen Intern Med 19:90–94. https://doi.org/10.1111/j.1525-1497.2004.20631.x

Druss BG, Marcus SC, Olfson M, Pincus HA (2004) Listening To Generic Prozac: Winners, Losers, And Sideliners. Health Aff 23:210–216. https://doi.org/10.1377/hlthaff.23.5.210

Duhigg C, Kocieniewski D (2012) Apple's tax strategy aims at low-tax states and nations. The New York Times

Economic Benefits of the Patent System (2010) ALRC. https://www.alrc.gov.au/publication/genes-and-ingenuity-gene-patenting-and-human-health-alrc-report-99/2-the-patent-system/economic-benefits-of-the-patent-system/

EFPIA (2019) The pharmaceutical industry in figures. EFPIA

EFPIA (2023) The pharmaceutical industry in figures

Ekpu VU, Brown AK (2015) The economic impact of smoking and of reducing smoking prevalence: review of evidence. Tobacco Use Insights 8:TUI.S15628. https://doi.org/10.4137/tui.s15628

Emanuel EJ, Emanuel LL (1992) Four models of the physician-patient relationship. JAMA 267:2221–2226. https://doi.org/10.1001/jama.267.16.2221

European Economy Series (2015) The 2015 ageing report: economic and budgetary projections for the 28 EU member states (2013–2060). European Commission

Eurostat Demography of Europe (2024) edition

Fagerlund N, Rasmussen SB (2005) AstraZeneca: the first abuse case in the pharmaceutical sector. Compet Policy Newsl 3

Faunce TA, Lexchin J (2007) "Linkage" pharmaceutical evergreening in Canada and Australia. Aust N Zeal Health Policy 4. https://doi.org/10.1186/1743-8462-4-8

Faunce T, Vines T, Gibbons H (2008) New forms of evergreening in Australia: misleading advertising, enantiomers and data exclusivity: Apotex v Servier and Alphapharm v Lundbeck. J Law Med 16:220–232

Feldman R (2018) May your drug price be evergreen. J Law Biosci 5:590–647. https://doi.org/10.1093/jlb/lsy022

Feldman WB, Rome BN, Raimond VC et al (2021) Estimating rebates and other discounts received by Medicare part D. JAMA Health Forum 2:e210626. https://doi.org/10.1001/jamahealthforum.2021.0626

Flume M, Bardou M, Capri S et al (2018) Approaches to manage 'affordability' of high budget impact medicines in key EU countries. J Market Access Health Policy 6:1478539. https://doi.org/10.1080/20016689.2018.1478539

Frick M, McKenna L (2019) A pharma view on Delinkage and new models for biomedical innovation: an interview with Marc Destito from Otsuka Pharmaceutical. Treatment Action Group. https://www.treatmentactiongroup.org/resources/tagline/tagline-fall-2018/a-pharma-view-on-

delinkage-and-new-models-for-biomedical-innovation-an-interview-with-marc-destito-from-otsuka-pharmaceutical/. Accessed 1 Jan 2024
Fulgham J (2018) Homeopathy. Sciencebasedmedicine.org. https://sciencebasedmedicine.org/reference/homeopathy/
Gallus S, Muttarak R, Martínez-Sánchez JM et al (2011) Smoking prevalence and smoking attributable mortality in Italy, 2010. Prev Med 52:434–438. https://doi.org/10.1016/j.ypmed.2011.03.011
Gamage D (2019) Five Key research findings on wealth taxation for the super rich. SSRN Electron J. https://doi.org/10.2139/ssrn.3427827
Garcia MI, Pygall A, Roy B (2022) Under the antitrust spotlight: patent litigation. Stephenson Harwood LLP. https://www.shlegal.com/insights/under-the-antitrust-spotlight-patent-litigation. Accessed 1 Jan 2023
Gleeson D, Moir H (2014) Explainer: evergreening and how big pharma keeps drug prices high. The Conversation. https://theconversation.com/explainer-evergreening-and-how-big-pharma-keeps-drug-prices-high-33623
Goodchild M, Nargis N, Tursan d'Espaignet E (2017) Global economic cost of smoking-attributable diseases. Tob Control 27:58–64. https://doi.org/10.1136/tobaccocontrol-2016-053305
Grandjean P, Landrigan PJ (2014) Neurobehavioural effects of developmental toxicity. Lancet Neurol 13:330–338. https://doi.org/10.1016/s1474-4422(13)70278-3
Greenberg J (2019) Skeptic of Elizabeth Warren's plan says 10 European countries scrapped wealth taxes. @politifact. https://www.politifact.com/punditfact/statements/2019/may/10/joel-griffith/some-countries-ditched-wealth-taxes-what-might-mea/. Accessed 1 Jan 2024
Gualano MR, Bert F, Scaioli G et al (2014) Smoking ban policies in Italy and the potential impact of the so-called Sirchia law: state of the art after eight years. Biomed Res Int 2014:1–6. https://doi.org/10.1155/2014/293219
Hargreaves B (2019) The scale of generic uptake in the major markets. Outsourcing Pharma. https://www.outsourcing-pharma.com/Article/2019/11/01/Top-countries-by-generics-share-of-market
Harris R (2017) R&D costs for cancer drugs are likely much less than industry claims, study finds. NPR. https://www.npr.org/sections/health-shots/2017/09/11/550135932/r-d-costs-for-cancer-drugs-are-likely-much-less-than-industry-claims-study-finds#:~:text=Richard%20Harris-,R%26D%20Costs%20For%20Cancer%20Drugs%20Are%20Likely,Than%20Industry%20Claims%2C%20Study%20Finds&text=iStockphoto%2FGetty%20Images-,A%20study%20of%20chemotherapy%20medicines%20produced%20by%2010%20companies%20found,cost%20in%20research%20and%20development
Harrison C (2008) News analysis. Nat Rev Drug Discov 7:112–113. https://doi.org/10.1038/nrd2516
Harvard Health Publishing (2017) Do not get sold on drug advertising–Harvard Health. Harvard Health. https://www.health.harvard.edu/medications/do-not-get-sold-on-drug-advertising
Haucap J, Stiebale J (2016) How mergers affect innovation: theory and evidence from the pharmaceutical industry. Handle.net
He AJ (2014) The doctor-patient relationship, defensive medicine and overprescription in Chinese public hospitals: evidence from a cross-sectional survey in Shenzhen city. Soc Sci Med 123:64–71. https://doi.org/10.1016/j.socscimed.2014.10.055
Health OECD (2015) Focus health spending 2015. OECD Health
Heather Bresch (2016) Testimony of Mylan CEO Heather Bresch before the United States house of representatives committee on oversight and government reform
Henig RM (2013) Young Americans are sicker than ever. Psychol Today. https://www.psychologytoday.com/us/blog/cusp/201312/young-americans-are-sicker-ever. Accessed 1 Jan 2024
Henschke C, Sundmacher L, Busse R (2013) Structural changes in the German pharmaceutical market: Price setting mechanisms based on the early benefit evaluation. Health Policy 109:263–269. https://doi.org/10.1016/j.healthpol.2012.12.005
Hernandez I, San-Juan-Rodriguez A, Good CB, Gellad WF (2020) Changes in list prices, net prices, and discounts for branded drugs in the US, 2007-2018. JAMA 323:854. https://doi.org/10.1001/jama.2020.1012

Himmelstein DU, Woolhandler S (2016) The current and projected taxpayer shares of US Health costs. Am J Public Health 106:449–452. https://doi.org/10.2105/ajph.2015.302997
Hoen E (2017) Growing consensus on importance of delinkage in pharmaceutical R&D. Delinkage. https://delinkage.org/growing-consensus-importance-delinkage-pharmaceutical-rd/. Accessed 1 Jan 2024
Hoen E (2020) Time for new pharmaceutical-innovation models. Med Law Policy. https://medicineslawandpolicy.org/2020/02/time-for-new-pharmaceutical-innovation-models/
Huang C-C, Frentz N (2014) What really is the evidence on taxes and growth? Center on Budget and Policy Priorities. https://www.cbpp.org/research/what-really-is-the-evidence-on-taxes-and-growth
Huet N (2014) France uses tax to put pressure on hepatitis C drug prices. Reuters. https://www.reuters.com/article/france-deficit-gilead/france-uses-tax-to-put-pressure-on-hepatitis-c-drug-prices-idUSL6N0RV27X20140930. Accessed 1 Jan 2024
I-MAK (2015) Patent challenges in five countries dispute validity of Gilead's claims to Hep C drug patents that block treatment for up to 59 million people. PR Newswire https://www.prnewswire.com/in/news-releases/patent-challenges-in-five-countries-dispute-validity-of-gileads-claims-to-hep-c-drug-patents-that-block-treatment-for-up-to-59-million-people-504402391.html. Accessed 1 Jan 2024
I-MAK (2018a) How excessive pharmaceutical patenting is extending monopolies and driving up drug prices
I-MAK (2018b) Major win for patients as Brazil rejects a key patent on Gilead hepatitis C Drug and European court of justice opinion Denies patent extension to Gilead's HIV Drug. I-mak.org. https://www.i-mak.org/2018/05/04/brazil-rejects-key-patent-eu-denies-patent-extension/. Accessed 1 Jan 2024
IMS Institute (2016) Price declines after branded medicines lose exclusivity in the U.S. IMS Institute for Healthcare Informatics
Institute for Health Metrics and Evaluation (2017) Findings from the global burden of disease study 2017
Institute of Medicine and National Research Council (2013) U.S. health in international perspective: shorter lives, poorer health. The National Academies Press, Washington, DC
International Generic and Biosimilar Medicines Association (2019) Trade Principles: Generic and Biosimilar Medicines
Islami F, Torre LA, Jemal A (2015) Global trends of lung cancer mortality and smoking prevalence. Trans Lung Cancer Res 4:327–338. https://doi.org/10.3978/j.issn.2218-6751.2015.08.04
Jahnsen K, Pomerleau K (2017) Corporate income tax rates around the world, 2017. Tax Foundation
Janssen Pharmaceutical Companies of Johnson & Johnson (2019) Transforming lives, advancing hope–2019 Janssen U.S. transparency report. https://transparencyreport.janssen.com/_document/janssen-2019-transparency-report?id=00000186-0e8d-da28-a1fe-9edd7e550001
Jeantet M, Lopez A, Destais N (2014) Evaluation médico-économique en santé. Inspection Générale des Affaires Sociales (IGAS)
Johnson G, Brough WT (2019) Big pharma is abusing patents, and it's hurting Americans. CNN Business. https://edition.cnn.com/2019/09/12/perspectives/drug-patents-abuse/index.html
Kaeding N, Pomerleau K (2019) Sen. Warren's Wealth Tax Is Problematic. Tax Foundation. https://taxfoundation.org/warren-wealth-tax/
Kelland K (2015) Gilead faces challenge to European patent on pricey hep C drug. Reuters
Kennedy J (2019) The link between drug prices and research on the next generation of cures. itif.org. https://itif.org/publications/2019/09/09/link-between-drug-prices-and-research-next-generation-cures/
Keown A (2018) A small Group of Pharma Companies is Making the bulk of medicines necessary for developing countries. BioSpace. https://www.biospace.com/article/a-small-group-of-pharma-companies-is-making-the-bulk-of-medicines-necessary-for-developing-countries/. Accessed 1 Jan 2024
Kertscher T (2019) 20% of health costs are for prescription drugs? Presidential candidate Amy Klobuchar's claim is close. @politifact. https://www.politifact.com/truth-o-meter/state-

ments/2019/feb/22/amy-klobuchar/20-health-costs-are-prescription-drugs-presidentia/. Accessed 1 Jan 2024

Kesselheim AS, Avorn J, Sarpatwari A (2016) The high cost of prescription drugs in the United States. JAMA 316:858. https://doi.org/10.1001/jama.2016.11237

Key S (2017) In today's market, do patents even matter? Forbes. https://www.forbes.com/sites/stephenkey/2017/11/13/in-todays-market-do-patents-even-matter/

Khokhar B, Weathers S, Joseph Mattingly T (2022) Direct-to-consumer advertising and the advancement of the quadruple aim: a narrative review. JACCP: journal of the American college of. Clin Pharm 5:459–466. https://doi.org/10.1002/jac5.1599

Kirzinger A, Lopes L, Wu B, Brodie M (2019) KFF Health tracking poll—February 2019: prescription drugs. The Henry J. Kaiser Family Foundation. https://www.kff.org/health-reform/poll-finding/kff-health-tracking-poll-february-2019-prescription-drugs/

Knowledge Ecology International (2015) Support for the Delinkage of the Costs of R&D and the Price of Medicines. https://www.keionline.org/book/support-for-the-delinkage-of-the-costs-of-r-d-and-the-price-of-medicines. Accessed 1 Jan 2024

Knowler WC, Barrett-Connor E, Fowler SE et al (2002) Reduction in the incidence of type 2 diabetes with lifestyle intervention or metformin. N Engl J Med 346:393–403

Komendant E (2019) Pharmaceutical patent abuse: to infinity and beyond! Association for Accessible Medicine. https://accessiblemeds.org/resources/blog/pharmaceutical-patent-abuse-infinity-and-beyond

Koyuncu DrA (2023) Germany to enact new law with significant changes to drug pricing and reimbursement rules. Inside EU Life Sciences. https://www.insideeulifesciences.com/2023/07/05/germany-to-enact-new-law-with-significant-changes-to-drug-pricing-and-reimbursement-rules/

Koyuncu DrA, Aretz DrM (2024) Germany again to reform drug pricing and reimbursement laws—with "confidential reimbursements prices" that impede international reference pricing. Inside EU Life Sciences. https://www.insideeulifesciences.com/2024/02/16/germany-again-to-reform-drug-pricing-and-reimbursement-laws-with-confidential-reimbursements-prices-that-impede-international-reference-pricing/

Kupferschmidt K (2010) Germany moves to lower drug prices. Can Med Assoc J 183:E77–E78. https://doi.org/10.1503/cmaj.109-3759

Labonte R (2015) Medical tourism isn't always a fair deal for developing countries. The Conversation. https://theconversation.com/medical-tourism-isnt-always-a-fair-deal-for-developing-countries-37691

LaMattina J (2013) India's solution to drug costs: ignore patents and control prices–except for home grown drugs. Forbes

Larkin I, Ang D, Steinhart J et al (2017) Association between Academic Medical Center pharmaceutical detailing policies and physician prescribing. JAMA 317:1785–1795. https://doi.org/10.1001/jama.2017.4039

Le News (2016) Swiss parliament rejects tobacco advertising ban. Le News. http://lenews.ch/2016/12/08/swiss-parliament-rejects-tobacco-advertising-ban/. Accessed 1 Jan 2024

Le News (2017) Government stops tax rises on Swiss cigarettes. Le News. http://lenews.ch/2017/03/01/government-stops-tax-rises-on-swiss-cigarettes/. Accessed 1 Jan 2024

Ledley FD, McCoy SS, Vaughan G, Cleary EG (2020) Profitability of large pharmaceutical companies compared with other large public companies. JAMA 323:834. https://doi.org/10.1001/jama.2020.0442

Lee C (2018) Chinese Healthcare trends: rising hospital privatization. Collective Responsibility. https://www.coresponsibility.com/chinese-healthcare-trends-rising-hospital-privatization/

Leonard K (2016) Could universal Health care save U.S. taxpayers money? US News & World Report. https://www.usnews.com/news/blogs/data-mine/2016/01/22/could-universal-health-care-save-us-taxpayers-money

Li Y (2019) The stock market's gain in the last 10 years is one of its best runs since the 1800s. CNBC. https://www.cnbc.com/2019/03/15/the-stock-markets-gain-in-the-last-10-years-is-one-of-its-best-runs-since-the-1800s.html

Li Y, Xu J, Wang F et al (2012) Overprescribing in China, driven by financial incentives, results in very high use of antibiotics, injections, and corticosteroids. Health Aff 31:1075–1082. https://doi.org/10.1377/hlthaff.2010.0965
Llor C, Bjerrum L (2014) Antimicrobial resistance: risk associated with antibiotic overuse and initiatives to reduce the problem. Therapeutic Adv Drug Safety 5:229–241. https://doi.org/10.1177/2042098614554919
Lowe D (2021) Novartis loses the Glivec patent fight in India. Science.org. https://doi.org/10.1126/blog-post.3400
Luthi S, Owermohle S (2019) "Patent thicket" bill caught in tug-of-war over drug pricing reforms. POLITICO. https://www.politico.com/news/2019/10/25/patent-thicket-bill-caught-in-tug-of-war-over-drug-pricing-reforms-056858
Mack K (2006) Reforming inequitable conduct to improve patent quality: cleansing unclean hands. Berkeley Technol Law J 21:147–175. https://doi.org/10.2307/24119536
Macmillan Cancer Support (2019) Prehabilitation for people with cancer: principles and guidance for prehabilitation within the management and support of people with cancer
Maddox J, Randi J, Stewart WW (1988) "High-dilution" experiments a delusion. Nature 334:287–290. https://doi.org/10.1038/334287a0
Mahdavi E (2017) Patents and the pharmaceutical industry. Calif Manag Rev. https://cmr.berkeley.edu/2017/05/patents-and-pharmaceuticals/
Makary MA, Overton HN, Wang P (2017) Overprescribing is major contributor to opioid crisis. BMJ 359:j4792. https://doi.org/10.1136/bmj.j4792
Marschang S (2019) UK action on AMR: pushing for an antibiotic de-linkage model. EPHA. https://epha.org/uk-action-amr-antibiotic-delinkage-model/. Accessed 1 Jan 2024
Massarani L (2024) Brazil to breaks patent on Merck's AIDS drug. Business & Human Rights Resource Centre. https://www.business-humanrights.org/en/brazil-to-breaks-patent-on-mercks-aids-drug. Accessed 1 Jan 2024
Matthews D (2014) Optimistic facts and charts that show the world is getting much, much better. Vox. https://www.vox.com/2014/11/24/7272929/global-poverty-health-crime-literacy-good-news
McBride W (2012) What is the evidence on taxes and growth? Tax Foundation. https://taxfoundation.org/research/all/federal/what-evidence-taxes-and-growth/
McCorvey JJ (2015) How drug company Gilead outpaces its competitors—and common diseases. Fast Company. https://www.fastcompany.com/3041565/how-drug-company-gilead-outpaces-its-competitors-and-common-d
McDermott E (2019) Bipartisan agreement that drug prices are a problem (and patents are complicated) could mean changes for pharma. IPWatchdog. https://www.ipwatchdog.com/2019/05/08/bipartisan-agreement-drug-prices-problem-patents-complicated-mean-changes-pharma/id=109068/. Accessed 1 Jan 2024
McGuire T (2019) Do high local taxes really hurt economic growth? Kellogg Insight. https://insight.kellogg.northwestern.edu/article/local-tax-policy-economic-growth
McMichael AJ (2013) Globalization, climate change, and human Health. N Engl J Med 369:94–96. https://doi.org/10.1056/nejmc1305749
Medicines Patent Pool (2020) Global Licence Overview. https://medicinespatentpool.org/what-we-do/global-licence-overview/licences-in-the-mpp/. Accessed 1 Jan 2024
Meletiadis N (2018) Public private partnerships and constitutional law. Routledge
Mikulic M (2024) Global pharmaceutical R&D spending 2010–2024. Statista. https://www.statista.com/statistics/309466/global-r-and-d-expenditure-for-pharmaceuticals/
Miller SM, Russek FS (1997) Fiscal structures and economic growth: international evidence. Econ Inq 35:603–613. https://doi.org/10.1111/j.1465-7295.1997.tb02036.x
Minnella EM, Carli F (2018) Prehabilitation and functional recovery for colorectal cancer patients. Eur J Surg Oncol 44:919–926. https://doi.org/10.1016/j.ejso.2018.04.016
Mofffatt M (2019) The economic effect of tariffs. ThoughtCo. https://www.thoughtco.com/the-economic-effect-of-tariffs-1146368

Mokdad AH, Mensah GA, Krish V et al (2019) Global, regional, national, and subnational big data to inform Health equity research: perspectives from the global burden of disease study 2017. Ethn Dis 29:159–172. https://doi.org/10.18865/ed.29.s1.159
Moon S (2019) Price transparency in medicines markets–scrutinizing evidence behind the claims. Health Policy Watch. https://healthpolicy-watch.news/price-transparency-in-medicines-markets-scrutinizing-evidence-behind-the-claims/. Accessed 1 Jan 2024
Morris MC, Evans DA, Tangney CC et al (2006) Dietary copper and high saturated and trans fat intakes associated with cognitive decline. Arch Neurol 63:1085. https://doi.org/10.1001/archneur.63.8.1085
Mouterde A-L, Bocquet F, Fusier I, Paubel P (2016) Hepatitis C: how has France limited the expenses related to new treatments? Expert Rev Pharmacoecon Outcomes Res 16:655–657. https://doi.org/10.1080/14737167.2016.1247696
Mozaffarian D, Stampfer MJ (2010) Removing industrial trans fat from foods. BMJ 340:c1826–c1826. https://doi.org/10.1136/bmj.c1826
Mozaffarian D, Katan MB, Ascherio A et al (2006) Trans fatty acids and cardiovascular disease. N Engl J Med 354:1601–1613. https://doi.org/10.1056/nejmra054035
Mühlau P (2021) Middle class squeeze? Social class and perceived financial hardship in Ireland, 2002-2012. Econ Soc Rev 45:485–509
Mullaney T (2014) I have no qualms about taking Gilead's $84,000 drug. MarketWatch https://www.marketwatch.com/story/i-have-no-qualms-about-taking-gileads-84000-drug-2014-04-22. Accessed 1 Jan 2024
Murray CJL (2013) The state of US Health, 1990-2010. JAMA 310:591. https://doi.org/10.1001/jama.2013.13805
National Cancer Institute Drugs Approved for Melanoma (n.d.). https://www.cancer.gov/about-cancer/treatment/drugs/melanoma
Nawrat A (2019) From evergreening to thicketing: exploring the manipulation of pharma patents. Pharm Technol. https://www.pharmaceutical-technology.com/features/pharma-patents-manpulation/
Neumann PJ, Cohen JT (2018) QALYs in 2018—advantages and concerns. JAMA 319:2473. https://doi.org/10.1001/jama.2018.6072
Nicastri E, Bevilacqua N, Schepisi MS et al (2009) Accuracy of malaria diagnosis by microscopy, rapid diagnostic test, and PCR methods and evidence of antimalarial overprescription in non-severe febrile patients in two Tanzanian hospitals. Am J Trop Med Hyg 80:712–717. https://doi.org/10.4269/ajtmh.2009.80.712
OECD (2017a) Health resources–pharmaceutical spending–OECD data. The OECD. https://data.oecd.org/healthres/pharmaceutical-spending.htm#indicator-chart
OECD (2017b) Tackling antimicrobial resistance ensuring sustainable R&D: final note prepared by OECD, WHO, FAO and OIE
OECD (2018) The role and design of net Wealth Taxes in the OECD. OECD tax policy studies, no. 26. OECD Publishing
OECD (2019) Social inequalities in Health and Health systems. OECD Health Policy Studies. OECD Publishing, Paris
OECD (2022) Health resources–Health spending–OECD data. Organisation for Economic Co-operation and Development. https://data.oecd.org/healthres/health-spending.htm
OECD (2023) Health at a glance 2023. OECD Publishing
OECD (2024) Corporate tax statistics database. OECD. https://www.oecd.org/en/data/datasets/corporate-tax-statistics-database.html
Office of Policy, Performance and Evaluation Early Childhood Education. CDC Archive (n.d.). https://archive.cdc.gov/#/details?q=early%20childhood%20education&start=0&rows=10&url=https://www.cdc.gov/policy/hi5/earlychildhoodeducation/index.html
Organisation Mondiale De La Sante (2015) WHO report on the global tobacco epidemic, 2015: raising taxes on tobacco. WHO

Outterson K, McDonnell A (2016) Funding antibiotic innovation with vouchers: recommendations on how to strengthen a flawed incentive policy. Health Aff 35:784–790. https://doi.org/10.1377/hlthaff.2015.1139

Oxford J, Kozlov R (2013) Antibiotic resistance–a call to arms for primary healthcare providers. Int J Clin Pract 67:1–3. https://doi.org/10.1111/ijcp.12334

Papanicolas I, Woskie LR, Jha AK (2018) Health care spending in the United States and other high-income countries. JAMA 319:1024–1039. https://doi.org/10.1001/jama.2018.1150

Parasrampuria S, Murphy S (2022) Trends in prescription drug spending, 2015–2021. Office of the Assistant Secretary for Planning and Evaluation, U.S. Department of Health and Human Services, Washington, DC

Paris V, Docteur E (2008) Pharmaceutical pricing and reimbursement policies in Germany. OECD Health Working Papers. https://doi.org/10.1787/228483137521

Passiglia F, Calandri M, Guerrera F et al (2019) Lung cancer in Italy. J Thorac Oncol 14:2046–2052. https://doi.org/10.1016/j.jtho.2019.05.019

Pategou J (2019) The marriage of big pharma and biotech. Drug Dis Dev. https://www.drugdiscoverytrends.com/the-marriage-of-big-pharma-and-biotech/

Pearl R (2017) Why patent protection in the drug industry is out of control. Forbes

Phelan M, Cook C (2014) A treatment revolution for those who can afford it? Hepatitis C treatment: new medications, profits and patients. BMC Infect Dis 14. https://doi.org/10.1186/1471-2334-14-s6-s5

Plüss JD (2019a) Push for drug pricing transparency strikes a nerve with industry. SWI swissinfo.ch. https://www.swissinfo.ch/eng/world-health-assembly_push-for-drug-pricing-transparency-strikes-a-nerve-with-industry/44969974. Accessed 1 Jan 2024

Plüss JD (2019b) WHO adopts watered-down resolution on drug transparency. SWI swissinfo.ch. https://www.swissinfo.ch/eng/world-health-organization_who-adopts-watered-down-resolution-on-drug-transparency/44995340. Accessed 1 Jan 2024

Pomerlau K, Potosky E (2016) Corporate income tax rates around the world, 2016. Tax Foundation

PopulationPyramid.net (2024a) Population pyramids of the world from 1950 to 2100–world 1962. PopulationPyramid.net. https://www.populationpyramid.net/world/1962/

PopulationPyramid.net (2024b) Population pyramids of the world from 1950 to 2100–world 2019. PopulationPyramid.net. https://www.populationpyramid.net/world/2019/

PopulationPyramid.net (2024c) Population pyramids of the world from 1950 to 2100–world 2029. PopulationPyramid.net. https://www.populationpyramid.net/world/2029/

PopulationPyramid.net (2024d) Population pyramids of the world from 1950 to 2100–Europe 2029. PopulationPyramid.net. https://www.populationpyramid.net/europe/2029/

Prasad V, Mailankody S (2017) Research and Development spending to bring a single cancer drug to market and revenues after approval. JAMA Intern Med 177:1569. https://doi.org/10.1001/jamainternmed.2017.3601

Preidt R (2015) World's population is getting sicker, study shows. Healthday.com. https://www.healthday.com/health-news/neurology/world-s-population-is-getting-sicker-study-shows-700144.html. Accessed 1 Jan 2024

President's Cancer Panel (2008) Meeting summary: environmental factors in cancer. https://deainfo.nci.nih.gov/advisory/pcp/archive/pcp1208/summary.pdf

Pruitt-young S (2021) In China, kids are limited to playing video games for only 3 hours per week. NPR. https://www.npr.org/2021/08/30/1032489883/china-kids-video-games-limits

Public Eye (2017) Lack of transparency of R&D costs. https://www.publiceye.ch/en/topics/medicines/patents-and-access-to-med/transparency. Accessed 1 Jan 2024

Rafols I, Hopkins MM, Hoekman J et al (2014) Big pharma, little science?: a bibliometric perspective on big pharma's R&D decline. Technol Forecast Soc Chang 81:22–38. https://doi.org/10.1016/j.techfore.2012.06.007

Rand LZ, Kesselheim AS (2020) An international review of Health technology assessment approaches to prescription drugs and their ethical principles. J Law Med Ethics 48:583–594. https://doi.org/10.1177/1073110520958885

Reinaud F (2022) Pharma prices continue to rise in the US—or do they? Pharm Technol. https://www.pharmaceutical-technology.com/pricing-and-market-access/pharma-prices-us/?cf-view
Ritchie H, Rodés-Guirao L, Mathieu E, et al (2024) Population growth. Our World in Data. https://ourworldindata.org/world-population-growth#note-3. Accessed 1 Jan 2024
Roediger A (2019) Why transparency in drug pricing is more complicated than it seems. World Econ Forum. https://www.weforum.org/agenda/2019/10/transparency-drug-pricing/
Rome BN, Kesselheim AS (2020) Transferrable market exclusivity extensions to promote antibiotic development: an economic analysis. Clin Infect Dis 71:1671–1675
Rome BN, Egilman AC, Kesselheim AS (2022) Trends in prescription drug launch prices, 2008-2021. JAMA 327:2145. https://doi.org/10.1001/jama.2022.5542
Roser M, Ortiz-Ospina E (2013) Income inequality. Our World in Data. https://ourworldindata.org/income-inequality
Roth Z (2005) The monopoly factory. Washington Monthly https://washingtonmonthly.com/2005/06/01/the-monopoly-factory/. Accessed 1 Jan 2024
Roughead EE, Harvey KJ, Gilbert AL (1998) Commercial detailing techniques used by pharmaceutical representatives to influence prescribing. Aust N Z J Med 28:306–310. https://doi.org/10.1111/j.1445-5994.1998.tb01953.x
Russo R, Scafato E (2006) Fumo e Salute: Impatto Sociale e Costi Sanitari. [Smoking and Health: Social and Health Costs]
Ryan M, Sood N (2019) State drug pricing transparency Laws: numerous efforts, Most fall short. USC Schaeffer. https://healthpolicy.usc.edu/research/state-drug-pricing-transparency-laws-numerous-efforts-most-fall-short/
S.2210–110th Congress (2007–2008) (2007) Medical Innovation Prize Act of 2007
Saez C (2019) Several ministers of Health speak up for drug market transparency, lower prices at WHA side event–Health policy watch. Health Policy Watch. https://www.healthpolicy-watch.org/several-ministers-of-health-speak-up-for-drug-market-transparency-lower-prices-at-wha-side-event/. Accessed 1 Jan 2024
Safer D (2000) Are stimulants overprescribed for youths with ADHD? Ann Clin Psychiatry 12:55–62. https://doi.org/10.3109/10401230009147088
Sagonowsky E (2017) Pharma's pervasive "evergreening" is driving prices up, study says. Fierce Pharma. https://www.fiercepharma.com/pharma/pharma-s-pervasive-evergreening-driving-prices-up-study-says
Sandoval R, Belausteguigoitia I, Hennis A (2016) The case of tobacco taxation: where we are and how to accelerate its use for public health. Rev Panam Salud Publica 40:200–201
Sarnak DO, Squires D, Kuzmak G, Bishop S (2017) Paying for prescription drugs around the world: why is the U.S. an outlier? PubMed 2017:1–14
Shapiro C (2000) Navigating the patent thicket: cross licenses, patent pools, and standard setting. Innov Policy Econ 1:119–150. https://doi.org/10.1086/ipe.1.25056143
Shaw B, Mestre-Ferrandiz J (2020) Talkin' about a resolution: issues in the push for greater transparency of medicine prices. Pharmacoeconomics 38:125–134. https://doi.org/10.1007/s40273-019-00877-3
Shaw B, Mestre-Ferrandiz J, Klein Wassink E (2023) Profitability in the global pharmaceutical industry: a contested space. ISPOR | international Society for Pharmacoeconomics and outcomes research. https://www.ispor.org/conferences-education/conferences/past-conferences/ispor-europe-2023/program/program/session/euro2023-3786/130819. Accessed 1 Jan 2024
Shaxson N (2011) 10 reasons we should tax corporations. The Guardian
Shepherd JM (2018) Consolidation and innovation in the pharmaceutical industry: the role of mergers and acquisitions in the current innovation ecosystem. J Healthcare Law Policy 21
Shrank WH, Hoang T, Ettner SL et al (2006) The implications of choice. Arch Intern Med 166:332. https://doi.org/10.1001/archinte.166.3.332
Silver JK, Baima J (2013) Cancer prehabilitation. Am J Phys Med Rehabil 92:715–727. https://doi.org/10.1097/phm.0b013e31829b4afe
Smith BL (2012) Inappropriate prescribing. American Psychological Association

Smith C (2022) The consequences of New York's proposed beverage tax. Citizens Against Government Waste. https://www.cagw.org/thewastewatcher/consequences-new-yorks-proposed-beverage-tax

Spellberg B (2011) Combating antimicrobial resistance: policy recommendations to save lives. Clin Infect Dis 52:S397–S428. https://doi.org/10.1093/cid/cir153

Stender S, Dyerberg J, Astrup A (2006) High levels of industrially produced trans fat in popular fast foods. N Engl J Med 354:1650–1652. https://doi.org/10.1056/nejmc052959

Stevens P, Ezell S (2020) Delinkage debunked: why replacing patents with prizes for drug development won't work. itif.org. https://itif.org/publications/2020/02/03/delinkage-debunked-why-replacing-patents-prizes-drug-development-wont-work. Accessed 1 Jan 2021

Streif F (2015) Tax competition in Europe–Europe in competition with other world regions? Discussion paper no. 15-082. ZEW-Center for European Economic Research

Stubbington T (2019) Global debt surges to highest level in peacetime: world's major economies have debts on average of more than 70% of GDP. @FinancialTimes. https://www.ft.com/content/661f5c8a-dec9-11e9-9743-db5a370481bc

Taber JM, Leyva B, Persoskie A (2015) Why do people avoid medical care? A qualitative study using National Data. J Gen Intern Med 30:290–297. https://doi.org/10.1007/s11606-014-3089-1

Tax Policy Center (2020) How do taxes affect the economy in the long run? Tax Policy Center. https://www.taxpolicycenter.org/briefing-book/how-do-taxes-affect-economy-long-run

Teitelman R (2019) Big pharma can't resist big mergers. Here's why. Barron's online. https://www.barrons.com/articles/pharmaceutical-companies-mergers-51550430327

Tett G (2014) Which middle class, which squeeze? @FinancialTimes. https://www.ft.com/content/c34696d6-8ec4-11e3-b6f1-00144feab7de. Accessed 1 Jan 2024

The Campaign for Sustainable Rx Pricing The Truth About Big Pharma's Patent Abuse (n.d.) CSRXP. https://www.csrxp.org/the-truth-about-big-pharmas-patent-abuse/

Tirrell M (2017) Johnson & Johnson lifts lid on drug pricing data, shows 3.5% net hike in 2016. CNBC. https://www.cnbc.com/2017/02/27/johnson-johnson-lifts-lid-on-drug-pricing-data-shows-35-net-hike-in-2016.html

Toole AA (2012) The impact of public basic research on industrial innovation: evidence from the pharmaceutical industry. Res Policy 41:1–12. https://doi.org/10.1016/j.respol.2011.06.004

Top 10 Pharmaceutical Companies in China (2017). Bizvibe. https://www.bizvibe.com/blog/pharmaceuticals-and-biotechnology/top-10-pharmaceutical-companies-china/

Torrey T (2010) Doctors firing or dismissing patients. Verywell Health. https://www.verywellhealth.com/can-my-doctor-fire-or-dismiss-me-as-a-patient-2615017

Trading Economics (2019) Country list government debt to GDP. Tradingeconomics.com. https://tradingeconomics.com/country-list/government-debt-to-gdp

Traynor K (2014) Effectiveness, costs weigh on HCV treatment decisions. Am J Health-Syst Pharm 71:1156–1157. https://doi.org/10.2146/news140051

Tsevat J, Moriates C (2018) Value-based Health care meets cost-effectiveness analysis. Ann Intern Med 169:329. https://doi.org/10.7326/m18-0342

Turpin C, Tomkins A (2007) British government and the constitution : text, cases and materials. Cambridge University Press

U.S. Office of Management and Budget (OMB) President's Budget: Historical Tables, 1934–2029 (Table 2.2) (n.d.)

UN Global Crisis Response Group (2023) A world of debt: a growing burden to global prosperity. unctad.org. https://unctad.org/publication/world-of-debt

UNCTAD (2023) Competition law enforcement issues raised by monopsonies

UNITAID (2016) An economic perspective on delinking the cost of R&D from the Price of medicines

Urban Institute (2019) Soda Taxes. Urban Institute. https://www.urban.org/policy-centers/cross-center-initiatives/state-and-local-finance-initiative/state-and-local-backgrounders/soda-taxes

Vaird AD (2019) Wealth taxation: an overview of the issues. American Enterprise Institute. https://www.aei.org/wp-content/uploads/2019/11/Wealth-Taxation-An-Overview-of-the-Issues-Revised-Nov-9-2019.pdf?x85095

Vanka P (2024) U.S. health expenditure as GDP share 1960-2022 | Statista. Statista. https://www.statista.com/statistics/184968/us-health-expenditure-as-percent-of-gdp-since-1960/

Waked I, Esmat G, Elsharkawy A et al (2020) Screening and treatment program to eliminate hepatitis C in Egypt. N Engl J Med 382:1166–1174. https://doi.org/10.1056/nejmsr1912628

Wang EEL, Einarson TR, Kellner JD, Conly JM (1999) Antibiotic prescribing for Canadian preschool children: evidence of overprescribing for viral respiratory infections. Clin Infect Dis 29:155–160. https://doi.org/10.1086/520145

Warburton DER, Nicol CW, Bredin SS (2006) Prescribing exercise as preventive therapy. Can Med Assoc J 174:961–974. https://doi.org/10.1503/cmaj.1040750

West MA, Wischmeyer PE, Grocott MPW (2017) Prehabilitation and nutritional support to improve perioperative outcomes. Curr Anesthesiol Rep 7:340–349. https://doi.org/10.1007/s40140-017-0245-2

Whelan CT, Nolan B, Maitre B (2016) Polarization or "squeezed middle" in the great recession?: a comparative European analysis of the distribution of economic stress. Soc Indic Res 133:163–184. https://doi.org/10.1007/s11205-016-1350-1

WHO (2015) The Doha declaration on the TRIPs agreement and public Health. World Health Organization. https://www.who.int/medicines/areas/policy/doha_declaration/en/

Why pharmaceutical companies are on a shopping binge (2019) The Economist. https://www.economist.com/the-economist-explains/2019/01/14/why-pharmaceutical-companies-are-on-a-shopping-binge

WIPO Reasons for Patenting Your Inventions (n.d.). www.wipo.int. https://www.wipo.int/sme/en/ip_business/importance/reasons.htm

Wolff EN (2010) Rising profitability and the middle class squeeze. Sci Soc 74:429–449. https://doi.org/10.1521/siso.2010.74.3.429

World Health Organization (2024) Patient safety rights charter. World Health Organization

World Health Organization Global Health Expenditure database (2024) Current health expenditure (% of GDP) | data. data.worldbank.org. https://data.worldbank.org/indicator/SH.XPD.CHEX.GD.ZS?view=chart

Worldometer World Population Clock (n.d.) Worldometer. https://www.worldometers.info/world-population/

Wu J, Cheng CW-C (2020) Into the Woods: a biologic patent thicket analysis. J Intellect Prop 19:93

Wynter-Blyth V, Moorthy K (2017) Prehabilitation: preparing patients for surgery. BMJ:j3702. https://doi.org/10.1136/bmj.j3702

Yang EJ, Galan E, Thombley R et al (2020) Changes in drug list prices and amounts paid by patients and insurers. JAMA Netw Open 3:e2028510. https://doi.org/10.1001/jamanetworkopen.2020.28510

Yebyo HG, Aschmann HE, Puhan MA (2018) Finding the balance between benefits and harms when using statins for primary prevention of cardiovascular disease. Ann Intern Med 170:1. https://doi.org/10.7326/m18-1279

Zucman G (2014) Taxing across Borders: tracking personal wealth and corporate profits. J Econ Perspect 28:121–148. https://doi.org/10.1257/jep.28.4.121

The Biopharma Challenge

4

4.1 How Is the Pharmaceutical Market Worldwide Like?

The worldwide prescription drug market is estimated at $1.28 trillion in 2022 (EFPIA 2023). Geographically, this figure is split among North America at 52% of the world pharmaceutical sales, followed by Europe at 22%, China at 8%, and Japan at 5%. The rest of the world adds to roughly 13% (EFPIA 2023). For the layperson, this distribution will surely seem odd. How does a country of 332 million have 52% of the world pharmaceutical sales in a world of 8.1 billion people, with pharmaceuticals being such an individual and universally needed item? Development is not the answer, as Japan with 125 million people represents only 5% of sales, and the EU 22%.

Not only are there regional differences in access but also in levels of consumption, pricing, penetration of generics, and in the amount of the value of each pack of pharmaceuticals that reaches the manufacturer. Many of these differences are politically influenced or resulting from market dynamics other than the quality of a product and patient need. For example, even inside Europe, the share of generic prescriptions is extremely diverse (e.g., 83% in Germany vs. 18% in Luxembourg) (OECD 2023).

The world pharmaceutical market is dominated by European and US-based companies, but is quite fragmented, as the leader captured less than 8% of the total world market in 2022. The top 50 most profitable companies worldwide contain two pharmaceutical multinationals: Pfizer and Johnson & Johnson at the 34th and 37th positions, respectively (CompaniesMarketCap Companies ranked by earnings n.d.). In 2022, US-based Pfizer became the first pharmaceutical company in history to earn annual revenue above $100 billion (Dunleavy 2023). Right behind were Johnson and Johnson (US) with $95 billion, Roche (Switzerland) with $66 billion, and Merck (US) with $58 billion (Dunleavy 2023). While large, pharmaceutical companies were nevertheless relatively smaller than the other companies in healthcare, with the largest one, Pfizer, making it only to tenth place on the list of largest

H. Falcão et al., *Pharma, Prices and Power*, Future of Business and Finance,
https://doi.org/10.1007/978-3-031-93933-4_4

companies in healthcare (Reiff 2024). Leading the list comes CVS Health, a company that makes money mostly distributing pharmaceutical products, with $315.2 billion in revenues.

4.2 The Activities of Biopharma Business and Their Challenges

The business of biopharma consists of a set of very specific activities, many of which are challenging and have significant impact on drug prices. Below, we examine these activities in more detail.

4.2.1 Drug Discovery and Development

Drug discovery involves identifying molecular targets associated with a disease and molecules that interact with them, to influence the disease progression or symptoms, with acceptable toxicity and risks. **Drug development** tests and establishes the selected molecule's suitability as a drug. The objectives of drug development are to ensure the absence of unacceptable toxicity (such as carcinogenic effects or impacts on fertility), understanding the benefits and side effect profiles of different doses, and demonstrating the incremental benefits as compared to current treatments.

Drug discovery is a costly endeavor, with clinical trials accounting for half of the expenses and the remaining costs largely attributed to preclinical drug discovery and post-trial approval processes (EFPIA 2023). In 2021, the pharmaceutical industry's R&D expenditures exceeded an estimated US$150 billion (EFPIA 2023), securing its position as the leader in research costs relative to net sales at 12%, which starkly contrasts with the average of under 5% across all other industries (EFPIA 2023). Despite the significant financial investment, exact R&D costs remain a topic of debate, as highlighted in Chaps. 1 and 3.

The development journey is not only becoming increasingly expensive, but it is also slow, complex, and filled with setbacks. The process of bringing a new drug to market typically takes 12–13 years and has a high failure rate (99.98–99.99%) as only 1–2 drugs are successfully developed out of every 10,000 substances tested in labs (EFPIA 2023). Even among the subset of drugs that progress to Phase I trials—the initial stage of testing in humans—only 5% will ultimately receive marketing authorization to be sold (Moreno and Pearson 2013).

Despite these challenges, drug development efforts have grown significantly, with 16,181 drugs reported to be in development in 2019, a 68% increase from the 9605 drugs in 2009 (Pharma Intelligence 2019). However, while the number of molecules available for patent is growing, R&D spend efficiency has been decreasing over time.

To counteract this growing inefficiency trend, companies have been experimenting with a range of approaches. One of the most effective ones so far has been hiring the best scientists, putting them in small discovery teams, giving them clear direction and appropriate resources, and then leaving them alone to do the work (Campbell et al. 2018). The role of smaller units or smaller companies in discovery and development cannot be overstated. Companies with revenue below half a billion dollars or less than $200 million in R&D spend represent 70% of late-stage pipeline drugs in phases II or III (IQVIA 2019).

Industry regulation is another important piece of the development process. Companies conducting studies to launch a new medicine have to comply with strict rules, known as good clinical practice (GCP), providing international ethical and scientific quality standards for designing, recording, and reporting trials that involve the participation of human subjects. Compliance and regular inspections as to GCP standards provide public assurance that the rights, safety, and well-being of trial subjects are protected, and that clinical-trial data are credible (EUR-Lex Clinical Trial Directive (Directive 2001/20/EC) n.d.; EUR-Lex GCP Directive (Directive 2005/28/EC) n.d.).

4.2.1.1 Challenges in Collecting Good Data

Pharmaceutical companies collect data on their new drugs through clinical trials, which are the largest cost in drug developments. Given that clinical trials can be costly and time-consuming, companies try to walk the thin line between compliance, safety, efficiency, and profitability. As such, most companies strategize which clinical trials to run or not, to increase their odds of getting approved, supporting their target price, or minimizing data collection costs. This revenue focus has been triggering Governments to distrust and thus increase its data demands to protect themselves against biased or suboptimal data on new drugs. Unfortunately, such additional data demands increase Pharma costs and creates new challenges.

First, some new drugs target tiny populations, exponentially increasing the cost and time of collecting more data as it is harder to find patients. Given the small target population, such extra trials will represent a more considerable relative cost against low-expected profits. And that is if the drug gets approved and reimbursed. Even considering the orphan status benefits, the profit equation gets riskier with every demand for more data.

Then, pharmaceutical companies compete with one another to move fast and gain a first-mover advantage when launching a new treatment. Once doctors and hospitals like and get comfortable with a treatment, they only prescribe a new competing medication if it offers significantly better benefits and lower risks. As a result, being the first-mover treatment translates into a profitable and sticky market barrier. To gain such advantage and protect their innovations, companies file for patents as soon as possible, which also starts the patent clock about a decade before launching the drug in major markets. Any extra clinical trial or data requirements could delay market entry and reduce patent exclusivity for months or years, thus significantly risking a drug's profit potential.

Finally, pharmaceutical companies try to come in early to increase their odds of securing a higher price than the competition. Those who opt for thorough clinical trials and showing complete data sets take longer to initiate P&R negotiations than those who don't and thus are disadvantaged. Once a direct competitor succeeds in getting their drug approved with less mature data, it reduces the P&R evaluation of the original compliant company. In most P&R negotiations, the Payer relies on a comparable drug (a.k.a., comparator) as the standard of care (SOC) and a reference to gauge and quantify the improved clinical value of the new drug under negotiation. This comparison influences the price premium the new drug is likely or not to get. If the new drug shows significantly increased value versus the comparator, it gains negotiation leverage to secure a relatively high price. However, if the benefit is considered minor or marginal, the Payer may even choose not to reimburse the drug or pay a discount versus the comparator.

Imagine a new drug A with a clinical value 25% above the current comparator (called drug C) who is doing their best to comply with the Payer's data requirements, spending millions of euros and years ensuring mature data on its benefits and safety. It is running a trial with two arms: one with patients taking drug A and the other drug C. In the meantime, there is another manufacturer trialing a competitor product for the same indication (drug B, worse than A, but better than C). That trial is also a two-arm trial against drug C, but was started after and still has immature data.

Now, imagine that the manufacturer of drug B decides to gain a competitive edge by rushing to market. Despite its incomplete data, it will likely be approved and at a premium price over drug C, given B's superior clinical value. Because drug B's data is not fully mature, its price will be discounted from its potential; however, it managed to become the new official standard of care in the country.

A few months later, the first company launches drug A, with evidence of superior benefit over the old comparator, drug C, but without similar data against drug B. From a procedural standpoint, the situation of drug A when being assessed is no different from the scenario where the manufacturer had on purpose chosen an old, obsolete drug to compare drug A against (to ensure it would demonstrate a benefit). Drug A will be considered not to have any demonstrated benefit against the standard of care. As a result, drug A will be priced below its value, and may fail to penetrate a market dominated by drug B as well as if it had been the first one to market.

Note that drug B's manufacturer took the right decision from a pricing perspective. Had they waited for drug B's trial to provide more complete data, they would be the ones not having the trial against the new and better standard of care. Instead, it will be drug A's shareholders who will likely be upset and punish their CEO for not pursuing P&R negotiations with incomplete data before the competition.

So pharmaceutical companies face the following clinical data dilemma: do I delay my market entry to comply with the higher data demands and increase my chances that the Payer will correctly value my new product and run the risks above? Or do I try my luck with incomplete data to get to market earlier but risk losing trust and angering the Payer for not collecting good data on purpose, which is the usual Payer interpretation?

4.2.1.2 Different Criteria Everywhere

Not only are companies competing with others as described above but they are playing in different matches running simultaneously. For example, companies must consider their evaluation by the US Food and Drug Administration (FDA), the European Medicines Agency (EMA), the Japanese Pharmaceuticals and Medical Devices Agency (PMDA), and the remaining MA or DAs worldwide.

Given these authorities' different requirements, companies must sometimes sacrifice one for the other, as it is quite hard or too expensive to satisfy them all. For example, the FDA and US Payers are more amenable to launches on orphan diseases using Phase 2 data; but its lack of Phase 3 data will be heavily penalized in Europe. So do we launch after our successful Phase 2 trial in the USA, or start our Phase 3 trials to launch in Europe as well? The tension is that having good Phase 2 data strongly signals to competitors that it is worth investing to create a very similar and thus competing drug, which is often done. Therefore, to wait until completing a Phase 3 trial would increase the risk of competitors with larger resources catching up, and risk losing the highly rewarding US Market. It would also mean preventing patients from benefiting from the drug in the interim and its resulting revenue.

4.2.1.3 Competition, Patents, and Similar Drugs

As it is usually described, pharmaceutical companies enjoy the monopoly of a patented drug over the Payer, for an inordinate amount of time (for as long as their patent lasts). However, that perception is not accurate. Patents protect the exact same molecule from being used by other manufacturers, but do not prevent competitors from, once aware of the promising results of Phase 1 and 2 trials, creating me-too molecules. These are often very similar to the first one in structure, often identical in function, but just different enough that they do not violate the first drug's patent.

Me-too drugs are easier and cheaper to do as the research from the first company points competitors into a promising direction. Competitors run trials with their molecules, comfortably knowing there is a very large likelihood of success. These two drugs often—but not always—don't have therapeutic equivalence, that is, they cannot be interchangeable by the Payers. However, once Payers have alternatives for their patient's needs, they can escape the Pharma's patent monopolistic power.

So, are me-toos good or bad? Depends on who you ask. For Pharma companies investing in drug discovery and bringing innovative breakthroughs the patent system wants to reward, me-too drugs are a tremendous challenge. For Pharma with larger capabilities to deliver from trial to launch, they are a great shortcut for success. Me-toos are also beneficial to provide alternatives and reduce prices for Payers and patients on the short-term, though it is unknown if me-toos create any undesirable long-term consequence.

4.2.2 Drug Manufacturing and Supply

Drug manufacturing refers to the production of pharmaceutical drugs ready to be shipped to wholesalers, hospitals, or pharmacies by pharmaceutical companies. Manufacturing, like clinical trials, is highly regulated by agencies such as the FDA (in the US) and EMA (in Europe). Their role is to carefully monitor compliance with good manufacturing practice (GMP) regulations, and ensure that the drug was manufactured properly, is safe for use, and has the ingredients and strength it claims to have. In addition, pharmaceutical companies must record batch manufacturing and distribution histories, in case there are any issues later, and carry routine inspections to record, but also investigate, any significant GMP deviations and ensure GMP enforcement. While necessary, this quality control adds to the cost of any medication.

Aside from the regulation cost, drug manufacturing is becoming more expensive as the R&D frontier increasingly involves biologic drugs, which represented 40% of all drugs approved in the USA in 2022 alone, up from a sum total of 27% since 2014 (de la Torre and Albericio 2023). Chemical drugs (synthesized through chemical reactions) are simpler in structure and have been giving way to the more complex biologic drugs (produced by living organisms). Biological drugs (e.g., antibodies and fusion proteins) are relatively more expensive to produce, given how their immunogenicity,[1] adverse events, and efficacy can be affected by even the slightest process change. As a comparison, while a chemical (small molecule) facility costs $30–100 million to build, the investment required to build a large-scale biologic facility that can properly handle the additional biologic drug complexity is $200–500 million.

4.2.3 Engagement with Regulatory Authorities

Regulatory authorities like the EMA and the FDA have three distinct and important societal functions: delivering scientific advice, evaluating and authorizing drugs, and monitoring safety. When it comes to evaluating and authorizing drugs, manufacturers must provide the regulatory authorities with data on the drug's effects and other relevant information[2] for their review. Given that just about every drug has risks as well as benefits, a drug is only approved if it shows evidence of effective, safe, and quality benefits to the target population that outweigh its known or potential risks. For example, a drug intended to treat patients with a life-threatening disease for which no other therapy exists may be considered to have benefits that outweigh the risks even if those risks would be considered unacceptable for a condition that is not life threatening.

Regulators consider any uncertainties that may result from imperfect or incomplete data when evaluating the clinical data submitted by the drug maker. Generally, the agency expects the submission of at least two well-designed clinical trials to ensure that the findings from the first trial are not the result of chance or bias.

[1] Immunogenicity is the undesirable ability of a substance to be detected by the body's immune system as a foreign object and provoke a reaction, typically an antibody response.

[2] The data submitted by companies in their application must include a range of information, including the way the drug is manufactured, its effects in laboratory studies, benefits and side effects observed in patients, and how risks will be managed, as well as the proposed information to be provided to patients and doctors.

However, convincing evidence from one clinical trial may be enough when involving rare diseases or when multiple trials may not be feasible. Companies must also provide strategies for managing risks, such as an approved drug label, which clearly describes the drug's benefits and risks and how the risks can be detected and managed. In more serious cases, a drug maker may need to implement a Risk Evaluation and Mitigation Strategy (REMS).

Regulatory authorities process applications in a bit over a year, including some back and forth with the manufacturer. In the end, 25% of applications are rejected, representing an additional time and risk for manufacturers to consider when developing and bringing a drug to market. Regulators have tried to reduce these costs by providing scientific advice when manufacturers request for guidance. Following such guidance reduces the chances of being rejected to 15%.

Once a drug has been authorized for use, the regulatory agencies constantly monitor its safety and take action if new information indicates that the drug is no longer as safe and effective as previously thought.

4.2.4 Access

Medicines that are granted a marketing authorization can be marketed and sold. However, before a drug is made available to patients, in Europe, for example, Pricing and Reimbursement (P&R) negotiations must take place at the national and/or regional levels. To ensure national access, the manufacturer must produce a submission dossier tailored to the specific regulations of each country, to be appraised by the local authorities. Producing such a dossier is not a minor task.

Based on the dossier, the Payer (the institution that will potentially pay for the drug) will decide whether it wants to reimburse the drug and under which conditions. P&R negotiations are highly structured and country-specific. There is, however, a general thread: first a State-affiliated scientific body performs a scientific evaluation of the drug to quantify or qualify the absolute clinical benefit the drug brings to different types of patients, and relative to competing drugs already reimbursed in the country. Their scientific assessment defines "how good the drug is" or its perceived clinical value in that country and becomes the basis for the price negotiation between the Payer's pricing commission and the Manufacturer. It may also define to which patient subpopulations the drug should be available or if it should be taken before or after other available and related treatments, and thus establishes the drug's sales volume and revenue in that country.

Payers and Manufacturers usually have differing perceptions of a drug's clinical value. While the manufacturer is expected to be positively biased toward the value of their drug, the State-affiliated scientific bodies are expected to be objective and neutral in their assessments. However, scientific assessments in some Markets have become more negatively biased, probably to provide the Payer with legitimacy to negotiate lower prices.

In the subsequent negotiation, the Payers' pricing commissions demand concessions and discounts from the manufacturer to match the scientific assessment, mitigate any perceived risks, and still obtain extra discounts. The manufacturer usually resists at least some such demands. They engage in plenty of complex discussions and intense price negotiations until a deal is reached. If there is no deal, in most countries the drug will not be reimbursed by that Payer and local access to it will become extremely limited, except in countries like Germany, where there are subsequent steps to help the parties reach agreement (e.g., arbitration).

Having the price, the reimbursable population, and hence the revenue of a product determined by a single negotiation is, of course, risky. A less successful negotiation will thwart the pharmaceutical company's investment expectations in this last stage, creating yet another risk for them to consider when deciding to invest in developing a new drug. This is not a minor risk: even when a drug is reimbursed in Europe, its initial patient population is partially restricted 82% of the time, and their prices are negotiated down. Besides, on average, only 45% of EMA-approved drugs are reimbursed across the EU (Newton et al. 2023). Germany tops the list (1st) by reimbursing 88% of drugs, with France (6th) only reimbursing 67%, and Norway, a wealthy country with a welfare state, is close to the average at 47%.

4.2.4.1 Inappropriate and Abusive Access Processes and Stakeholders

Some countries in Europe have created rigorous P&R processes to determine access of pharmaceutical products, such as Germany, France, the UK, and others. Their overriding mission is to provide first an objective measure of a drug's fair value for stakeholders in their country, and then to reimburse based on said value at a balanced point that is both manageable to the Payers and agreeable by the manufacturer.

The scientific evaluation part of these processes is serious, technically competent, and comprehensive. Unfortunately, in several countries they started becoming biased against Pharma during the last decade.

A larger problem, however, lies in the subsequent P&R negotiation process. Payers have been overtly abusing their monopsony power through aggressive and value-destroying win-lose tactics. Such tactics often involve distorting the scientific valuation, threatening not to reimburse, or imposing extremely unfavorable conditions or onerous clauses onto Pharma. We examine some examples below as we categorize the tactics into price-control tactics (direct or indirectly imposing a discount relying on the pharmaceutical company's lack of credible good alternatives), market access tactics (credibly threatening to worsen a drug's sales to gain discounts), and P&R process tactics (tailoring a biased process to gain power). Ultimately, they all lead to reduced prices and differ only in how they attempt to do so.

Price-Control Win-Lose Tactics (Direct or Indirect Imposition of Discounts)

1. **Sales caps**: In this tactic, Payers negotiate with pharmaceutical companies to establish a maximum number of units for which they will pay. Any units consumed beyond this limit are provided free of charge. Initially introduced to control off-label usage of drugs (using a drug for a purpose not approved by

regulatory authorities), and to provide budget predictability to the Payer, the practice has evolved into a mechanism for also setting artificially low unit limits, leading to additional disguised discounts. For example, in France, Italy, and Spain, Payers push pharmaceutical companies to agree to caps below the expected usage, decreasing per-unit costs with each additional free product consumed. Some governments may also indirectly encourage physicians to switch patients to capped drugs to access free treatments.

2. **Drug expenditure fixed envelope with payback** (Italy, France): In this tactic, a government sets a maximum budget for spending on pharmaceutical drugs, typically approved by the parliament. When the total expenditure for drugs exceeds this budget, the government requires pharmaceutical companies to reimburse the excess amount, often based on their market share. For example, if the agreed budget is exceeded by $10 million and a company holds 1% of the market share, they would reimburse $100,000 to the government.
3. **Targeted taxes or legislation**: Governments may impose additional taxes, specifically on pharmaceutical profits, on top of other standard corporate taxes. For example, the UK introduced a 26% tax on pharmaceutical profits in 2023.
4. **Price moratoriums** (most countries): This tactic involves prohibiting pharmaceutical companies from increasing the prices of their drugs, even when it would be fair to update them to account for inflation. As a result, these nominal price freezes effectively translate into an automatic discount over time as the real (not nominal) price of the drugs diminishes. In a similar vein, in the UK and Sweden, the price reward for each unit of quality of life delivered by a treatment (cost-effectiveness or affordability threshold) has remained stagnant for the past two decades, despite all the accumulated inflation.
5. **Mandatory discounts** (Germany, Italy, Spain): Governments use their legislative power to impose automatic discounts on drug prices, often as a percentage of the list price, even before the P&R negotiation begins or at its outset. These discounts are mandatory and apply to various medications, irrespective of their initial list prices. For instance, in Germany, a 7% discount was mandated in 2024, while Italy imposes a 10% discount requirement.

Market Access Win-Lose Tactics (Credibly Threatening to Worsen a Drug's Sales)

1. **Prior authorization** (Spain, Italy, Austria, France): Physicians must provide detailed patient information to Payers before prescribing certain drugs. Given increased administrative burdens, this requirement often results in reduced prescriptions, even when the treatment may have been the most suitable for a patient. Again, the mere threat of being put on such a list may compel pharmaceutical companies to give more discounts.
2. **Reducing the number of patients eligible to the drug (France, Italy, Spain, UK):** the label proposed by EMA can be reduced by the Payer. For example, the EMA can authorize the drug for all adult patients suffering from a given disease but the Payer can restrict the reimbursement to the sub-population of patients

whose treatment with a cheaper drug (typically generic) has failed or is proven to have too many side effects for this patient.

3. **Preferred drug lists**: Payers (sick funds) financially incentivize physicians to prescribe specific patented drugs over others based on economic considerations. This tactic creates a conflict of interest, as it can sway physicians away from the best clinical considerations for the patient toward the financial interests of the physician. The threat of deprioritizing a medication can be the final push necessary for pharmaceutical companies to give an extra discount.
4. **Christmas legal scares on physicians**: In Germany, certain health funds send letters to physicians during the Christmas season, starting legal action by what the funds claim to be excessive prescription costs, when they exceed arbitrarily and not shared low-cost limits. This tactic forces doctors to waste their Christmas season preparing their legal defense with a lawyer and learn to prioritize patients who require cheaper treatments over those who need more expensive therapies.
5. **Compulsory licensing**: This tactic relies on threats of revocation of a pharmaceutical patent under certain conditions. Suppose pharmaceutical companies fail to meet specific government requirements, such as lower prices for essential medications. In that case, the government can revoke their patent rights and allow generic, and thus cheaper, drug versions from other manufacturers.
6. **Fast-track approval of competitors (branded competitors, generics or biosimilar drugs)**: Cheaper competing drugs may receive expedited approval to enter the market and bring their significantly lower prices as quickly as possible, forcing the incumbent pharmaceutical company to reduce its prices as well or risk losing the market completely. A Payer may threaten to use this tactic against pharmaceutical companies to pressure them into giving more discounts.

P&R Process Win-Lose Tactics (Unilaterally Defining the Rules of the Process)

1. **Setting overly demanding burden of evidence**: Payers reward drugs with higher prices if they demonstrate bringing higher benefits to patients and the healthcare system. Hence, a drug demonstrating better result than the most widely used current treatment receives a higher valuation than a drug that would be compared to an older, less used treatment. However, if the burden of evidence is overly demanding, it becomes extremely difficult, if not impossible, for the treatment to prove its benefits. Thus, it has to settle for further discounted prices. For example, in the UK, a drug's benefit is calculated over the next decades of a patient's life. In practice, the Payer demands that the manufacturer bring data to support the benefit over decades. It is impossible to comply with such a request as a drug would need a 20-year trial, be outdated, and be out of patent by the time it reached the market, thus failing to reach patients for those many years. Generally speaking, Payers disregard the feasibility of producing the data they request and then evaluate the data as insufficient, demanding significant discounts over the treatment's price. In a more positive light, we can say that Payers force pharmaceutical companies to provide discounts today to buffer them from

all conceivable risks As not all risks materialize, Payers get free money just by setting overly demanding burdens of evidence.

2. **Pooled procurement processes (Benelux, Nordic countries, Southern countries)**: Some countries collaborate to negotiate drug prices collectively, reducing the pharmaceutical company's alternatives and thus enhancing their bargaining power as a single buyer.
3. **Delayed reimbursement** (most EU countries): Except for Germany and select drugs in France with the Early Access program, patient drug access is typically delayed by 6–18 months in Europe after EMA approval. By controlling the reimbursement timing, Payers implicitly threaten to delay a drug's market entry, thus hurting a pharmaceutical company's profitability or pressuring them into unfair discounts in exchange for a standard access speed to the market or sometimes just to be granted a meeting with the authorities.
4. **Constant price-Down renegotiations**: Governments engage in continual renegotiations with pharmaceutical companies to secure lower drug prices. For instance, in France, the Minister of Finance may demand strong cost reductions for the year from the Economic Committee for Health Products (CEPS), which then demands additional discounts, such as 20% more, from the top-selling pharmaceutical companies. After some back-and-forth, discounts may land at or below their initial request, causing price uncertainty for pharmaceutical firms. Similarly, countries like Spain, Belgium, Italy, and Germany frequently opt for short-term agreements lasting only 2–3 years to create opportunities for frequent price-down renegotiations. They have recently started proposing automated contract renewals in unfavorable conditions, which may be better and more predictable for manufacturers than going through another renegotiation.
5. **Same or lower prices, never up:** Under this win-lose practice, when a drug proves effective for a new indication, its price is reassessed. If the benefits for the new indication are deemed lower than for the original use, the drug's price is reduced proportionally. However, if the benefits are determined to be higher, the price remains unchanged. In short, if a drug provides greater overall value to society in a new indication, it will not be compensated for its additional value. At best, its price will remain stagnant, perpetuating an inequitable pricing structure.

The above win-lose tactics involve the Payer abusing its power to set the rules of the game, to influence the market to its advantage and contrary to creating a level playing field, and to force discounts independent of what is fair or valuable. Another tactic is to use them collectively. Payers jump from one tactic to another whenever the pharmaceutical company has a good argument against one of the tactics. A Payer will use its wide array of win-lose tactics to keep the pharmaceutical company guessing and find its weakest link until the negotiation reaches the Payer's desired price.

These tactics are widespread even in the P&R negotiations of countries known for their rigorous scientific assessments of drug efficacy and pricing and that end up reimbursing many innovative drugs. Despite the abundant use of such win-lose tactics, these countries can be considered Pharma innovation "friendly" when compared to another group, those that, despite being rich and scientifically sophisticated nations (e.g., Norway), often employ less sophisticated, win-lose negotiation processes, which essentially boil down to: "*Give me [extreme discount number] or I will walk away, and there will be no point talking any further.*" These requested discounts are often extreme, illegitimate, and much lower than what other countries pay, resulting in a wide number of no-agreements, with the obvious negative impact on patients' health. To make matters worse, these Governments then blame the lack of agreement on the "greedy Pharma."

4.2.5 Lobbying Institutions

Given all the regulations pharmaceutical companies face—not just the ones that apply to all industries but also those concerning patents, clinical trials, manufacturing, registration, price setting, tax, and more, biopharma associations invest a good deal of money to defend their interests.

Lobbying groups exist in Europe and the USA, with significant presence in both regions. In the USA, the industry spends large sums of money on lobbying and campaign contributions, like many other industries, to have a say on legislative outcomes and continued access to power (Wouters 2020). Especially given that the interests of health insurers, for example, often oppose those of Pharma, such as wanting to lower pharma prices, and they spend far more on lobbying than drug manufacturers (Welsh and Young 2017), pharmaceutical companies are at risk if they just sit on the sides passively. The fact that the largest companies in healthcare are US-based non-Pharma companies testifies that this risk and struggle are real.

4.2.6 Engagement with Healthcare Providers and Marketing

Pharmaceutical companies are often criticized for marketing directly to doctors and it may in fact be one of the most controversial activities of Pharma. This kind of marketing is highly debated as it can both provide educational value on the latest medical advances but also pressure or mislead doctors to write unnecessary or even harmful prescriptions.

Marketing activities can in fact serve an educational purpose that is much needed. When not deceptive, marketing activities can make physicians aware of the latest drugs available for their patients at a time of information overload. A new drug enters the market approximately every four working days. For example, 51 new drugs were approved annually by the FDA between 2013 and 2018 (Baedeker et al. 2019). It is almost impossible for a doctor to stay on top of them all, especially given that this information is highly technical, hard to find, and complex to digest. Unfortunately, medical associations or other disinterested organizations have not really stepped up to bear the burden of educating doctors on how to help their patients. This space is left to the pharma companies, which presents a conflict of interests.

Doctors share the inherent human tendency of being resistant to change. There is inertia in their prescribing habits. They may be satisfied with the effectiveness of the medications they are familiar with. It can feel risky to switch to a supposedly better treatment, especially before colleagues have done so, because it entails potentially managing different side effects, different dose management and the new drug may not prove to be better as the data reports. Finally, some of this resistance to change may derive from doctors' lack of confidence when comparing different drugs or reading about clinical trials. Statistical illiteracy in doctors is an unfortunate and documented reality (Gigerenzer and Gray 2013), which makes education on new products very much needed, though it also means that doctors are more easily fooled by biased education than we expect.

Studies documenting the underuse of beta blockers, cholesterol treatment, and aspirin for heart attack and coronary artery disease patients illustrate the lack of success in translating research findings into medical practice. That happens even in oncology: across Europe, more than 50% of patients with Chronic Myeloid Leukemia continue to be treated with a 1st generation agent while the 2nd generation of products have demonstrated better survival (Shen et al. 2020). Medical delay in learning about and prescribing new drugs limits the full public health benefits of these innovations (Lenfant 2003). In fact, some studies have found that when quality of care standards for medication management are not followed, 50% of the time it is because an indicated medication has not been prescribed, while prescription of inappropriate medication represents only 3% of cases (Higashi et al. 2004).

A dedicated one-to-one session to explain and answer questions that helps doctors learn in the convenience of their office (a.k.a. detailing) can be a positive exercise if done properly. Companies have increasingly abandoned questionable sales tactics, and adopted codes of conduct to properly inform drug benefits to unaware physicians, helping their patients and all stakeholders in the system. Conversely, some pharmaceutical representatives are paid to sell as much medication as possible, and their financial incentive system may encourage win-lose, but effective, sales moves.

Another issue is the cost of this marketing system compared to other ways companies promote their products. Physically going to physician offices means that a representative only sees 4–5 doctors each day, and they get very little time with each. Besides, much like the lobbying effort, such investment can be a waste of money as the players pay increasing amounts of money to compete and eventually stay in the same place.

As a result, companies are moving to more targeted online education and away from drug reps who pay personal visits, and, given the reputation of pharmaceutical reps, this may not be a bad thing, if MDs are still getting educated. Pharmaceutical companies have to publicly disclose any expenses associated with healthcare professionals which accounted for most of their promotional spending and increased between 1997 and 2016 from $15.6 billion to $20.3 billion, including $5.6 billion for prescriber detailing, $13.5 billion for free samples, $979 million for direct physician payments (speaking fees, meals) related to specific drugs, and $59 million for disease education (Schwartz and Woloshin 2019).

In the USA and New Zealand only, pharmaceutical marketing also includes direct to consumer advertising (DTC). From 1997 through 2022, US DTC prescription drug advertising increased from below $1 billion to $8.1 billion, with a shift toward advertising high-cost biologics (Adams 2023; Kux 2010).

In sum, as we look at the above biopharma activities, we see how many of them create significant costs and uncertainties that, directly or indirectly, impact the pricing of medication. While some of them are inherent to any business, and others to the specific delicate nature of pharmaceuticals, others may be the result of suboptimal healthcare practices and could be avoided to reduce the overall cost of getting the best drugs to patients.

4.3 Competitors for Pharma's Revenue

Pharmaceutical companies usually do not sell or supply directly to consumers, but rather rely on intermediaries, each of whom adds to the final drug cost and reduces the potential profits of the manufacturer. Within each country, different players take a bite out of the pie of the price of a pharmaceutical. For example, in Europe, one-third of the price of a drug ends up in the hands of government, pharmacists, and wholesalers, leaving approximately 67% with the manufacturer.

In the US market, the situation is, in general, more unfavorable to Pharma. More than 90% of drugs are distributed through wholesalers, who then supply pharmacies, hospitals, clinics, and nursing homes, with three particular wholesalers accounting for more than 90% of the market (Seeley 2022). Wholesalers negotiate discounts with manufacturers and then compete for contracts with providers and pharmacies (Seeley 2022). One study found that for every $100 spent on drugs in the USA by patients and insurers together, $58 goes to manufacturers ($15 is net profit and $17 for drug production costs), $19 accrues to insurers ($3 of which is net profit), pharmacy benefit managers (PBMs) end up with $5 ($2 net profit), pharmacies keep $15 ($3 net profit), and wholesalers keep about $2 (30 cents net profit). Thus the total net profit on the $100 is $23, of which $15 is captured by the manufacturer and the remaining $8 by intermediaries (Sood et al. 2017). Notice that each manufacturer in the fragmented pharma industry keeps $15 on their few products, while the consolidated intermediaries make $8 on every drug, which explains why they are some of the largest companies in the world. The fight for a higher share of the drug price is a challenge for Pharma.

4.3.1 Drug Supply and Parallel Trade

While not a problem in the USA, pharmaceutical companies have to worry about parallel trade impacts on the supply dynamics in the European market. Parallel trade is the term for the resale of pharmaceuticals between countries, which happens when countries price similar drugs differently—to the detriment of pharmaceutical companies (Kyle 2009). The EU's parallel importation and trade laws allow drugs to be sold freely—thus, traders can buy from countries where the price was negotiated to be lower and resell the drugs for a profit in countries where the price is higher. It is unlawful for a pharmaceutical company to do anything specific to prevent parallel trade, which undercuts their ability to reap the negotiated profits in countries that have negotiated to pay more (Elvidge 2009).

Take, for example, a situation where the negotiated list price in Portugal is much lower than the price in Germany. A German wholesaler would be incentivized to buy the entire Portuguese stock to sell in Germany, at or slightly below the German price, profiting at the expense of the manufacturer discount to Portugal—and creating a shortage for Portuguese patients (Portugal Resident 2012). Parallel trade harms every player except the resellers who trade cross-border. Government does not save money, manufacturers lose money, and patients lose access to drugs. The solution would be to exclude drugs from parallel trade or have a single EU price.

4.4 Pharma's Reputation

In a 2023 Gallup ranking of the public esteem of 25 US industries, the pharmaceutical industry ranked last in terms of how respondents felt about it (Saad 2023). No other industry is held in lower esteem. Eighteen percent of Americans reported a positive view of drug makers, while 21% reported feeling neutral, and 60% reported a negative view. This is despite the response of pharma in quickly developing a COVID-19 vaccine. Pharma came in even behind industries that are often vilified in the media for their poor customer service (airlines), pollution (oil & gas) or greed (banking and legal sectors).

It is surprising that such a rich global industry has been unable to improve its reputation despite its products being responsible for improving our most important asset, our health. Pharma seems to be hated and vilified in diametrical opposition to how doctors and nurses are loved and esteemed.

Independently of the reason, once Pharma is reputed as the evil healthcare actor, Governments feel entitled to rationalize their win-lose negotiation behavior and even illegal decisions as legitimate moves against the "greedy" Pharma. Doctors and just about anyone else have become afraid of supporting Pharma for fear of being labeled as supporting the "enemy," independently of the merits of each particular case. This silence or discrediting of opposing voices give extreme power to a few government officials to make biased healthcare decisions without the impartial input of doctors or other segments of society.

Such isolated and negatively biased decision-making creates an environment of distrust and permissiveness that leads to suboptimal negotiation processes and poor healthcare decisions, especially as they increasingly center around price only, rather than a drug's total value and cost to society. This negative reputation limits Pharma's negotiation ability to build trust, which in turn reduces their ability to argue for their interests, suggest or invite new options, or claim the legitimacy or veracity of their arguments without inviting suspicion and thus a negative response.

4.4.1 Why Is Pharma's Reputation So Bad?

We believe there are many factors contributing to this bad reputation.

One factor is that Pharma is corporate, technological, industrial, and profit-oriented, as opposed to natural and pure. Pharmaceuticals are perceived as very dangerous and Pharma as ill-intended. Meanwhile, herbal treatments without trials for efficacy or safety and known to cause side effects are esteemed as safe and natural—despite "natural" often meaning being a diluted plant poison or being a molecule occurring in food sources but taken in very high dosages. Despite pricing them at several fold, the price of off-patent drugs, the producers of these products are not perceived as pursuing profit, nor is the advertising of "*improving immune function*" perceived as misleading.

Another factor is that people don't have a direct relationship with Pharma. The closer most people are of interacting with Pharma is when taking pharmaceutical products as patients. However, they do it through their physician, with whom they develop a personal relationship. Not surprisingly, if the pharmaceutical products don't meet the usually high expectations of instant cure, most patients will directly blame the product and pharma. When it does, many patients often see it as merit of their medical doctor.

Besides these factors that Pharma has no responsibility over, there are other factors where Pharma has a contribution. As we have seen in the several pharma activities, there are ethical grey zones that also contribute to the ill-reputation. For example, lobbying makes Pharma, in the eyes of most people, as being cozy with politicians. Marketing directly to doctors to increase sales raises the very valid question on whether doctors' prescribing is being wrongly influenced. The two largest factors behind Pharma's terrible reputation, however, are probably the negative media coverage it has, and pricing.

4.4.2 Pharma Is Bad at Marketing Pharma

Pharma's success in the past decades is not a prevailing narrative, and yet the case is easy for us to make. Longevity has increased over the past 40+ years, despite the fact that the global prevalence of diabetes has nearly tripled since 1990 (with 200 million people living with diabetes in 1990 to 830 million in 2022), and the global prevalence of obesity among adults more than doubled since 1990 (World Health Organization 2024a) to 16% of adults in 2022 (World Health Organization 2024b). Drug treatments are not the only source of life expectancy improvement, of course, but they represent a share of it.

Some researchers have argued that biomedical innovation has indeed been the principal cause of recent improvements in health (Fuchs 2010). To get more specific, between 2000 and 2009, the improvement in population-weighted mean life expectancy at birth seen across 30 OECD countries was 1.74 years. Medicines are estimated to have contributed to 73% of this improvement once other factors are taken into account (income, education, immunization, reduction in risk factors, health system access) (Lichtenberg 2014). That is, a total of 1.27 years of added *mean* life expectancy in only 10 years.

It is also the case that death rates for non-communicable diseases, including cancer, declined nearly 20% in the EU, Australia, Canada, and Japan from 2000 to 2012 (World Health Organization WHO Mortality Database n.d.). In addition, the five-year relative survival rate for all cancers diagnosed in 2004–2010 increased to more than 68% from 49% during the late 1970s (American Cancer Society 2015).

Drugs also generate economic benefits through productivity gains from people being healthy enough to work. The decline in cancer deaths observed between 2000 and 2011 has been estimated to have resulted in $127 billion in productivity gains (Hanly et al. 2014). It should be noted, however, that these kinds of analyses are very challenging. For example, the use of antihypertensive drugs to prevent deaths from stroke or heart attacks will cause people to live longer and hence die from other diseases, like cancer, which will typically entail their own costs. All considered, pharma has done a phenomenal job delivering on its societal mission of helping people live healthier and longer lives, but the high prices and abuses have dominated the news headlines.

4.4.3 Negative Media Sells

The low reputation rankings are not all that surprising in light of the media's focus not on pharma's increased life expectancy and productivity gains but on scandals, fines, ethical transgressions, and prices. From one drug maker forced to pay a $20 million SEC fine over bribery in China (Robinson 2016) to another pulling a painkiller from the market due to cardiovascular risks and problems with data reporting (Neilan 2004), to yet another raising the price of a critical medication from $13.50 to $750 (Pollack and Huetteman 2016), there is a long stream of negative news headlines. More recently, of course, there was the catastrophic opioid epidemic (Meier 2018), but that has been more the nail on the coffin of Pharma's terrible reputation than the cause of it.

A great example of this negative bias is how the development of the COVID vaccines was met by the media and general public. The fact that the vaccines were created in record time by Pharma workers working overtime was not given credit; the fact that several of these vaccines worked so well was taken for granted, and those that did not work well were seen as "fiascos." The fact that they saved millions of lives was disregarded. The economic benefit of the vaccines in allowing societies to resume its normal life was barely mentioned or publicly recognized.

Instead, the headlines focused on how costly the vaccines were—between 3 to 30 euros—and on the side effects of the vaccine. Later on, the focus turned to how they "did not work as well," omitting that it was not the vaccines that had disappointed, but the virus that had mutated. No mainstream media we know mentioned that the side effects of the vaccines (such as the myocarditis) were generally similar but weaker effects of the Covid viral infection, caused by our immune system's reaction to either the vaccine or the infection. In the media, the price of the vaccine was never compared with its economic benefits, to other everyday items of the same price, or to the intangible values of safety, health, and freedom.

Life expectancy increases are boring statistics that give people at best a tiny warm feeling for a second, and then are quickly forgotten or taken for granted. Thus, it is more profitable for the media to characterize Pharma as a villain responsible for financial distress, manipulation, bankruptcy, and patients left behind because of greed, because these news are personal, get eyeballs, and sell. Moreover, it is very convenient for Governments, as it gives them more clout to negotiate aggressively with Pharma. Nowhere does that accused greed get discussed more than in the realm of drug pricing.

4.4.4 The Tension Between Patient and Profit

Most industries face a tension with its customers on the topic of pricing, where their interests do not match. Companies try to minimize this tension by explaining the legitimacy of their prices in their clients' eyes (e.g., better quality, new materials, higher detail, additional functions, inflation, etc).

In reality, most companies in most industries price their products based on competitive pressure or willingness to pay (WtP), the gold standard of pricing strategy in business education. Willingness to pay can of course be extremely problematic if applied to some specific pharmaceutical products if patients cannot do without them, as it would be akin to taking the patient's life as a hostage. It would disrespect the deeper social contract between pharma and patients, summarized in the expression: "just because you can doesn't mean that you should" (Kerr 2016). In Pharma, pricing at the patient's willingness-to-pay would be an abusive pricing strategy and healthcare systems are prepared to resist it. It still happens in some out-of-pocket markets and it may happen in some fringe situations, as we will see below.

Even without willingness-to-pay pricing, the tension in Pharma pricing is manifold higher than other industries, as it deals with life and health. The United Nations Universal Declaration of Human Rights states that "everyone has the right to a standard of living adequate for the health and well-being of himself and of his family" (United Nations 2018). Any threat to our health is perceived, rightly so, as a direct threat to our life. As such, most countries believe that health is a public good or a basic right, which leads many to think it should be free. Yet, as a society, we delivered the responsibility over our pharmaceutical health to the private sector, which works through institutions designed to make a profit.

From an innovation perspective, this allocation of our pharmaceutical needs to the private sector seems to be working well. Most current research on pharmaceuticals is led by private players. In 2018, the pharmaceutical industry invested $102 billion in research. That same year, the entire budget of the US-based National Institutes of Health (NIH), the world's largest public medical research agency, was $35.4 billion (Schulthess et al. 2022). It was the private sector that succeeded with the quick development, testing, and production of COVID-19 vaccines. Conversely, crucial research expected from public institutions to understand and fight the epidemic quickly, that should have been carried out by public institutions immediately, such as quantifying the impact of using masks, or data-driven best practices on how to use masks and other anti-infectious measures, took too long to be produced, and was done sporadically.

Being mostly private, pharmaceuticals follow private incentives and where profits can be made. In the past, research investments were directed toward the most prevalent diseases as these promised the biggest markets and highest revenue. However, since Payers worldwide started to signal a higher willingness to pay for drugs tackling orphan diseases or for high visibility ones, such as cancer, diabetes, dementia, etc., the pharmaceutical innovation focus shifted toward these new higher-priced treatments.

Widespread theories claim that pharma is hiding cures to several chronic diseases to keep patients on a more profitable maintenance medication for years. That is, however, not compatible with the current pricing model: if a pharma company could, for instance, cure cancer with a single pill, they would be able to obtain very high prices from governments, because the price of pharmaceuticals is calculated based on the full treatment cost (be it a single pill or a life-long treatment) and as a function of the clinical benefit.

The market is also very competitive and fragmented. As soon as a trial gives great results, competitors immediately start running trials using similar molecules. That is why we have so many competing drugs in Pharma. If one company tried to keep a single-pill treatment hidden to protect a life-long treatment, a competitor would not have such qualms and would bring the single pill treatment to gain market share from the lengthier treatment. No company wants to risk losing the potential profit from a breakthrough drug to another player. Given the system incentives, when Pharma finds effective treatments, they want to bring them to market as quickly as possible.

What sometimes happens is when products are licensed and priced to be used for a short period, and then some companies get patients to use it for longer periods. That happens mostly in psychotropic drugs, as in the case of the Opioid epidemic.

4.4.4.1 How About When It Is Patients or Profit?

When it comes to making decisions, Pharma caters to the interests of both patients and its shareholders, but not Payers, despite society expecting them to do so. Most times, the interests of patients and shareholders are aligned (e.g., when developing the best possible drugs, providing access to all patients in need, etc.), so it is easy for Pharma to make decisions putting patients first.

Sometimes, the interests of these two groups are at odds. In these moments, our experience is that most people working in pharmaceutical companies put patients first in their decisions, consistent with why they joined the industry and what motivates them to show up to work every day. However, a few times pharmaceutical employees convince themselves that they are putting patients' interests first, when they are actually favoring their shareholders' or organizational interests.

Like in any other business, pharmaceutical companies are challenged daily with managing the difficult balance between the socially oriented desire to do the right thing and the shareholder pressure to grow and increase profits. Unfortunately, this constant tension exposes pharmaceutical companies to misguided individuals or unrestrained corporate cultures and a few eventually succumb to the money altar, and deviate from a balanced approach. The never-ending pressure to show growing profits every quarter, under present-day loose regulation, has resulted in several companies, including some in the pharmaceutical sector, to fudge numbers, cut corners, adopt illegal or unethical practices, or lose sight of their public mission. Those are the ones that hit the news and raise outrage against the industry.

While we must constantly fight against the negative outcomes from delegating our pharmaceutical innovation needs to the private sector, how can we prevent, minimize, or eliminate them? Experts and researchers agree that it is hard to know if businesses are indeed more unethical today or if they are just more scrutinized and we more aware and justifiably intolerant of such practices than before (Karlsson et al. 2017). Can we ever expect perfection, i.e., a system that delivers what we want (e.g., a high rate of innovation at affordable costs) without any occasional failures (e.g., zero ethical abuses)?

4.4.5 Are There Drug Pricing Abuses? If So, Why?

Drug pricing has become a focal point of healthcare policy. In America, 8 out of 10 people surveyed have said that the cost of drugs is "unreasonable" (Kirzinger et al. 2019). Why so?

We will look at the dramatic and interesting story of the EpiPen, that made headlines back in 2016, by raising its prices sixfold. EpiPen is a device that injects epinephrine, an effective and lifesaving drug for those experiencing a severe and potentially deadly allergic reaction (e.g., anaphylactic shock), which occurs most in children. Originally developed by Merck KGaA in 2007, the EpiPen, normally sold in a pack of two, cost approximately $100. It was later acquired and improved by Mylan, a large generics manufacturer, which gradually raised the price to $608 by 2016 in the USA (Kerr 2016; Khazan 2016), while costing $85 in France and $69 in the UK (Khazan 2016; Paton and Kresge 2020).

The raise in EpiPen's US price was much higher than other pharmaceuticals, and led to a public outcry, governmental hearings, and investigations for antitrust violations. Mylan started lobbying to include EpiPen on the US federal list of preventive medical services, which would require employers and insurers, but not patients, to pay for it. Mylan's CEO Heather Bresch suggested that health insurers should absorb the price increase. When questioned about EpiPen, she pushed for a discussion of the whole pricing system in the USA, which was seen as a disingenuous move to push the spotlight away from Mylan. Meanwhile, contributing to the outrage, Bresch received a cumulative 670% raise (Kerr 2016).

Mylan tried to patch its damaged reputation with the promise of a $300 generic EpiPen plus discounts and free devices for patients who had to pay list price, which again was seen as disingenuous by many. The generic version was still three times more expensive than the pre-acquisition EpiPen price and the discounts came with anti-competition conditions that benefited Mylan. Mylan became a poster case for pharmaceutical industry's abuses and negative reputation (The Editorial Board 2016), which includes other notorious cases such as Martin Shkreli from Turing Pharmaceuticals that rose the price of Daraprim from $13.50 to $750 per tablet overnight, and eventually ended in jail.

The EpiPen story is a terrible story of Pharma pricing. However, the reality may be much more nuanced than the simplistic "greedy CEO who increased prices because she was unethical" story we saw on TV. At closer look, we see a fascinating, nuanced story that includes so many aspects of what is wrong in pharmaceutical pricing in the USA. Let's take a closer look then.

To start, the EpiPen is not a pharmaceutical product but rather a drug-device combination, and thus under a different regulation. The device injects an old, generic, out-of-patent pharmaceutical (epinephrine). It also has a long patent that prevents competitors from copying the device's exact format. In addition, the FDA rejected applications for slightly different devices that avoided the EpiPen patent considering them as too different to be an EpiPen generic. Without an EpiPen generic, pharmacists had no cheaper substitute for EpiPen prescriptions. We can say that, in a way, the regulator created a quasi-monopoly for EpiPen.

That quasi-monopoly increased in 2015, when Sanofi's competitor device Auvi-Q was recalled due to dosage safety concerns. EpiPen still faced competition from the much cheaper though lesser-known epinephrine injector Adrenaclick. However, parents feared it was harder to use and thus an inferior device to save their children's lives when in distress, and thus stayed loyal to and reinforced EpiPen's quasi-monopoly.

By then, however, EpiPen already cost $461 vs. $509 for Auvi-Q, both up from $241 when Auvi-Q was launched 3 years earlier (Herper 2016). From 2012 to 2015, prices doubled (Herper 2016), when competition was expected to make them fall. How could that be? Product Benefit Managers (PBMs) in the USA threaten not to list (e.g., not offer to patients) a product or to only list it with high copays, if the company does not give them large percentage-based rebates (Herper 2016). These threats are stronger when PBM can pivot toward competing products and, if implemented, can significantly hurt sales. Hence, Pharma companies have found that the best way to accommodate the PBM demands is by raising list prices so they absorb the large percentage-based rebates without sacrificing profits.

Heather Bresch stated that Mylan got a net price of $274 or 45% of the $608 list price for two EpiPens in 2016 (Pollack 2016), up from when Mylan received a net of $87 or 88% of the $99 list price in 2008. Despite the threefold net price increase, as the list price increased, the net price percentage fell by almost half. Sanofi, the Auvi-Q producer, blamed Mylan for giving such large rebates to restrict access to Auvi-Q (Staton 2017). True or not, PBMs seem to trigger pharmaceutical price increases, maybe even more when there is competition.

In 2016, the co-pay for EpiPen was $73 or 12% of the $608 list price. During that year, many employers attempted to save money by shifting their employees to healthcare plans with larger deductibles, increasing their co-pays, and thus exposed them to a larger share of the high EpiPen list price.

Here is another ethical dilemma now faced by healthcare plans regarding the sale of high deductible plans. While high-deductible plans seem unfair to high-need patients (net beneficiaries), without them, insurers would bear the cost spikes alone, which would be politically much more acceptable for society. This would mean that plan costs would rise across the board. With the co-pay increases to patients, high-deductible plans share with patients the financial impact of patient/doctor choices for more expensive products, as well as of the increasing pharmaceutical prices. In this way, healthcare plans can keep the prices of their plans more affordable and will not be alone fighting increased drug costs.

Mylan manufactures 7500 generics, and EpiPen is their largest grossing one. As a generics manufacturer, Mylan likely had little to no negotiation power against PBMs or other stakeholders across the rest of its portfolio. However, the EpiPen device patent gave it quite a bit of negotiation power over its price. Bresch, possibly after years being the weaker party when negotiating with PBMs, may have seen for the first time the opportunity to play the same negotiation game branded drugs play (e.g., higher prices, higher rebates).

Besides, Mylan had invested in improving the EpiPen device engineering and making it available at high-need public locations (e.g., schools) for free for emergency uses. Bresch probably saw Mylan adding enough value to patients, and was less concerned with the impact on healthcare plans, who often squeezed her on the rest of her generic portfolio. Given EpiPen's patent, she may have rationalized that EpiPen only cost a fraction of what a regular branded-drug costs, and thus was doing nothing wrong or out of the ordinary, but rather claiming a fair return on her investment and benefit to patients.

Given the new information, was Heather Bresch a greedy and unscrupulous CEO or thoughtful and patient-focused she claimed to be? Let's first adopt some perspective-taking, a best practice in negotiation, and put ourselves in Heather Bresch's shoes to see how she saw her decisions based on information from her many interviews or statements.

Potential Mylan's Perspective

1. EpiPen's list price increases were designed to deliver higher percentage-based rebates to PBMs and have the balance paid by healthcare plans, not patients. Only a few US patients with high deductibles would pay for it, as such plans were a novelty in 2016. According to Bresch, 90% of patients paid less than $50 for their EpiPens.
2. The EpiPen pricing strategy aimed to reduce patient co-pays, as only by offering PBMs the highest possible rebates, would they place EpiPen in the highest tiers of their formularies, which allow for lower copays (The Wall Street Journal 2019). Mylan could offer high rebates by increasing its list price, as it did, or at the expense of its profit margin. It tried the first assuming it was not going to harm patients significantly.
3. EpiPen is not a pharmaceutical, but rather a device carrying one. As such, the EpiPen price was still significantly below what was generally considered appro-

priate for a medical device in the US Market (Henschke and Redberg 2018; Sifferlin 2018).[3]

4. The US and European EpiPen price comparison unfairly singled out EpiPen as if it were an outlier. Instead it reflects a normal US-EU medical device price difference. For example, drug-eluting cardiac stents[4] cost $340 in Germany vs. $1400 in the USA (Wenzl and Mossialos 2018a, b), and other medical devices presented even higher differences.
5. Mylan invested US$1 billion to improve the EpiPen device, increase public awareness over anaphylactic shock, lobby legislators, and donate EpiPens. This investment reduced the amount of anaphylactic shock deaths, which reflects EpiPen's added benefits to patients.
6. Mylan had no monopoly to push people out of therapy as patients could switch to Adrenaclick, at half of EpiPen's cost. It is not EpiPen's fault if competing products were inferior. If anything, it is a testament to EpiPen's superiority as a product and the recognition of Mylan's value add.
7. The accusations of negotiation power abuse are unfair. When generic manufacturers, who mostly offer commoditized, and thus highly substitutable, products, have low negotiation power against PBMs or healthcare plans and are bullied into lowering their prices, no one complains about negotiation power abuses. When other medical devices or patent-protected pharmaceuticals leverage their patents to enhance their negotiation power, no one complains about patent abuses. Why was EpiPen being unfairly singled out when everyone else was doing the same?
8. The accusations of anti-competitive moves by Sanofi were dismissed by the High Court (Leonard 2023).

Our perspective-taking shows that Bresch did not see herself as an "evil greedy Pharma CEO taking advantage of patients in need." Instead, the simplistic evil Mylan's story sold by the media, politicians, and other healthcare stakeholders can also be a great smokescreen for the contributions of others to the larger problem (Lopez 2016), which we examine below:

1. **Sanofi** chose to price Auvi-Q at parity with EpiPen, even matching its price raises until it eventually became more expensive than EpiPen, despite having an inferior product as evidenced by its later removal from the market. Sanofi claimed that it had to raise prices because it was stuck in a rebate competition with Mylan, and thus could not keep prices low. If so, Mylan was equally stuck

[3] Medical devices' prices were less regulated, raised more often (e.g., after new versions), and cost much more than the EpiPen's price in 2016. Only by 2018, did the medical devices' pricing and lack of regulation catch the public attention.

[4] Drug-eluting stents (DES) are thin, vascular prostheses coated with a slow-release medication to reopen and maintain open coronary arteries narrowed by arteriosclerosis. These stents help prevent blood clots from forming within the stent, providing an effective treatment for coronary artery disease.

competing with Sanofi and, if this argument is true, Sanofi competition gave Mylan little choice but to raise EpiPen's prices as well.
2. **PBMs**'s negotiated for percentage-based rebates, and as such pushed absolute list prices up (Lopez 2016), as shown by Mylan's decreasing EpiPen's price share (from 88% in 2008 to 45% in 2016).
3. **Someone(s)** was getting $334 out of each EpiPen's $608 list price sold to patients on high deductible plans. Agreements between retailers, wholesalers, and PBMs are confidential, so we don't know how they split the total $334 amount. Meanwhile, PBMs's profits doubled in the 2 years (2014–2016), without significant changes in business activities.
4. **FDA's** regulation on generic devices at the time prevented generics from entering the market. Similarly, its slow processes on generic evaluation (median of almost 4 years) prevent many generics from reaching the US market (Lupkin 2016).
5. **Physicians** could have prescribed alternative devices instead of just EpiPen.
6. **Healthcare plans** started offering large deductible plans, cheaper to employers, not patients, who were left exposed if in need of high-cost treatments.
7. **Employers** started choosing large deductible plans to cover their workers at lower costs.

While Bresch's choices were influenced by the multifaceted dynamics with different stakeholders as seen above, Mylan still leveraged its negotiation power to maximize profits. And while her choices deserve scrutiny, the other healthcare actors were doing much of the same. The difference in the EpiPen case is that Mylan for once had significant more negotiation power than its counterparties and stakeholders, and used it effectively as many others have done against Mylan in the past. Another difference is that Mylan's one power lever, EpiPen, involved children's lives, and Bresch seemingly failed to anticipate the impact of using her power in this context. So our answer is that the healthcare problem is much deeper than CEOs morals and greediness.

In a system dominated by win-lose negotiation interactions, individuals think selfishly and rationalize their subsequent unethical power-based choices by blaming others: "*Why should I not leverage my negotiation power to improve my profits, when everyone else is selfishly doing the same whenever they can?*" One does not need an evil mind or heart to harm patients and their families. The aggregation of many, small, inconsiderate, selfish contributions of several players in a system made dysfunctional by win-lose negotiations is sufficient to cause such harm. In fact, we would go as far as saying that: A big chunk of the evil and pain caused in the world today is a consequence of win-lose negotiations.

The EpiPen story should have led to a deeper system examination, as Bresch seemingly intended. It should have exposed the series of win-lose negotiations and value-negative services and actors, and hopefully led us to confront the real problem and collaborate toward much better solutions.

Unfortunately, it seems that the lesson taken from the EpiPen story was the simplistic idea that "It was caused by yet another evil greedy Pharma CEO." If that is the lesson, then US citizens' health and money will be dependent on Pharma CEOs being better at balancing "how greedy" they must be. On one end, there is the public demanding low CEO greediness, but on the other, there are shareholders demanding high CEO greediness. What is the sweet spot? Maybe if Heather Bresch had been less greedy, and settled for a lower price, let's say the $520 of years prior, it would have never made the news. But would the EpiPen affordability be OK at $520?

The individualization or personification of the problem is satisfying as we can put a face to the misdeed felt or done, and punish them. However, when we do so at the expense of a systemic look at the problem, such as the structural forces and dynamics that shape individual decisions, we will be limiting ourselves to cosmetic changes or punishments. Given the complexity of our health system, we need to appreciate its stakeholders' goals, strategies, and negotiation interactions to accurately diagnose organizational pressures or failures that lead individuals to make or get away with bad decisions. Finally, much like climate change, game theory, or the prisoner's dilemma, we must examine each actor's interaction effects on the others as they shape choices and behaviors that, while logical to the individual, are detrimental to the collective or the system.

On the other hand, if we assume that our health and healthcare costs should not be dependent on the lack of greed from CEOs or rest solely on individual change, but rather on broader systemic change, we can start asking equally broader questions:

1. Should a non-innovative life-saving drug and a slightly innovative device costing $35 to produce be sold for $608? Should a minor improvement on the device grant it a decades-long patent when there is only a short time from design to market?
2. Should the FDA approval process take years? And in doing so, delaying a product launch and thus reducing the patent-intended rewards for innovation or the entry of competitors after patent expiry?
3. Should an expensive, patent-protected pen have the validity of only 1 year? If epinephrine expires, then shouldn't the epinephrine, instead of the whole device, be replaced?
4. Should it be allowed to sell in packs of two, instead of individual pens?
5. Should PBMs negotiate for rebates, not price decreases? Should those rebates be passed only to Healthcare plans, while the resulting price increases and higher copays are passed on to patients?
6. Should middlemen receive $334 for distributing a pen to patients? Should their payment be a percentage of the value of the product? Why? What incentives does that generate?
7. Should public opinion be shocked when the $608 bill falls on a few patients, but OK when it falls on a healthcare plan, thus falling on all patients through raises in their premiums?
8. Which are the value-positive activities in this system? Which ones are value-negative? How much value are the value-negative providers extracting from the system?

And the list can go on as we attempt to diagnose our healthcare system's real weaknesses and areas for improvement to promote superior pricing dynamics and positive consequences to our collective health.

4.4.6 Price Evolution and Popular Perception

Despite its particularities, the EpiPen case well illustrates many of the US healthcare system problems. If we step back from our focus and availability bias over the few, flashy, yet horrible pharma pricing stories, we find a more boring, yet positive situation. While most people see list prices increasing higher than the inflation rate, after off-invoice discounts, rebates, statutory payments under the Affordable Care Act, and patient coupons, the average price charged by manufacturers—the net price—is increasing at a much slower pace than list prices (Scott et al. 2020). In fact, in many European countries, net prices are actually falling (Reinaud 2022).

In the USA, list prices have little financial impact on most insured patients, except for those in high deductible plans, as spending is capped regardless of list prices. At Medicare Part D, which covers approximately 60 million individuals in the USA,[5] the 2023 standard benefit included a deductible of $505, and a 25% coinsurance up to $4660 of patient spending. For example, a $4660 treatment would have an insured patient pay $1544, or 33% of the total bill, which includes the $505 deductible plus the 25% coinsurance of the remaining amount ($1039). As many patients take several treatments, after $7400 of out of pocket spending until 2024, the coinsurance drops from 25% to 5%. Things will change in 2024 and beyond, with the new IRA, a topic we will develop further later in this chapter.

In Europe, the situation is different due to P&R negotiations. As seen previously, a drug's clinical benefit is assessed by national payers, which gives them a significant power advantage to negotiate whether the drug will be available, to whom, and at which price. Furthermore, negotiated prices at launch are unchangeable, not corrected for inflation, and bound to be reduced at a pre-set renegotiation date, usually every 2 years. The only time drug prices increase in Europe is when new drugs are launched and negotiate higher prices to reward their superior clinical value, compared to existing, less-effective drugs.

As seen earlier, European drug prices are significantly lower than in the USA and it is hard to imagine a sufficient rate of investment and innovation if the USA were paying European prices as well. In fact, many see the USA indirectly subsidizing pharmaceuticals in Europe and the rest of the world.

It is therefore somewhat surprising that Europeans also consider the price of their drugs too high, probably as they benchmark not against US prices but rather against generic drugs with prices negotiated down to the minimal limit needed to ensure manufacturing and still heavily subsidized (Euronews 2022). As in the COVID

[5] Medicare Part D covers oral drugs and provides health insurance for Americans aged 65 and older as well as some younger people with disability status or specific diseases, such as end stage renal disease and amyotrophic lateral sclerosis.

vaccine pricing example, many Europeans thought that the vaccine should have been free or at most priced at cost, instead of Pharma profiteering from the plight of the people in the midst of a pandemic.

For many Europeans, the higher the need, the cheaper a drug should be, so everyone who needs it must have access to it. While that makes some sense at a healthcare system copay level, it does not translate well into the manufacturer pricing and as an incentive to innovation. And yet, Payers and politicians operate under the incentives of their electorates. That tension between pricing based on value or on need represents one more challenge for Pharma.

As we will see in the next pages, this popular perception is exactly the opposite of the pricing system used in Europe, which creates a profoundly negative, and in our perspective unfair, perception of drug pricing in Europe.

4.4.7 Drug Pricing Seems Cruel to the Layperson, But Is It?

One key reason behind Pharma's negative reputation is drug pricing. It is hard for anyone to stay indifferent when hearing stories of patients suffering or dying for lack of access to expensive drugs. Either patients die due to non-reimbursement, or healthcare systems pay exorbitant prices to treat a single patient.

It is important, however, to differentiate high prices from abusive ones and understand the rationale for drug pricing. For example, US authorities recently approved a $2.1 million gene therapy to treat spinal muscular atrophy (SMA),[6] making this the most expensive drug to date. Such a high price tag has generated much criticism—but is it abusive? Spinal muscular atrophy is a rare and deadly disease caused by a genetic defect that weakens a person's muscles so dramatically that they become unable to move, and eventually breathe. This life-saving therapy, high as it is, may not be an irrational number nor an abusive one after all.

The implicit deal between governments and the pharmaceutical industry, first by the USA after World War II (Magee 2019), and later spread to Europe, was: government wants to advance healthcare research and not only provide the cheapest, stagnant care with the current technology. This developmental rationale stemmed from the US WWII victory being credited to the R&D of the atomic bomb. Within a few years, the USA created the most potent weapon the world had ever seen, enabling it to win the war without further combat. Had the USA spent those resources sending more conventional troops and weapons against Japan, the estimated additional American casualties was numbered in the millions (Cox 2021).

As the war ended, governments diverted their war resources to population-benefiting efforts. The USA opted to invest it in developing new therapies that would win the war on disease, and thus chose to fund academic research, instead of building public hospitals where patients would be eternally treated with 1940s' technologies. This choice turned the USA into the largest healthcare R&D funder worldwide and the driving force behind our biomedical technological progress for

[6] The therapy is aimed at patients younger than 2 years old and with a mutation of a specific gene.

decades, until other governments eventually joined the R&D effort. While all that, R&D has not yet created the ultimate weapon to win the war on disease, its progress has been phenomenal, particularly since WWII a few diseases have been eradicated, others are expected to be soon, and many diseases became treatable (Breene 2017; Roser et al. 2014).

Governments fund pharmaceutical R&D in two ways. First and most straightforward, they directly fund some academic pharmaceutical research. Second, users temporarily pay high patent-protected price premiums for new and improved drugs to reward successful R&D from the private sector.

Indeed, governments do not have the money to fund and absorb the risk of all desired R&D activity given its inherent high failure rate (as seen in Chap. 3). Hence, governments outsource the cost of failure when they encourage pharmaceutical companies to fund R&D in exchange for paying them high prices for good drugs. If the R&D fails, as most do, governments pay nothing. This outcomes-based approach increases R&D activity while reducing the government's risk at a cost of temporary high prices for the eventual R&D success. Without that reward, investors will reject taking on the big R&D risk, and move their money to another industry with better returns. In sum, for this innovation system to be well funded, drugs cannot be priced based on the cost of producing pill, but rather based on their clinical value in filling an unmet health need for society.

Different countries value clinical value in different ways. Some countries (e.g., the UK) follow cost-effectiveness, where drugs are priced roughly based on how many extra years of quality life (QALY) they provide. Drugs providing one extra year of quality life are reimbursed if they cost the system less than £30,000. Note that this £30,000 threshold was set in 2000 and not inflation adjusted since then, in the majority of cases. In other markets, the value of life is less quantified, but the logic is similar: good drugs save lives and Payers pay. Payers pay much less for less good drugs. Not-good drugs are not reimbursed or sold, and their manufacturers shoulder the cost of failure.

This system mostly makes sense. What should be the UK price of a curative drug for a deadly disease that kills young children? Answer in the case of a 1 year old baby boy: £30,000 per year of high quality of life gained x the additional life expectancy of a healthy 1 year old baby boy in the UK born on 2020 (Buxton 2022) or 86.3 years $\approx$ £2.5 million. This would be the most expensive drug so far, but it grants the boy a full life to old age, and thus the highest possible benefit to an individual.[7] With this investment, where children's lives are saved at £2.5 million each, governments have financed the development of technology that can save every child born with SMA forever. It is a success that drugs like these are developed, and the price we pay is what allows that to happen. A few years after the patent expires, generics hopefully enter the market and make the treatment significantly more accessible by reducing its prices by 80% or more. New and better treatments follow, continuing the cycle of innovation and improvement of our quality of life.

[7] One could consider a higher social benefit in the case of drugs against contagious diseases, which indirectly save several lives but are actually priced lower than in this example.

This doesn't imply all pricing is justifiable or fair. Problems happen when the system does not work as planned and diverts from the drug's real clinical value. For example, such deviations happen when Payers emit negatively biased clinical evaluations or make unfounded extreme discount demands or threats to negotiate a lower-than-deserved price or when Pharma submits biased dossiers or reduced patient and sales forecasts to negotiate a higher-than-deserved price for its drug.

Value pricing, described above, is highly correlated with the willingness to pay *of the Payer,* not the patient. Between two drugs competing for the Payer's limited budget, a Payer often prefers the drug that brings the most value to its patients and pays more for those that bring more value. To the outside, this system seems based on willingness to pay, when in fact it isn't, as the parties are pricing based on an agreed upon value-based system.

We can differentiate the two approaches if we consider the Buyer's alternatives when setting a new drug price. When the Payer has competing drugs for the same disease (modern drugs, that are effective and carry expensive price tags) the new drug price tends to be higher than when the Payer only has old, ineffective and cheap drugs available.

This happens because the comparators are the main basis of calculating value in many healthcare systems, not willingness to pay. If it was based on willingness to pay, then Pharma would ask Payers to pay more when their patients had no good treatments available, which is not what happens. Willingness to pay pricing could be misunderstood for treatments of high unmet need cases affecting particularly vulnerable populations (e.g., cystic fibrosis). In these rare cases, Payers have an additional interest to pay a premium to incentivize Pharma to invest in such indications.

Also, in a full willingness to pay system, the competition of the modern drugs in the same indication should push their prices down, while the single old drug should enjoy a monopoly-like high price. Instead, what we find in most healthcare systems is a pricing system rooted in the value comparison of available treatments. This value-based pricing system underscores that pricing is not driven by Pharma's goodwill but rather by a structured approach that doesn't rely on willingness to pay.

It is also very important to highlight that the system works under the understanding that healthcare systems, rather than individual patients, will cover the costs. In a developed society, it's expected that individuals shouldn't go without or have to bear the cost of innovative treatments on their own—a principle that, if violated, signals a failure in the healthcare system.

Prices can be deemed inappropriate for various reasons. While uncommon outside of the USA, the manufacturer could be demanding an undeservedly expensive price for its new, high unmet need, unique drug from a low-power Payer who cannot say no. Alternatively, Pharma could be negotiating based on an overestimated value or non-representative data, as when drugs fail to replicate the benefits seen in clinical trials ran with non-representative groups of patients. Payers outside the USA protect themselves from these risks by only paying for observed outcomes or demanding discounts to buffer for every eventuality. These risk-transfer moves unfairly shift all risk to Pharma, given that a drug's uncertainty is intrinsic to the disease, research, or P&R process and often not the manufacturer's fault.

While Pharma can be criticized for its shortcomings, high drug prices don't necessarily mean a flaw in Pharma's approach. So, to what extent are high Pharma prices a wrongdoing? Are Pharma and Payers pricing life-saving benefits in an unfair way? How absurd is it to value one extra year of high-quality of life at £30,000, and thus a full life at £2.5 million? Actually, there are several examples outside Pharma that value life at around the same or much above the £2.5 million (equivalent to US$3.3 million or €3 million) price tag, such as:

1. The cost of seatbelts for passengers in school buses values life at $2.8m (Tengs et al. 1995).
2. Banning asbestos in roof coatings puts the value of a life at $5.2m.
3. The flammability standards for children's clothing are reported to cost companies $15m per life saved.
4. The cost to strengthen buildings in earthquake-prone areas is reported at $18m per life saved.

The above examples have clear differences and nuances compared with pharmaceuticals. Still, while £2.5 million seems outrageous at first, it is not at odds with how we value saving lives across the board. This extreme price tag for a drug becomes more palatable when we factor in the value-based system's ability to calibrate prices according to a drug's life-enhancing or life-saving value, the steep, confidential discounts offered to European Payers, and how an innovative drug's benefits are then captured in perpetuity as they become much cheaper with time and eventually stepping stones for future innovations.

Unfortunately, it is hard to convey such pricing complexities to an average audience, which are then often absent from the mainstream media. Instead, much of the negative news or stories we discussed earlier reinforce that drug pricing worldwide is based on willingness to pay or that Payers are being blackmailed even when companies properly pursue a price within the national pricing rules. Pharma negligence in showing its side of the story publicly enables the persistence of its negatively biased image around the world.

4.4.8 Sales or Negotiation Tactics Have Been Dangerously Aggressive

We propose to start this subchapter on sales and negotiation tactics by looking at the worst recent example of Pharma we know of. Unfortunately, worst examples stick to memory, and they tend to contaminate the reputation of entire industries.

The OxyContin example in the USA illustrates how overly aggressive or unsupervised sales tactics can cause serious problems or even cross ethical or legal lines. In 2018, Massachusetts joined more than two dozen other states in suing Purdue Pharma, the makers of OxyContin, for "the harm they inflicted in our state" by helping to drive the opioid crisis (Podolsky et al. 2019) and provided plenty of information on OxyContin sales tactics from 1996 to 2001 (Van Zee 2009):

1. Over 40 national pain-management and speaker-training conferences were held at resorts in Florida, Arizona, and California, where over 5000 physicians, pharmacists, and nurses were recruited and trained for Purdue's national speakers' bureau. It is well-documented that this type of event influences physician prescribing habits even though physicians do not believe it does (Van Zee 2009).
2. Purdue's OxyContin marketing plan targeted the highest opioid-prescribing physicians nationally. They identified the least discriminate prescribers with large numbers of chronic-pain patients, who could ultimately yield the most revenue for the company (Van Zee 2009).
3. A lucrative bonus system encouraged sales representatives to do whatever was needed to increase sales of OxyContin in their territories. In 2001, in addition to the average sales representative's annual salary of $55,000, bonuses averaged $71,500 (from $15,000 to nearly $240,000) (Van Zee 2009).
4. A patient starter coupon program provided patients with a free limited-time prescription for a 7- to 30-day supply. By 2001, when the program was ended, approximately 34,000 coupons had been redeemed nationally (Van Zee 2009).
5. Purdue trained its sales representatives to carry the message that the risk of addiction was "less than one percent." These studies did not cover the scenario where opioids were used daily for a prolonged time in treating chronic pain (Van Zee, 2009).

Purdue Pharma was not alone. Since 1997, over 100 financial settlements between drug companies and governments have resulted in $11 billion in fines for off-label or deceptive marketing practices (Schwartz and Woloshin 2019). The deliberately orchestrated opioid crisis with its tens of thousands of victims and growing has been a horrible and inexcusable development of abusive practices (National Institute on Drug Abuse 2024). As far as we know, OxyContin is one of, if not the worst case where the tension between patients and profits swung completely in the wrong direction.

Despite the repulsion such cases create on us, only a subset of physicians are actually involved in rogue practices. A sales executive involved in the opioids scandal claimed that "98% of your business is going to come from 2% of your doctors." Only a very small subset of doctors were "willing to play the game," and he and his team had to search far and wide to find them and get their bonuses (Kabani 2020).

It is reassuring to learn that 98% of doctors were isolated from or resistant to such aggressive sales tactics, and this anecdote helps us right size the problem on the doctors' end. No such absolution for the salespeople from these pharmaceutical companies though. And yet, it is easy to see why in extreme cases, the lure of profit could push normal people into such behaviors. Ultimately, these salespeople were applying tactics commonly used in many other industries (e.g., timeshare sales, used car dealerships, payday loans, etc.), not appreciating how in Healthcare such aggressive tactics can easily turn unethical and have deeper consequences.

4.5 How Can Things Be Improved?

When one reads about the opioid horror story, a common take-away is: "*Wow, look at how terrible Pharma is.*" or perhaps "*That's what happens when corporations are allowed to take over our healthcare.*"

If asked: "What could have prevented this from happening?" Answers could be: "*If those people were not that evil,*" or "*By not having private companies in healthcare,*" or "*By having more free-market competition in Pharma,*" or "*By punishing these criminals hard enough that no one does similar things again*" or still "*There is nothing that could have been done. When evil people get together, that's it.*" Unfortunately, none of these suggestions are likely to prevent similar behavior in the future, nor in opioids nor anywhere else in Pharma.

We know that the Opioid crisis was preventable because it did not occur elsewhere, despite the drugs' presence in many other countries. Patients did not get addicted to opioids by taking prescription opioids. Why was that?

If we take some of the above answers, the conclusion is that US doctors and US sales reps are more evil than German or French ones? Or that American patients are mentally weaker, unable to fight pain on their own, or just more prone to addiction? Hypotheses that claim that pharma workers are evil or some patients are weak are, in our view, silly, offensive, and wrong. Outside of the USA, countries prevented patients from becoming addicted to prescription drugs through regulation demanding shorter treatments, no automatic refills, no direct-to-consumer advertising, prescription drug monitoring programs (PDMPs) to prevent doctor-shopping, and so forth (Brink et al. 2022).

In sum, the different results came from differences among the systems. To avoid a future drug-induced crisis, we should appreciate that most people, in the private or public sectors, will misbehave if they perceive the risks to be small and the rewards high. As such, prevention must involve designing better environments, incentives, and rules to achieve better results. To illustrate this point, let's check how feasible it is that listed pharmaceutical companies can change a few of their most criticized behaviors on their own.

Common criticism #1: Pharma companies' fiduciary duty with shareholders is not aligned with its mission or common good. Indeed, companies can try to align the two by sacrificing short term gains and upholding their mission, which can result in gains in reputation, relationships (e.g., Payers), and worker motivation. This alignment can significantly increase productivity and profits, which aligns shareholders' interests with those of the broader community.

However, there are company decisions for the common good that drop profits. For example, asking for prices lower than a drug's value in P&R negotiations. If a company were to do that, the impact on profits would be dramatic. After all, a 10% reduction in price leads to a 66% reduction in profits in a company with 15% profit margin. The company's share price would plunge, making investors furious and willing to sack management. Even if investors were also on board with decisions for the common good, the share price drop would open the door for a hostile takeover that would financially hurt the socially conscious investors. The new management would likely reinstate the previous, profit-making policy of aggressive pricing, secure superior prices in P&R negotiations, and be seen as a success to be emulated in the industry.

Common criticism #2: If Pharma make most of its money in developed markets, why not drastically lower its prices to developing ones? Because any company would take a big risk in doing so. Not only would it risk parallel imports into their key markets, but Payers of developed markets would use these lower prices as references in their P&R negotiations.

Common criticism #3: Pharma could do more to increase the common good by running trials on more representative patient populations (e.g., older patients with multiple pathologies). That approach would require larger trials and investments, and the outcomes would be looked at unfavorably by physicians, who would likely focus on absolute survival times without diving into the clinical trial population details. Running longer trials to acquire more mature data could help, but we already examined before how that would enable competitors to rush to market to become the new standard of care, drastically reducing the drug's profitability despite its more accurate data.

This little exercise is our attempt to illustrate how hard it is for individuals in listed companies to make choices that diminish share price and profits. At every turn, it seems that no good deed will go unpunished by competitors. So, do we believe that nothing can be done to improve the status quo? Not at all. Quite the contrary. We even wrote a book on the topic!

We believe that the people are not the problem, and if we want Pharma to act in ways that would bring even more benefit to society, we should seek solutions considering the competition between Pharmaceutical companies. We also suggest putting aside the pharma negative lens when searching for improvements to our healthcare.

4.5.1 Pharma Prices Are Highly Controlled

Regular reports put pharma at the center of a coming storm with headlines such as: "Public health systems face growing challenges to cope with the increasingly high prices of the new medicines." (Morgan et al. 2020) Is the system in fact being brought to its knees by pharma pricing?

Pharma costs are not out of control. They are actually declining in the EU (now even faster given the high inflation) and flat in the USA compared with other healthcare costs. For all of the outsized attention pharma receives, its share of the healthcare budget is just 15% and relatively stable over the past 15 years, if not decreasing. This means 85% of healthcare spending is not drug-related.

The EU has a wide range of tools to control its drug expenditures (Carone et al. 2012). All EU Member States have lists specifying which pharmaceuticals will be reimbursed based on the outcome of their P&R negotiations. Most negotiate drug prices strictly using comparators plus a premium or discount based on value differential. Then, during P&R negotiations, Payers demand pharmaceutical companies to:

1. Give discounts or rebates
2. Set caps or envelopes that entitle Payers to claim free or almost free products after reaching a pre-agreed volume
3. Pay back a share of revenue if national budget ceilings for drugs are exceeded (in 2023 in the UK, the percentage of payback in addition to usual taxes was 26.5%)
4. Agree to risk sharing arrangements which trigger lower prices or refunds if certain pre-agreed conditions are not reached and
5. Accept price freezes and cuts imposed unilaterally by governments (850mio worth of price cut in France in 2023)

EU market entry restrictions delay patient access for months to consider P&R decisions. Most EU member states monitor at least some prescription behavior and volume through electronic prescriptions. Physicians are mandated, fined, or receive financial incentives to follow prescription guidelines, quotas, targets, and budgets, with a focus on generics in at least 11 EU member states. Most EU member states offer prescribing advice and support, patient education campaigns, patient co-payments, differentiated reimbursement rates for essential, chronic, and other drugs, as well as excessive out-of-pocket payment protection to vulnerable groups. In sum, many aspects of Pharma, including drug prices, are very much in control.

Surely, as the Opioid crisis in the USA has proven, the system can improve, but it is *relatively* well controlled already, at least in Europe. What do we mean by *relatively*? Well, given that we want to solve healthcare problems, we should look at the whole of healthcare.

4.5.2 Different Levers to Improve Healthcare Outcomes

One way to reduce treatment costs and increase its benefits is by reducing inappropriately prescribed pharmaceuticals, and other value-negative costs. In fact, for lack of pharma-like quality checks, medical treatment more broadly varies tremendously in quality, but being diffuse, distributed, or nuanced, such variance is little known, hard to identify or blame. According to Gerd Gigerenzer, hospitals and doctors everywhere are subject to conflicts of interest which cause practice variability (Gigerenzer and Gray 2013) and harm patients, such as:

1. In Germany, the rate of breast-conserving surgery conducted under similar conditions varied widely (from 0–100%) in 78 clinics, suggesting that treatments were based neither on the best science nor on women's preferences.
2. Eight percent of the children in one region in Vermont had their tonsils removed, while in another area, 70% underwent the same procedure.
3. In Maine, the proportion of women who have had a hysterectomy by the age of 70 varies between communities from less than 20% to more than 70%.

4. In Iowa, the proportion of men who have undergone prostate surgery by age 85 ranges from 15% to more than 60%.
5. In Brazil, 55% of births are by c-section (Rudey et al. 2020), compared to 21% worldwide (Betran et al. 2021), with part of the variance explained by doctors trying to optimize and plan their schedules and increase their profits in detriment of the less expensive, faster recovery, but more time-consuming natural birth process.

As we can see, more healthcare or an overtreatment bias are not always better. In the United States, regions with high utilization and expensive care show slightly worse mortality outcomes, perceived access, and patient satisfaction (Hall 2015).

Unfortunately, doctors and hospitals are subject to conflicting interests when their patient care decisions can increase their earnings, such as when operating under fee-for-service systems (e.g., additional payment for each test, treatment, or even injectable drugs in the US). Services for which physicians get little pay from health insurances (e.g., talking to patients or making home visits) are discouraged, whereas those that increase the flow of income (e.g., surgery and imaging) are encouraged. The ones that give in to the money temptation become value-negative providers as they forego the best patient care and overprescribe for profit's sake.

Defensive medicine is another source of overtreatment bias, which involves the practice of prescribing a suboptimal or unnecessary test or treatment only to protect the physician or hospital against the risk of malpractice lawsuits. According to Gerd Gigerenzer, 93% of 824 US physicians at high risk of litigation reported practicing defensive medicine moves, such as ordering unnecessary CTs, biopsies, and MRIs, or prescribing more antibiotics than medically indicated (Studdert et al. 2005). Defensive medicine also appears in discrepancies between doctors' recommendation to patients versus to their own families. In Switzerland, for instance, the rate of hysterectomy in the general population is 16%, but among doctors' wives and female doctors it is only 10% (Domenighetti et al. 1993). Defensive medicine may become the rationalization for profit-motivated decisions, as the doctor's interests diverge from the patient's well-being.

No one seems to be ever sued for overtreatment or defensive medicine, even if it costs millions to the system, and risks unnecessary harm to tens of thousands of patients. These value-negative providers make for few and less attractive headlines as the bad stories are reduced to boring statistics. Notwithstanding, they cause great harm and losses, and fixing it can be a great way to improve our healthcare.

It is important to reinforce that reducing overtreatment and defensive medicine would be a great way of reducing pharmaceuticals costs: We would be reducing the money spent on pharmaceuticals on patients they bring the least benefit. Given the scale of overtreatment and defensive medicine, the impact would be significant.

4.5.3 Patent Expiration Could Contribute More to Lower Costs

Another way of reducing pharmaceutical costs without reducing care would be to optimize the switch to generics and biosimilars after patent expiration and ensure there is enough generic competition. Many OECD countries have low generic penetration, despite complaints over high drug prices, and there lies opportunity.

Some countries have taken effective measures to increase the benefit of generics and biosimilars, such as demanding that prescriptions indicate the molecule name, not its brand, or that pharmacists carry competing drugs and show all their prices to patients. Countries that have adopted similar measures have seen an increase in the use of generics and a drop in prices. Countries that avoid such measures, some unpopular with physicians, patients, or pharmacists, fail to take full benefit of patent expiration.

4.5.4 Some Wealthy Nations Could Stop Free-Riding on the Patent System

The patent system rewards the innovator for a limited period by granting exclusivity, after which the innovation falls into public domain, benefiting humankind forever (see Chap. 3). In Pharma, it is the developed nations who pay most if not all of the patent price premium for the innovation. After the patent expires, generics come in, and the innovation is sold worldwide, cheaper, and in perpetuity.

This system benefits poor nations who, without contributing to the innovation, eventually gain access to it, even if many years later than other countries, and too late for the patients during that wait. While one could claim that poor countries are free-riding the innovation funded by developed nations, there seems to be a tacit international agreement, though much debated, that this seems to be an acceptable arrangement for now.

Unfortunately, some wealthy countries free ride the patent system acting as if they were poor countries, such as when they dedicate only 10% of their healthcare expenses to pharmaceuticals vs. the 18% OECD average). Despite being scientifically advanced, these countries were for years reluctant to set up their HTA systems and relied on win-lose purchasing processes that ignored a drug's clinical value, squeezed suppliers, and focused on securing the lowest possible price. When the manufacturer stops lowering prices to match the country's extreme and baseless demands, the drugs are denied reimbursement. Consequently, these countries have very low reimbursement rates for innovative drugs. For example, Norway's reimbursement list is 1/3 that of Germany's and still below the Czech Republic's, despite having three times the GDP per capita of the latter.

Wealthy nations with much lower reimbursement rates may have a higher threshold for new drugs and have the freedom not to reimburse them. There are, however, challenges to this perspective. One is the lack of drug evaluation. If they had an HTA system with unique criteria that disqualified certain drugs, the above argument would make more sense. A second challenge is that they are interested in the drugs, but only if they are cheap enough, which often means cheaper than what other similar countries pay for them. A third challenge is that their P&R negotiation approach, sometimes limited to a letter saying: "Your price is too high," does not carry the competence expected from a Government responsible for its citizens' lives. Finally, whenever available, generics are reimbursed in these Markets, thus showing that the country wanted the products all along, but chose to free-ride the patent game, taking advantage of manufacturers and other wealthy nations.

Surely, each country has the freedom to reimburse or not any drug they like. They should, however, not free-ride, as it abuses and weakens the system by overburdening a smaller number of countries. One way to counter this loophole would be for wealthy nations to always pay a period of branded price before enjoying the generic price or be unable to buy the generic at all, thus distributing the patent price premium burden and allowing Pharma to accept lower launch prices over a higher volume or have a EU-wide price. Probably those free-riding countries will not accept such an idea, or will find creative ways to bypass it, unless through some external pressure from its peers. Until then, this is another challenge for Pharma.

4.5.5 Clinical Data Could Be Used More Effectively

Despite being very expensive to acquire, much clinical data is either biased, lacking, or misunderstood. To inform medical decision-making, demonstrate respect to trial participants, and maintain public trust in clinical research, it is critical that complete reporting of trial evidence is made available in an easily accessible and unbiased way. Unfortunately, there are many shortcomings to that ideal.

A well-known shortcoming is publication or dissemination bias: researchers, journal editors, or publishers from any field of science have a bias to publish studies that show positive results. Negative or null research findings are either not published, or only selectively published, which lead to an overrepresentation of positive studies. In the case of pharmaceutical research, this overrepresentation can distort the accepted scientific truth about a drug's effectiveness or safety, and our understanding about it.

Besides the bias, some researchers or pharmaceutical companies may tactically manipulate a drug's clinical data by reporting only favorable trials; only the favorable part of the trial data; or cherry-picked data to draw a particular conclusion. These biases and tactics help researchers get published, but also help Pharma create stronger, though misleading, cases about the value of their drugs. The result is that healthcare professionals and policymakers cannot make fully informed decisions based on the entire body of relevant research.

To combat such bias, initiatives such as the AllTrials campaign have been calling for "all past and present clinical trials to be registered and their full methods and summary results reported" (AllTrials 2013). The European Commission has also called for investigations on the extent and impact of dissemination bias, and recommendations to overcome incomplete or selective access to trial results. Today, laws mandate that clinical trial sponsors and institutions register protocols and report study results in an official database (ClinicalTrial.gov). Such initiatives have increased the number of sponsors disclosing three quarters of their trials, compared with less than half for non-industry sponsors (Baronikova et al. 2019). Among the top 50 pharma companies, 26 publicly committed to the disclosure of trials data.

But mere transparency isn't enough. Statistical literacy is needed as well. Surprisingly, most people, even in healthcare, cannot correctly interpret the data that was so costly to acquire. For example, in 1995, the UK Committee on Safety of Medicines issued a warning that third-generation oral contraceptive pills increased the risk of potentially life-threatening blood clots in the legs or lungs twofold; that is, by 100% (ABC News 2008). What was not clarified is that for every 7000 women who took the third-generation pill, only two had thrombosis. Indeed, it meant a 100% increase over the one in 7000 women taking the second-generation pill, but hardly the reason for panic. Instead, the "100% increase" news caused great anxiety, many stopped taking the pills, which led to 13,000 additional abortions in the following year at a cost of £4–6 million for the National Health Service. This case illustrates how even the basic difference between a relative (100%) and an absolute risk increase (1 in 7000) is not well understood by the general public.

Most people assume that physicians are statistically literate, but the few existing studies indicate that physicians fail even in their specialties. Gigerenzer reports that most physicians confuse an increase in 5-year survival rates in screening with a decrease in mortality, which has severe consequences. For example, let's imagine a hypothetical deadly disease that progresses slowly and where treatments are mostly ineffective but cause immense suffering.

In such a disease, screening means using exams to find this disease at an earlier stage, before it causes noticeable symptoms. Treatment can then start earlier. However, as treatment is mostly ineffective, patient mortality will not be improved by screening and by the earlier start of treatments. However, the 5-year survival rates will be improved. Why? Because the 5-year survival clock starts counting when the disease is **found, not when it starts to develop symptoms**.

Let's give an example: suppose that, if not screened, patients discover their disease at 67 years old due to symptoms and pass away at 71. With screening, they discover the disease at 65. Given that the treatment is ineffective, they still die at 71, but experience 6 years of treatment instead of four. Their mortality is the same, but the 5-year survival is 100% for the screened group as they "survived" for 6 years, and 0% for the non-screened group who all passed away within the 5-year mark.

This discrepancy creates the false impression that screening is beneficial. In reality, screening might worsen patients' quality of life by subjecting them to harsh, ineffective treatments from age 65 to 67. Doctors, focusing on 5-year survival rates rather than mortality, may advocate for screening and early treatments, believing it's best for their patients, without verifying if it actually improves mortality.

Doctors also do not understand how to determine the positive predictive value of a test (Gigerenzer and Gray 2013). As such, they test patients for very rare diseases, where most of the positive results come from false positives, not from patients really having the disease. They then interpret the tests as true positives, leading to unnecessary treatments and extreme anxiety in patients.

About a third of doctors overestimate benefits if expressed as relative risk reductions, as seen in the oral contraceptive pill example and often confuse concepts such as sensitivity and specificity.

Some medical schools are presently investing in statistical literacy, but most still produce physicians who lack the ability to understand evidence. Without statistical literacy in health, informed evidence-based medical decision-making will remain an illusion. Meanwhile, either due to biases, tricks, or statistical illiteracy, the conversation around a drug's value and safety are compromised.

4.5.6 What Would Have More Impact in Improving US Healthcare Costs?

The USA has several healthcare players that do not add medical value, but leverage their negotiation power to extract money from the system. That the largest companies in healthcare in the world are pharmacy benefit managers (PBMs) and healthcare plans that operate only in the USA is very telling. PBMs buy and sell pharmaceuticals, and healthcare plans buy and sell medical services. They are intermediaries that do not deliver clinical benefit, unlike pharmaceutical companies, hospitals, physicians, or nurses. Their wealth accumulation and several fold higher administrative costs over their European equivalents (e.g., sick funds) suggest where the US healthcare system could be drastically improved.

When you have a system, like in the USA, that rewards the use of power by value-negative providers, it leads to a positive feedback loop: the more power they have, the more they can leverage it to negotiate better deals and get more money, the more money they get, the more negotiation power they can buy, and the cycle continues. Unfortunately, all that money is effectively being sucked out of healthcare and taken from value-positive providers and patients, to pay for many jobs whose main activity is to fight other stakeholders instead of improving patients' lives.

There are, however, many books on this particular topic, and we consider it outside of our scope. Nevertheless, it is a tremendous challenge for Pharma to split its US revenues with so many value-negative actors.

4.5.7 The IRA: Danger Ahead for Pharma or a Long Coming Law

The Inflation Reduction Act (IRA) of 2023, championed by President Biden and passed solely with Democratic support against Republican opposition, represents a strategic challenge to the pharmaceutical industry. This legislation, upon closer look, reveals a calculated power-play by Biden to impose checks on Pharma. The pharmaceutical industry is justifiably concerned in the US market, and will need to strategize to either protect itself from or take advantage of the significant changes ahead.

What are the three key IRA provisions, which worry Pharma (Cubanski et al. 2023):

1. **Price increase limitation:** It forces manufacturers to provide rebates to Medicare to prevent its drug prices from increasing more than the inflation index.
2. **Reducing patient payments:** It redesigns Part D, capping patients' out-of-pocket drug costs at US$ 2000 per year and US$ 35 per month on insulin. To achieve this price capping, patients are exempt from catastrophic coverage, and Medicare drastically reduced its contribution from 80% to 20%. Part D plans (60%) and manufacturers (20%) must pay the rest of the catastrophic coverage, despite Plan D plans being prevented from increasing premiums beyond 6% annually (Cubanski and Neuman 2023).
3. **Lowering some drug costs:** It allows Medicare to negotiate the price of ten drugs every year, chosen among those most sold to Medicare and in the market for seven (small molecules) or 11 years (biologicals), starting 2026, if they still do not have any generic or biosimilar competition.

At first sight, the IRA looks pretty light and unambitious, and drafted only to curb potential abuses. It sets a logical cap on price increases after launch, it limits patient expenditure to what looks like a reasonable amount, and it proposes to lower the prices of only 10 drugs per year. Besides, these 10 drugs, having been in the market for many years, have already made a lot of money since their launch, and thus may have already been well rewarded for their clinical benefits.

We believe the US government anticipated that Pharma will likely react to the IRA in the same way it reacted to past moves to lower its prices: by saying that it would drastically reduce innovation, threatening that no new drugs will ever be created, that it is socialized medicine, and then challenge the legislation in courts. However, the IRA seems to have anticipated and been crafted to withstand this reaction from Pharma as seen by how the companies owning the 10 first products to negotiate have already filed lawsuits against the IRA, which are not going well (Landi 2023).

First, it isolates Pharma, as it mostly only hurts them among all healthcare stakeholders. Meanwhile the profits of PBMs, healthcare plans, physicians, and other stakeholders stay untouched, and may even benefit from the extra money in patients' pockets. As such, Pharma will likely be fighting this bill alone, looking like the evil, greedy player, while all remaining stakeholders will back up the IRA for how fair and excellent it is for patients.

Second, the provisions look extremely reasonable, logical, and simple. Pharma won't likely convince the public opinion, struggling with inflation, that the inflation cap is arbitrary and disregards value. The negotiation of drug provision only involves ten of the most sold drugs after many years in the market, which negotiation will lead to a new price based on the drug's clinical benefit to patients. Besides, it is a small discount as it applies only to the later years of the product. The patient expenditure limit of US$2000 demands an arbitrary 20% from Pharma, but voters will probably support that discount as people need fewer reasons when they are earning more.

Thirdly, the IRA may worsen Pharma's reputation and make it into a public enemy as it caters to the most vulnerable stakeholder, the patient, and thus gains the moral high ground. If Pharma challenges the IRA provisions through its expected reaction (speech: "diminished innovation, terrible for patients," plus action: block the IRA in courts), public opinion may vilify them. Why is Pharma against poor patients being protected with a US$2000 limit? Why exactly will a price decrease of only ten blockbuster drugs after seven or 11 years diminish innovation industrywide if they were fairly priced at launch and were to be replaced by generics soon after? Has Pharma been lying and taking advantage of us all along?

Meanwhile, the remaining stakeholders will criticize, from the safety of their corners, Pharma's greediness over such a light demand from the government.

4.6 Why Is Pharma Worried, and Rightly So

If price increases are kept in line with inflation, the 20% discount will expand healthcare access to many patients, and the price negotiations are limited to 10 drugs, why is Pharma so much against it? Isn't Pharma just being greedy?

Let's take a step back to understand the context before answering the questions. Former President Trump was very vocal against drug prices and about improving US healthcare. He was unhappy that US citizens paid more for drugs than Europeans, and that the system was overly complex and shady. He claimed to be on the verge of changing healthcare but did not deliver on his promises (Knight 2020). At the end of his term, Trump rushed a series of new healthcare rules (Sanger-Katz and Weiland 2020), and left saying: "*I just hope they keep it. I hope they have the courage to keep it, because the powerful drug lobby—big pharma—is putting pressure on people like you wouldn't believe*" (Sanger-Katz and Weiland 2020).

Trump's rules aimed at increasing the US healthcare system's transparency. Healthcare providers would have to disclose prices publicly. Pharma rebates to PBMs would end. Physicians would receive fewer incentives when prescribing drugs. Medicare would adopt European practices through the usage of international reference pricing, even if limited to 50 drugs. Overall, these rules would shine light on the system's financial transaction and minimize value-negative moves, while distributing the burden to all providers. For reasons we do not fully know or understand, the rules were quickly overruled by both courts and the Biden administration.

Trump's rules were probably his opening offer to negotiate with healthcare stakeholders, and if so, it was not a terrible one for Pharma. Many companies compensate the Europeans' aggressive pricing practices with high US earnings. To suddenly have the lower European prices influence US prices through its new adoption of international reference pricing would severely hurt Pharma's profits. However, a slow introduction of international reference pricing in the USA could give Pharma time and legitimacy to raise European prices and balance its accounts. Furthermore, the rules would have helped Pharma in their negotiation struggles with the PBMs. So while the rules would reduce Pharma prices and potentially its profits, they would be a systemic shake up more likely to eradicate value-negative practices, including those from Pharma and beyond.

However, the IRA seems pointed in the opposite direction. Once implemented, after the first 10 drugs, another 15 drugs will be negotiated in 2027, then another 15 part D and part B drugs in 2028, and so on. By 2028, Medicare would have negotiated the price of only 40 drugs, and initial launch prices may increase dramatically in response, for example. So why the fuss with the IRA?

The IRA provisions slowly but surely single Pharma out, while running small pilot projects and building legitimacy that the US government probably hopes to use to justify rapidly expanding the IRA provisions later on. In doing so, the IRA does not look at the system as a whole, and is not tackling other underlying flaws in the US healthcare system. The US healthcare system, as seen above, is heavily dependent on negotiations and has consistently rewarded those when they have more negotiation power. It is reasonable to expect that the best-selling drugs will be overpriced as these give Pharma the power to claim superior deals. Hence, the new US price negotiations of the best selling drugs will surely find at least a few cases of overpricing over the drug's clinical value, given their higher negotiation power to command higher prices.

Considering that there are approximately 19,000 drugs in the US market, what will happen when the US government believes they have enough blockbuster drug data to generalize it to all of them? The public upheaval following a few publicized drug overpricing cases may create a political environment conducive for the US system to move to a full HTA system. That change would not be necessarily bad for the USA, if PBMs and healthcare plans with their much deeper pockets allow it. In short, the fuss with the IRA is that it risks going only after Pharma, which is mostly a value-positive provider, and not solve the US healthcare woes.

Besides, there is a risk that PBMs will continue exerting their negotiation power on pharmaceutical manufacturers. The new US policy for negotiating drug prices will not give Pharma any leverage or legitimacy to increase or defend their prices in Europe. The lack of negotiation based on international reference pricing does not provide pharmaceutical companies with the argument that heavily discounted European prices reduce their earnings in the USA, so Europe will be free to continue its aggressive tactics. Given that the USA has been the lifeline for many pharmaceutical companies, Pharma will have no place to balance its earnings, and risk being squeezed from all directions.

That is not to say that there aren't efforts to tackle the PBMs' contribution to high drug prices. At the federal level, there are congressional bills on PBM reform pushing for higher transparency and other improvements that could help lower drug costs. The question is whether the power of the PBMs will allow these efforts to succeed. While these bills have garnered bipartisan and public support (Taylor 2023), they have yet not succeeded in being approved (Weixel 2024).

Another avenue for changing PBMs practices is the ongoing Federal Trade Commission (FTC) inquiry. In 2023, the new FTC chair issued a critical statement against PBMs and the FTC itself, discarding previous FTC endorsements of PBMs and highlighting an investigation into alleged wrongdoings, collecting 24,000 complaints from pharmacists, doctors, and patients (Khan 2023). This strong desire for change will be tested against the PBMs' formidable resistance.

Another imminent threat to Pharma is state-level initiatives to reduce drug costs. In 2023, over 300 state bills aimed at curbing high drug prices were introduced, with many already enacted. PBM practices are similarly targeted with over 100 bills proposed (Gattine and Reck 2023), and some passed into law. Many States have introduced concepts like Upper Payment Limits to cap drug prices, or are exploring drug imports from Canada, either as a genuine strategy or as leverage in negotiations for lower drug prices. Florida's Governor DeSantis, a former presidential candidate, is leading this charge, indicating the political appeal of reducing drug costs.

Healthcare has become a priority within the 2024 US elections (Vakil 2023), with all three candidates projecting an anti-Pharma stance. Pharma's poor reputation and the lack of transparency in US drug pricing make it a common target for all candidates (Cattan 2023).

In any case, and very importantly, all these actions to lower drug costs have not largely impacted Pharma stock prices (GlobalData Healthcare 2023), which may signal that the market believes that effective changes will be slow to come by, despite all these initiatives and all the bashing Pharma will take during the 2024 US presidential campaign.

4.7 Conclusion: A Tough Road Ahead for Pharma

Pharma gets most of the blame for healthcare funding challenges, but we hope this chapter has shown that this narrow focus is misplaced, and that the future can be brighter if we see the many avenues to reduce costs and improve our healthcare. After all, the majority of healthcare expenses are unrelated to pharma (85%), and there are plenty of misallocations of these funds. Even the significant savings that we should pursue by increasing generics penetration is small when compared to reducing or eliminating defensive medicine. But governments find it hard to influence patients, hospitals, and physicians, especially as they look for reelection, and, as mentioned above, it is much easier to attack pharma instead.

Very importantly, the situation is different within and outside the USA. In the USA, Pharma can be accused of several subpar actions and behaviors, made possible by looser regulation and lobbying. If our goal is to improve outcomes and sustainability, then we must target value-negative activities from Pharma but also from other healthcare actors that suck value through their negotiation power, some without really delivering clinical value.

Outside of the USA, specifically Europe, Pharma is tightly controlled, and yet it is still blamed for many healthcare problems and costs. Despite the widespread belief that pharma has the upper hand in P&R negotiations, it is governments who often have the power edge. Governmental agencies define the pricing and reimbursement rules, and don't reimburse an estimated one-third of drugs in Europe. For example, countries as wealthy and welfare-focused as the Nordics, despite being large exporters of pharmaceutical products, have low reimbursement rates and outdated P&R processes and negotiations supported by an anti-pharma sentiment fed to its population.

Many governments do not want to accurately assess a drug's true value because recognizing its worth means acknowledging the fairness of higher prices. Thus, some countries prefer to remain ignorant and adopt aggressive take-it-or-leave-it tactics to extract unfairly high discounts from Pharma. Given its bad reputation, it is hard for Pharma to ask for help from physicians, patients, or politicians, who fear being seen as pharma-friendly if they are seen as pushing their governments to reimburse needed drugs to its citizens.

Sometimes, pharma overcomes this power imbalance by creating an exceptional product that governments can't reject and must reimburse (e.g., the COVID-19 vaccine). Alternatively, they can rely on the USA and its higher reimbursement rates to finance their European commercial operation. Alternatively, though much less attractive, they can withdraw from the European market altogether or outsource to local players.

Many companies prefer to keep the European market because clinical trials are cheaper (patients and physicians cost less), and their patients can still be used in FDA submissions for the US market. Some companies have legacy relationships in Europe, which helps them get more reimbursement than companies without such history or relationships. Ultimately, there is a risk that if reimbursement rates are not sufficient, European patients may end up without access to certain critical drugs. The current US healthcare status quo is becoming increasingly unsustainable, and changes there can greatly impact European drug prices.

In sum, Pharma is facing increasing and externally imposed, yet not always value-adding, costs and risks that impact drug pricing and could start to shift the opportunity–cost equation of investors and innovators in the industry. Besides, the continued vilification of pharmaceutical companies may diminish their ability to deliver their main contributions to society—better drugs and broad access. There are already very challenging drugs to launch in Europe because of the low reimbursement prices. As a society, we need to ask if we prefer to have much cheaper access to the currently existing medication pool at the risk of reducing the development rate of new and better treatments for the future. It will be hard to have the best of both, as pharmaceutical companies can't afford to continue to invest, develop, and launch new breakthrough treatments at the same rate if they are not adequately financed.

That said, it does not mean we must accept things as they are and do nothing about it. On the contrary, much can be done to reduce waste, distrust, and misunderstandings in the industry, particularly in P&R negotiations between Governments and Pharma, as we shall see in Chap. 6.

References

ABC News (2008) Drug claims often misleading. https://abcnews.go.com/Technology/story?id=6034371&page=1

Adams B (2023) The top 10 pharma drug ad spenders for 2022. Fierce Pharma. https://www.fiercepharma.com/special-reports/top-10-pharma-drug-brand-ad-spenders-2022

AllTrials (2013) What does all trials registered and reported mean? https://www.alltrials.net/find-out-more/all-trials/

American Cancer Society (2015) Cancer facts and figures 2015. https://www.cancer.org/research/cancer-facts-statistics/all-cancer-facts-figures/cancer-facts-figures-2015.html

Baedeker M, Ringel M, Schulze U (2019) 2018 FDA approvals hit all-time high—but average value slips again. Nat Rev Drug Discov 18:90–90. https://doi.org/10.1038/d41573-019-00004-z

Baronikova S, Purvis J, Southam E et al (2019) Commitments by the biopharmaceutical industry to clinical trial transparency: the evolving environment. BMJ Evid Based Med 24:177–184. https://doi.org/10.1136/bmjebm-2018-111145

Betran AP, Ye J, Moller A-B et al (2021) Trends and projections of caesarean section rates: global and regional estimates. BMJ Glob Health 6:e005671. https://doi.org/10.1136/bmjgh-2021-005671

Breene K (2017) 7 deadly diseases the world has (almost) eradicated. World Econ Forum. https://www.weforum.org/agenda/2017/05/7-deadly-diseases-the-world-has-almost-eradicated/

Brink W, Pierce M, Amsterdam J (2022) What lessons from Europe's experience could be applied in the United States in response to the opioid addiction and overdose crisis? Addiction 117:1197–1198. https://doi.org/10.1111/add.15839

Buxton J (2022) Past and projected period and cohort life tables. Office for National Statistics. https://www.ons.gov.uk/peoplepopulationandcommunity/birthsdeathsandmarriages/lifeexpectancies/bulletins/pastandprojecteddatafromtheperiodandcohortlifetables/2020baseduk1981to2070

Campbell IB, Macdonald SJF, Procopiou PA (2018) Medicinal chemistry in drug discovery in big pharma: past, present and future. Drug Discov Today 23:219–234. https://doi.org/10.1016/j.drudis.2017.10.007

Carone G, Schwierz C, Xavier A (2012) Cost-containment policies in public pharmaceutical spending in the EU. SSRN Electron J. https://doi.org/10.2139/ssrn.2161803

Cattan N (2023) Trump and Biden have one thing in common: bashing big pharma. Bloomberg

CompaniesMarketCap Companies ranked by earnings. (n.d.). https://companiesmarketcap.com/most-profitable-companies/

Cox S (2021) H-057-1: operations downfall and Ketsugo—November 1945. Naval History and Heritage Command. https://www.history.navy.mil/about-us/leadership/director/directors-corner/h-grams/h-gram-057/h-057-1.html

Cubanski J, Neuman T (2023) Changes to Medicare part D in 2024 and 2025 under the inflation reduction act and how enrollees will benefit. KFF. https://www.kff.org/medicare/issue-brief/changes-to-medicare-part-d-in-2024-and-2025-under-the-inflation-reduction-act-and-how-enrollees-will-benefit/

Cubanski J, Neuman T, Freed M (2023) Explaining the prescription drug provisions in the inflation reduction act. KFF. https://www.kff.org/medicare/issue-brief/explaining-the-prescription-drug-provisions-in-the-inflation-reduction-act/#bullet01

de la Torre BG, Albericio F (2023) The pharmaceutical industry in 2022: an analysis of FDA drug approvals from the perspective of molecules. Molecules 28:1038. https://doi.org/10.3390/molecules28031038

Domenighetti G, Casabianca A, Gutzwiller F, Martinoli S (1993) Revisiting the Most informed consumer of surgical services: the physician-patient. Int J Technol Assess Health Care 9:505–513. https://doi.org/10.1017/s0266462300005420

Dunleavy K (2023) The top 20 pharma companies by 2022 revenue. Fierce Pharma. https://www.fiercepharma.com/pharma/top-20-pharma-companies-2022-revenue

EFPIA (2023) The pharmaceutical industry in figures

Elvidge S (2009) The rising problem of parallel trade. Life Science Leader. https://www.lifescienceleader.com/doc/the-rising-problem-of-parallel-trade-0001

EUR-Lex Clinical Trial Directive (Directive 2001/20/EC) (n.d.). http://data.europa.eu/eli/dir/2001/20/2022-01-01

EUR-Lex GCP Directive (Directive 2005/28/EC) (n.d.). http://data.europa.eu/eli/dir/2005/28/oj

Euronews (2022) Europe's energy crisis could cut production of cheap medicines. https://www.euronews.com/next/2022/09/29/european-pharma-companies-may-stop-producing-some-generic-drugs-amid-energy-crisis

Fuchs VR (2010) New priorities for future biomedical innovations. N Engl J Med 363:704–706. https://doi.org/10.1056/nejmp0906597

Gattine D, Reck J (2023) State house wrap-up: states continue to tackle high drug prices in 2023 session. NASHP. https://nashp.org/state-house-wrap-up-states-continue-to-tackle-high-drug-prices-in-2023-session/

Gigerenzer G, Gray JM (2013) Better doctors, better patients, better decisions : envisioning health care 2020. Mit Press

GlobalData Healthcare (2023) Half of top 20 biopharma company market cap impacted amid the IRA in Q3 2023. Pharm Technol. https://www.pharmaceutical-technology.com/analyst-comment/half-of-top-20-biopharma-ira-q3-2023/?cf-view

Hall A (2015) Regional patterns in medical technology utilization. BEA Working Papers 0126, Bureau of Economic Analysis

Hanly P, Soerjomataram I, Sharp L (2014) Measuring the societal burden of cancer: the cost of lost productivity due to premature cancer-related mortality in Europe. Int J Cancer 136:E136–E145. https://doi.org/10.1002/ijc.29105

Henschke C, Redberg RF (2018) Medical device Price differentials in the U.S. and Europe—rethinking Price regulation? Health Affairs. https://doi.org/10.1377/forefront.20181206.716970

Herper M (2016) The insurance rip-off at the heart of the EpiPen scandal. Forbes

Higashi T, Shekelle PG, Solomon DH et al (2004) The quality of pharmacologic Care for Vulnerable Older Patients. Ann Intern Med 140:714. https://doi.org/10.7326/0003-4819-140-9-200405040-00011

IQVIA (2019) The global use of medicine in 2019 and outlook to 2023. IQVIA Institute for Human Data Science. https://www.iqvia.com/insights/the-iqvia-institute/reports/the-global-use-of-medicine-in-2019-and-outlook-to-2023

Kabani M (2020) Alec Burlakoff: the rise and fall of a pharmaceutical opioid sales executive. CBS News. https://www.cbsnews.com/news/alec-burlakoff-rise-and-fall-of-a-pharmaceutical-opioid-sales-executive-60-minutes-2020-06-21/

Karlsson P-O, Rivera K, Aguirre D (2017) Are CEOs less ethical than in the past? strategy+business. https://www.strategy-business.com/feature/Are-CEOs-Less-Ethical-Than-in-the-Past

Kerr J (2016) How tremendous greed can Lead to the demise of a leader: the Mylan EpiPen debacle. Inccom. https://www.inc.com/james-kerr/the-mylan-epipen-debacle-how-tremendous-greed-can-lead-to-the-demise-of-a-leader.html. Accessed 1 Jan 2024

Khan LM (2023) Statement of chair Lina M. Khan Regarding the Policy Statement Concerning Reliance on Prior PBM-Related Advocacy Statements and Reports. Federal Trade Commission. https://www.ftc.gov/legal-library/browse/cases-proceedings/public-statements/statement-chair-lina-m-khan-regarding-policy-statement-concerning-reliance-prior-pbm-related. Accessed 1 Jan 2024

Khazan O (2016) Have you ever tried to buy an EpiPen? The Atlantic. https://www.theatlantic.com/health/archive/2016/08/epi-pens/497126/

Kirzinger A, Lopes L, Wu B, Brodie M (2019) KFF Health tracking poll—February 2019: prescription drugs. The Henry J. Kaiser Family Foundation. https://www.kff.org/health-reform/poll-finding/kff-health-tracking-poll-february-2019-prescription-drugs/

Knight V (2020) Back to the future: trump's history of promising a Health plan that never comes. KFF Health News. https://kffhealthnews.org/news/back-to-the-future-trumps-history-of-promising-a-health-plan-that-never-comes/

Kux L (2010) Direct-to-consumer prescription drug advertisements; presentation of the major statement in television and radio advertisements in a clear, conspicuous, and neutral manner. Fed Regist 75

Kyle MK (2009) Chapter 13–parallel trade in pharmaceuticals: firm responses and competition policy. In: International Antitrust law & policy: Fordham corporate law. Juris Publishing, Inc, pp 339–358

Landi H (2023) Trump, Biden HHS chiefs clash over impact of Medicare drug price negotiations. Fierce Healthcare. https://www.fiercehealthcare.com/payers/trump-biden-hhs-chiefs-clash-over-impact-medicare-drug-price-negotiations. Accessed 1 Jan 2024
Lenfant C (2003) Clinical research to clinical practice—lost in translation? N Engl J Med 349:868–874. https://doi.org/10.1056/nejmsa035507
Leonard M (2023) High court turns down Sanofi's EpiPen lawsuit against Mylan (2). Bloomberg Law. https://news.bloomberglaw.com/antitrust/supreme-court-turns-down-sanofis-epipen-lawsuit-against-mylan. Accessed 1 Jan 2024
Lichtenberg FR (2014) Pharmaceutical innovation and longevity growth in 30 developing and high-income countries, 2000–2009. Health Policy Technol 3:36–58. https://doi.org/10.1016/j.hlpt.2013.09.005
Lopez L (2016) Scrutiny of PBMs, Express Scripts grows with drug-price fury. Business Insider. https://www.businessinsider.com/scrutiny-express-scripts-pbms-drug-price-fury-2016-9. Accessed 1 Jan 2024
Lupkin S (2016) EpiPen controversy fuels concerns over generic drug approval backlog. KFF Health News. https://kffhealthnews.org/news/epipen-controversy-fuels-concerns-over-generic-drug-approval-backlog/. Accessed 1 Jan 2024
Magee M (2019) Code Blue. Atlantic Monthly Press
Meier B (2018) Origins of an epidemic: Purdue pharma knew its opioids were widely abused. The New York Times
Moreno L, Pearson AD (2013) How can attrition rates be reduced in cancer drug discovery? Expert Opin Drug Discovery 8:363–368. https://doi.org/10.1517/17460441.2013.768984
Morgan SG, Bathula HS, Moon S (2020) Pricing of pharmaceuticals is becoming a major challenge for health systems. BMJ 368:14627. https://doi.org/10.1136/bmj.l4627
National Institute on Drug Abuse (2024) Drug overdose death rates. National Institute on Drug Abuse. https://nida.nih.gov/research-topics/trends-statistics/overdose-death-rates
Neilan T (2004) Merck pulls Vioxx painkiller from market, and stock plunges. The New York Times
Newton M, Stoddart K, Travaglio M, Troein P (2023) EFPIA Patients W.A.I.T. indicator 2022 survey. IQVIA Inc
OECD (2023) Health at a glance 2023. OECD Publishing
Paton J, Kresge N (2020) Why the $600 EpiPen costs $69 in Britain. Bloomberg. https://www.bloomberg.com/news/articles/2016-09-29/epipen-s-69-cost-in-britain-shows-other-extreme-of-drug-pricing-itnvgvam. Accessed 1 Jan 2016
Pharma Intelligence (2019) Pharma R&D Annu Rev:2019
Podolsky SH, Herzberg D, Greene JA (2019) Preying on prescribers (and their patients)—pharmaceutical marketing, iatrogenic epidemics, and the Sackler legacy. N Engl J Med 380:1785–1787. https://doi.org/10.1056/nejmp1902811
Pollack A (2016) Mylan raised EpiPen's Price before the expected arrival of a generic. The New York Times
Pollack A, Huetteman E (2016) Martin Shkreli invokes the fifth amendment during grilling by congress. The New York Times
Portugal Resident (2012) Suppliers blamed for drug shortage. Portugal Resident https://www.portugalresident.com/suppliers-blamed-for-drug-shortage/. Accessed 1 Jan 2024
Reiff N (2024) 10 biggest Healthcare companies. Investopedia. https://www.investopedia.com/articles/markets/030916/worlds-top-10-health-care-companies-unh-mdt.asp
Reinaud F (2022) Pharma prices continue to rise in the US—or do they? Pharm Technol. https://www.pharmaceutical-technology.com/pricing-and-market-access/pharma-prices-us/?cf-view
Robinson M (2016) Glaxo to pay $20 million SEC fine over bribery in China. Bloomberg. https://www.bloomberg.com/news/articles/2016-09-30/glaxo-to-pay-20-million-sec-fine-over-bribing-chinese-officials
Roser M, Ochmann S, Behrens H, et al (2014) Eradication of diseases. Our World Data https://ourworldindata.org/eradication-of-diseases
Rudey EL, Leal M, do Rego CG (2020) Cesarean section rates in Brazil. Medicine 99:e19880. https://doi.org/10.1097/md.0000000000019880

Saad L (2023) Retail, pharmaceutical industries slip in public esteem. Gallup. https://news.gallup.com/poll/510641/retail-pharmaceutical-industries-slip-public-esteem.aspx
Sanger-Katz M, Weiland N (2020) A final try by trump to cut drug prices may stumble in court. The New York Times
Schulthess D, Bowen HP, Popovian R et al (2022) Correction: the relative contributions of NIH and private sector funding to the approval of new biopharmaceuticals. Ther Innov Regul Sci 57:170–171. https://doi.org/10.1007/s43441-022-00461-6
Schwartz LM, Woloshin S (2019) Medical marketing in the United States, 1997-2016. JAMA 321:80–96. https://doi.org/10.1001/jama.2018.19320
Scott C, Sabot E, Kirk K (2020) The myth of skyrocketing drug prices: a closer look at the US gross to net problem. PharmExec. https://www.pharmexec.com/view/myth-skyrocketing-drug-prices-closer-look-us-gross-net-problem. Accessed 1 Jan 2024
Seeley E (2022) The impact of pharmaceutical wholesalers on U.S. drug spending. www.commonwealthfund.org. https://www.commonwealthfund.org/publications/issue-briefs/2022/jul/impact-pharmaceutical-wholesalers-drug-spending
Shen S, Chen X, Cai J et al (2020) Effect of Dasatinib vs Imatinib in the treatment of pediatric Philadelphia chromosome-positive acute lymphoblastic leukemia: a randomized clinical trial. JAMA Oncol 6:358–366. https://doi.org/10.1001/jamaoncol.2019.5868
Sifferlin A (2018) What the Netflix documentary 'bleeding edge' gets right about the dangers of medical devices in America. Time. https://time.com/5346330/what-the-netflix-documentary-bleeding-edge-gets-right-about-the-dangers-of-medical-devices-in-america/
Sood N, Shih T, Van Nuys K, Goldman D (2017) Flow of money through the pharmaceutical distribution system. USC Schaeffer. https://healthpolicy.usc.edu/research/flow-of-money-through-the-pharmaceutical-distribution-system/
Staton T (2017) What if EpiPen price hikes were designed to crush rivals? Sanofi suit claims that, and much more. Fierce Pharma. https://www.fiercepharma.com/pharma/what-if-epipen-price-hikes-were-designed-to-crush-rivals-sanofi-suit-claims-and-much-more. Accessed 1 Jan 2024
Studdert DM, Mello MM, Sage WM et al (2005) Defensive medicine among high-risk specialist physicians in a volatile malpractice environment. JAMA 293:2609. https://doi.org/10.1001/jama.293.21.2609
Taylor NP (2023) PBMs run media blitz calling out practices of their peers, telling policymakers reforms can cut costs. Fierce Pharma. https://www.fiercepharma.com/marketing/pbms-run-media-blitz-calling-out-practices-their-peers-telling-policymakers-reforms-can. Accessed 1 Jan 2024
Tengs TO, Adams ME, Pliskin JS et al (1995) Five-hundred life-saving interventions and their cost-effectiveness. Risk Anal 15:369–390. https://doi.org/10.1111/j.1539-6924.1995.tb00330.x
The Editorial Board (2016) The EpiPen outrage continues. The New York Times
The Wall Street Journal (2019) How drug prices work | WSJ. YouTube. https://youtu.be/aeG2lWxYO_Y?si=jDcgXbWHAz3157i_. Accessed 1 Jan 2024
United Nations (2018) Universal declaration of human rights. Un.org. http://www.un.org/en/universal-declaration-human-rights/
Vakil C (2023) Seven issues that will define the 2024 election. The Hill. https://thehill.com/homenews/campaign/3853380-seven-issues-that-will-define-the-2024-election/
Van Zee A (2009) The promotion and marketing of OxyContin: commercial triumph, public Health tragedy. Am J Public Health 99:221–227. https://doi.org/10.2105/ajph.2007.131714
Weixel N (2024) Government funding bills leave out PBM changes as white house mulls reforms. The Hill. https://thehill.com/policy/healthcare/4507164-government-funding-bills-leave-out-phamacy-benefit-manager-industry-changes-as-white-house-mulls-reforms/
Welsh H, Young R (2017) How Leading U.S. Corporation Govern and Spend on State Lobbying. The Investor Responsibility Research Center Institute (IRRCi)
Wenzl M, Mossialos E (2018a) Prices for cardiac implant devices may be up to six times higher in the US than in some European countries. Health Aff 37:1570–1577. https://doi.org/10.1377/hlthaff.2017.1367

Wenzl M, Mossialos E (2018b) U.S. Hospitals Pay More Than European Hospitals for Cardiac Implants. The Commonwealth Fund. https://www.commonwealthfund.org/publications/journal-article/2018/oct/us-hospitals-pay-more-european-hospitals-cardiac-implants. Accessed 1 Jan 2024

World Health Organization (2024a) WHO factsheets: obesity and overweight. https://www.who.int/news-room/fact-sheets/detail/obesity-and-overweight

World Health Organization (2024b) WHO factsheets: diabetes. https://www.who.int/news-room/fact-sheets/detail/diabetes

World Health Organization WHO Mortality Database (n.d.). https://www.who.int/data/data-collection-tools/who-mortality-database

Wouters OJ (2020) Lobbying expenditures and campaign contributions by the pharmaceutical and Health product industry in the United States, 1999-2018. JAMA Intern Med 180:688. https://doi.org/10.1001/jamainternmed.2020.0146

P&R Negotiation Challenges

5

5.1 Who's the Enemy?

When Governments/Payers and Pharma meet for their P&R negotiations, they arrive overburdened by the many challenges we examined in the previous chapters. Besides carrying a uniquely heavy, complex, and ambiguous negotiation responsibility, each party approaches the structurally challenging P&R negotiations with several variables that hinder any negotiator's ability to find creative solutions or reach agreement:

1. They involve two powerful parties with several different interest groups, akin to a multiparty negotiation.
2. They don't trust each other.
3. They unintentionally created and are now stuck in a power-escalation dynamic.
4. They meet to discuss a few but highly politically relevant issues.
5. They involve large amounts of money and may dramatically impact people's lives.
6. They use a large volume of very complex data to assess a product's objective price with subjective or hard-to-predict value.
7. They are under significant constraints of time pressure, limited budgets, organizational targets, fiduciary responsibilities, media attention, public scrutiny, competitive dynamics, legal intricacies, etc.

When negotiations are structurally complicated, and P&R clearly qualifies as such, negotiators fail to diagnose the source of their challenges or failures as being structural, and wrongly blame their counterparties. Without understanding negotiation theory, negotiators see each other as the main threat to their goals instead of blaming the negotiation's structural difficulties. Psychological dynamics also contribute to this distorted blame game that turns negotiations into escalating and intractable conflicts between Payers and Pharma.

H. Falcão et al., *Pharma, Prices and Power*, Future of Business and Finance,
https://doi.org/10.1007/978-3-031-93933-4_5

Negotiators often fall into the bargaining trap and the zero-sum mindset, where most negotiators, ignorant of negotiation theory and other available processes, get trapped bargaining or fighting over extreme, opposing demands for the often wrongly assumed limited value available. This adversarial approach pushes negotiators into an "Us vs. Them" mentality, where we mistakenly see our counterparty as an adversary with ill intentions toward us, the victims. We then interpret and even experience our counterparties' moves as aggressive and illegitimate, while we believe ours, no matter how fierce, are only in self-defense.

When such dynamics happen, and especially if we feel threatened or distant from our goals, we feel an increased need to defend our side and augment our level of aggression, which we rationalize as for defensive purposes only. This escalation under the above biases builds up a distorted history of bad deeds done exclusively by the counterparty and frees us from ethical restraints in our future moves. The result is a substantial self-fulfilling prophecy, where escalating dynamics consistently impoverish negotiation outcomes and everyone's satisfaction.

Our experience advising and teaching thousands of individuals and negotiations across industries and geographies has taught us that when individuals negotiate in the above manner, it is not because they are inherently selfish or evil. Instead, when negotiators behave negatively toward their counterparties, it is because they cannot see collaboration leading to success, but rather that it makes them vulnerable, weak, or incurring significant losses, financial or reputational. In other words, they feel ignorant or helpless to protect their interests and to collaborate simultaneously, so they don't. Instead, they pursue their goals the way they know how to, and drop collaboration.

Indeed, for collaboration to take hold, we need much more than just good intentions; we also need knowledge and tools. Unfortunately, those are usually unavailable, so cooperation does not happen. In the end, negotiators conclude it did not occur because the others had bad intentions or were bad people instead of appreciating the difficulty of the above-mentioned structural negotiation challenges and the negotiators' joint inability to pursue collaborative negotiation processes.

5.2 Competition Blues: Blame the Game and the Players!

Imagine being a referee in a professional football match. At minute 15, the game is a model of fair play, so you take a break and tell the players to continue without you for the next 20 min. What level of violence do you expect to see upon your return? There is a significant chance that the match will be more violent. Would it be because the players don't know the rules? Or because they are intrinsically unethical? We don't think so.

Players want to win, and many will push their limits and that of the game in pursuit of success. Over and over, when a team loses, you hear their coach in post-match interviews moaning that the team lacked intensity on the ball or aggressiveness. In competitive games, if one team sticks to the rules, the other team might win by bending said rules. Lose enough games, and eventually, you lose your job. As a result, as one team increases its aggressiveness, the other feels the need to mimic. But if both teams play this way, they will seriously hurt each other without increasing their odds of winning the game. Their choices would become victims of a prisoner's dilemma, where the best decision for each team interacts negatively to create a horrible outcome for everyone.

Given this risk, many may argue ethically that their team should continue its fair play even when trashed by an adversary that breaks the rules without punishment. However, how would the club fans respond? They would eventually ask to fire the coach or players. So, while laudable, this can be another problematic and risky strategy to pull off, given the stakeholders' pressure and power.

Another argument is to expect neither team to break the rules. After all, no player wants a violent game or career-ending injuries. Unfortunately, most players would genuinely feel they were pushing the rules to their limits or paying it back because their competitors were clearly breaking the rules and "did so first." They will do it out of loyalty, to protect teammates, or by overconfidently underestimating the odds of being seriously injured. Without a referee to neutrally assess and curb the excesses of each side, competitive matches could quickly escalate into serious violence. Curiously, no one will know who started it or how they got to the undesirable outcome as they usually only see part of the picture. In this part, the others misbehaved and thus cannot connect the dots. Moreover, it is often not a single move that does it but several small ones that creep up and escalate as everyone is busy trying to win.

After returning from the coffee break, what if the referee furiously lectured the players on their lack of ethics, poor behavior, or how he could not trust them? This is an exercise in futility, which may clear the referee's conscience and shift blame, but ultimately change nothing.

Yet, we are not saying: "Blame the game, not the player." While we acknowledge the pressures and adverse outcomes of trying to win a poorly designed or poorly monitored game, we advocate for personal accountability. We believe that players have the responsibility to become masters of their game and make improved decisions to change it when it pushes people into negative behaviors and outcomes. We are saying: "Blame the game and the players. Then, focus on improving the game first, and then raise the bar for the players."

We hope the above analogy between football and organizational players helps illustrate our points. Athletes and organizations are both engaged in competitive games. Companies, governments, executives, or public officials who believe in fair play still have their performances unfairly compared with those of their more unethical competitors. They face many of the questions and challenges we posed above, which are hard to answer as many rules are loose enough to allow powerful and unethical players to get away with unfair practices. Unfortunately, for many, any behavior that helps them win is considered acceptable or even desirable, leading to a dangerous game of who can push the boundaries further without getting caught. For them, if it is not criminal, it may not be ethical, but it is also not unethical. This makes the competition and, thus, survival much more challenging for the ethical ones, whose stakeholders demand wins, but the players still need to learn how to win without mimicking the unethical competition.

In the corporate landscape of the twenty-first century, companies and individuals engage in ethical actions when it results in positive publicity, favorable sentiment, or improved morale, and may even make the eventual honest call and lose money in less-costly decisions. However, there is an expectation that companies and executives, usually measured by shareholder value, should still uphold ethical standards willingly, even if it means financial losses for them and their investors. The expectation extends to investors endorsing such costly decisions in the stock market against their short-term economic interests. These expectations could turn out similar to the referee returning to the game expecting to see nothing but fair play and lead to the misdiagnosis that the lack of fair play is caused exclusively by greed.

Corporations operate within a competition game and are fragile and susceptible to the dynamics above. It is up to the referee, the supporters, organizers, and players, but not only players, to channel their energies toward societal good; otherwise, the bad apples will outcompete the good ones and rise to the top. Once there, the bad apples set the tone and the example for future apples. And then, at every turn, the beautiful game becomes a bit less so.

The same reasoning applies to the Government or Payer side. Surely, Governments want to do what is best for their citizens and countries. Still, they respond to voting citizens instead of shareholders and face competition from opposing political parties. In a world with perfect information, fully informed citizens, and politicians collaborating for sound decisions, Governments would gain popular support and win elections to ensure the game improves everyone's lives. Sadly, this is not the world we live in. Fortunately, there are good apples on both sides, but unfortunately, there are also bad ones.

Given politics and public financial constraints, some voters want their Governments to bargain hard and squeeze company profits as much as possible. They are motivated by their ignorance of P&R processes, media and political misinformation, distrust of Big Pharma, and belief that Pharma freely and hugely overcharges without delivering value in return. Some voters suspect that P&R deals are confidential to hide bribes or other unethical practices between Pharma and public officials. Others believe Governments are friends with Pharma, colluding against patient interests, as seen in the anti-vaccine skepticism. As a result, Governments and politicians seem to be increasingly tough on Pharma to project a populist image and gain easy political wins, given that every voter cares about healthcare and its costs. We heard of politicians admitting that they were knowingly making a bad yet populist decision out of fear of presenting anything else to the parliament, angry voters, a populist media, and political rivals.

As previously discussed earlier in this book, most Governments have the dual healthcare role of defining the rules of the game and being an efficient Payer or manager of its services and products. The first role means instilling fair drug evaluation and pricing processes, a level-playing field, etc. The second role stems from a fiduciary duty to optimize the use of taxpayers' money. The conflict between the two functions is present in every governmental healthcare decision, and it feeds a significant conflict of interests, much like when corporations or executives need to balance business ethics and profits. It seems optimistic to expect politicians and public officials to make only ethical decisions, even when it risks being unpopular with voters, their political parties, or their careers. We are not saying that some will not, just that expecting they will always do it, despite high personal costs, seems too much.

When Corporations or Governments decide on an unethical course of action, they do not say to themselves, "This is the wrong thing to do, and I will do it!" rubbing their hands in anticipated pleasure. With the possible exception of some psychopaths, most people rationalize a reason to do what is convenient for themselves and their group. As seen in Chap. 2, most people facing such pressures will try to reassure themselves that their unethical move is ethical or not that bad. The higher the level of conflict between the two sides, the easier it becomes to fall prey to this rationalization! First, because the individual feels more comfortable doing so as the unethicality of the move is now balanced with the ethicality of protecting the group vs. the enemy. Second, because it becomes the socially accepted course of action inside each group, and we want peer approval.

Chapter 4 explored the prevailing negative sentiment toward the pharmaceutical industry. Governments are often pressured to adopt an anti-pharma stance if they wish to gain popular support and elections, and not doing so could be career-ending in some instances. Similarly, pharmaceutical companies are reluctant to lower prices (and profits) significantly if competitors don't, as they would otherwise face swift acquisition by competitors, who will then raise prices back up or higher. Meanwhile, the executive who first lowered prices risked having committed career suicide. These dynamics raise a crucial question: Can we blame them for acting the way they have been?

These competitive pressures on Government and Pharma set the stage for what we can expect from both. To solely chastise them for their morals is counterproductive. It creates false hopes without leading to positive change. Instead, we can tailor an environment where the parties have different goals and pressures that consistently push them toward collaboration.

5.3 P&R Negotiations "Unintended" Win-Lose Escalation

As seen previously, the negotiation tensions between Pharma and Payers are worsening. With the current rules rewarding innovation, they also encourage Pharma to keep launching newer, better, and more expensive drugs to deliver superior treatment to patients who until then only had worse but cheaper therapies. This innovation benefits patients and aligns with humanitarian goals but strains Payers financially. As Payers try to keep their healthcare budgets in check, they get stressed and risk-averse during P&R negotiations as they shift their attention away from the growing humanitarian benefits to their pharmaceutical bill.

One big challenge with P&R negotiations is that the parties are discussing a new drug's potential clinical value, which is technically and objectively hard to do. Despite the extensive data gathered during clinical trials, a new drug after launch may present new side effects, a lower efficacy, or other longer-term surprises. When the value of some new pharmaceutical products fails to materialize in practice, Payers distrust Pharma, their clinical trial methodologies, or their negotiation intentions. In contrast, Users doubt the Payers' ability to evaluate Pharma products successfully.

Historically, Payers were price takers and did not negotiate prices much. Then, they started to negotiate but were less equipped or sophisticated than the big pharmaceutical companies and could have done better. More recently, as Payers learned from past P&R negotiations, they accumulated and shared knowledge over Pharma negotiation tricks and win-lose moves. They have also been waking up to their own win-lose and power possibilities. As a result, Payers have been increasingly opting for win-lose actions or suboptimal, adversarial, or unethical negotiation calls. We are not here to blame anyone but to understand and seek solutions.

Public officials must deliver on their complex P&R negotiation mandate to balance health and budget while balancing their careers. While the scientific assessment is done by experts that evaluate the drug thoroughly, the negotiators carrying out the negotiation in some Markets are often not as knowledgeable and are overworked and understaffed. They would benefit from having more technical understanding of the drug under negotiation for them to negotiate optimally.

Not only are they not as familiar as they could be, but they are also aware that, on average,[1] pharmaceutical negotiators are much more familiar with the drug's data and potential implications. This makes them feel unsure, defensive, and unwilling to get off script, and more aggressive.

Furthermore, Payers see their P&R choices limited to (1) aggressively or manipulatively negotiate to reduce Pharma prices beyond what is truly legitimate, while risking providing less care if Pharma walks away (e.g., offer fewer innovative drugs), or (2) negotiate in a friendlier manner, conceding to Pharma when Pharma brings valid points, in this way not obtaining the best deals one could and being seen as weak or pharma-friendly by its peers. Which one would most anyone opt for?

Suppose a public official aggressively asks for a steep discount. In that case, there is a chance the pharmaceutical company will give it, and the negotiator is a hero or at least not a sucker. Suppose the company rejects the discount and walks away. In that case, the Payer negotiator can always blame the negotiation failure on the greediness of the pharmaceutical company. By doing so, the Payer's negotiator is again partially seen as a hero who fought as hard as possible to save public funds, thus mitigating the contrary perspective of the bureaucrat who is letting people die to save money. In contrast, if the public official negotiates collaboratively, there is a significant risk of people pointing fingers at the perceived naïve or corrupt Payer negotiator, even if the price agreed was fair and the deal good and the drug is made available to patients. It worsens if later news shows that the drug is cheaper in other countries or if in a subsequent negotiation a colleague obtains a much larger discount.

[1] With some exceptions. In some Pharmaceutical companies, especially after fusions and downsizing, Market negotiators can also be overburdened with too many tasks and not enough time to prepare for each negotiation.

Given the choices on the table, being tough on and attacking the high profits of wealthy Pharma corporations, many already hated by the public, seems the better headline for Payers and politicians, especially if they reach a deal at the end. If you are to be blamed for something, make sure you are blamed for doing the impossible to help your group. Most Payer negotiators have seen the more aggressive option as superior and safer, with the occasional cost of when desired drugs are not reimbursed and patients are negatively affected. To obtain more negotiation power, some Payers have worked to increase its public opinion tolerance over non-reimbursements. In these countries, the people more easily accept the rejection of innovative drugs and settle for subpar treatments, as Payers blame Pharma greediness for it.

Breaches in fair process, and concerns over future innovation are also other issues these Payers are incurring. Fair process violations are hard to prove and risk retaliation, and future innovation is a future problem that many countries don't worry about and don't mind free-riding other countries in the meantime. Payer negotiators are concerned with providing the best medication to its citizens now, reducing prices, saving face, and show group loyalty. Furthermore, given the hard fiscal and economic situation of recent times, investing for the future seems to have dropped in priority.

Given that choice and the win-lose history of many pharmaceutical companies, Payers have been escalating their win-lose actions, constantly searching for a negotiation edge they can leverage. They have been stricter in interpreting data, biased in their evaluations, frequently changing the rules of the P&R game, dismissive about additional value brought by innovative drugs, treating different medicines as commodities, and using other aggressive negotiation tactics when discussing prices.

While these pressures-and fear-based reactions are understandable, much as with the Pharma discussion above, they are far from good or ideal, even to Payers. Win-lose moves usually result in lower-value deals for all. When pharmaceutical companies experience the Payer's win-lose tactics, they grow distrustful of the system's fairness and grow hopeless about trying to play fair, especially if they see their competitors' win-lose moves paying off. Many Pharma negotiators vent that they feel like fighting against a rigged system, where fairness, scientific data, commercial common sense, and logical argumentation, not to say their interests, are rapidly ignored, and only power matters. Consequently, these companies often rationalize their growing adoption of win-lose moves as self-defense against Payers' abuses.

5.4 Where Is This Leading Us?

Payers have seen that win-lose works well enough for them. They have power, and when they use it, they have been getting better results than before. Most Pharma companies have preferred not to escalate the conflict or leave the countries that treat them poorly, as long as they can make some money. Voters hate the high profits from Pharma and often side with the Payers when problems arise. Why would Payers stop doing what seems to be working?

One answer is that they shouldn't stop. The Payers' win-lose strategies seem to be working well for them, especially as they adopt it simultaneously across many countries. European Payers currently have a sustainable power advantage over Pharma, which they use to obtain lower prices, even if it backfires a bit once in a while. One of the rare examples of it backfiring spectacularly happened during the early COVID-19 vaccine negotiations. Quickly obtaining enough vaccines was or should have been a clear priority over price, with each country in the world interested in the limited available resources. Hence, vaccine manufacturers, in this case, clearly had more negotiation power than the Governments.

Yet, we saw European countries maintain their price-focus and win-lose strategy as they joined forces partially to increase their negotiation power and demand that Pharma took responsibility for all liabilities under threats of breaking patents. This was a staggering display of power blindness, as European Governments ignored that they did not have the upper hand. As a result, Europe received vaccines relatively late, and instead of accepting that their own win-lose approach led to the delay, they consistently blamed the delays on the manufacturers (Deutsch and Wheaton 2021).

On most drugs, however, the Payers have more negotiation power and as such are currently discouraged to change to a more collaborative approach. As long as the USA adopts the market-based system with its free drug pricing, without referencing foreign prices, it will foot the bill for pharmaceutical innovation by itself. As a result, other Payers, such as European nations, can theoretically continue demanding extreme price reductions until they meet Pharma's marginal cost of supplying to them. If the USA decides to reference European prices or its government starts to negotiate medication prices more openly, the pricing and access of pharmaceuticals in Europe or other parts of the world will undergo a revolution.

Meanwhile, Pharma and Payers are distrustful of one another. Pharma leverages its exclusivity and information power, while Payers resort to their legislative and monopsony power. In such systems, plenty of expectations and peer pressure exist to negotiate win-lose. For example, HQs often interpret their collaborative negotiators as having conflicts of interest, Stockholm syndrome, or being weak.

Many may feel disheartened at this gloomy win-lose escalation and feel like giving up or writing it off as one of these vast institutional problems with no solution, at least none that an individual can help implement. Luckily, these win-lose behaviors have surfaced in a limited set of choices described above: (a) negotiate aggressively or manipulatively or (b) negotiate in a friendly manner, making concessions when the other brings good points. And yet, there is a third alternative, one where the parties actively negotiate and do so through win-win, non-power strategies and moves.

Win-win is a more arduous negotiation technique to master than win-lose, especially once a win-lose escalation dynamic is already in place, as in the case of P&R negotiations globally. As win-lose moves become the norm in an industry or environment, it requires a lot of fortitude and technical mastery for a negotiator to go against the grain and attempt win-win successfully. In sum, win-win is rare in P&R negotiations because it is hard to do. However, win-win can be highly beneficial, as it can reward positive behaviors, penalize bad practices, and improve outcomes for both Pharma and Payer. As Payers are used to and expect win-lose from Pharma, Pharma negotiators can stand out by negotiating win-win and showing commitment to crafting superior outcomes for Payers, Pharma, and other stakeholders.

Win-win negotiations can change the P&R game for the better. We have done it. We have seen it succeed several times. In the next chapter, we share how we did it, so you can either do it directly or, if you are not connected to these negotiations, at least push your country's P&R systems in a win-win direction. At the end of that road lies an improved, innovative, cheaper, and sustainable healthcare system that supports longer, pain-free lives.

Reference

Deutsch J, Wheaton S (2021) How Europe fell behind on vaccines. POLITICO. https://www.politico.eu/article/europe-coronavirus-vaccine-struggle-pfizer-biontech-astrazeneca/

What Can You Do Differently? 6

At this stage, you may be asking yourself: what can we do to fix the systemic problems faced by both Pharma and Payer? The answer can be multifaceted, and yet we wrote this book to highlight that a greatly overlooked and yet very promising answer is in the negotiation process. Improving negotiations is one effective way to reverse the adversarial interactions plaguing the current system and create a conducive platform to co-create ideas and agreements to get better drugs at cheaper costs to patients around the world.

Value-oriented negotiations can drive tailored, innovative solutions, crafted by experts on both sides. The solutions from different P&R negotiations and countries can be piloted at small cost, compete in the healthcare ideas' marketplace, and the best can percolate through the entire system to promote new, market-tested equilibria. This approach rejects top-down solutions driven by legislatures ignorant of the full impact of their decisions, or a power-driven attempt that turn some parties into losers. Instead, it offers the promise for a better future ahead.

6.1 The Typical Negotiation vs the Value Negotiation

To understand the difference between the typical negotiation between a Pharma representative and Payer and a value-based negotiation between them, we can examine what each might look like. Throughout this chapter, we present hypothetical P&R negotiation dialogues to illustrate key learning points. We approach the P&R negotiations from the perspective of the pharmaceutical company for a couple of reasons: it is the negotiation side we know best; and they have more freedom and potential incentives to change their negotiation approach.

H. Falcão et al., *Pharma, Prices and Power*, Future of Business and Finance,
https://doi.org/10.1007/978-3-031-93933-4_6

6.1.1 A Typical P&R Negotiation (from the Pharma Representative Perspective)

After pleasantries, you as the Pharma representative present your proposal for reimbursement of your new product, including a mandatory significant discount over your list price. The Payer opens by criticizing what they see as weaknesses in your new product, uncertainties in your data, and ambiguities in your product's value. When you attempt to show data or make reasonable arguments, for instance, how other payers around the world reacted to the same data, they become irrational, stubbornly insisting that you must increase the discount or be out of the market entirely. You realize your proposal will never be accepted. You offer a price reduction at your bottom line as dictated by headquarters.

But the Payer does not stop there. They repeat why your proposal was totally wrong from the start and again criticize your product and data. They do not budge from their position, even when you tell them you are not authorized to come anywhere close to their proposed numbers. They suggest ending the meeting until you to talk to your headquarters and come back with a more reasonable proposal. You leave the room frustrated and afraid of your phone call to headquarters, where you will ask permission for a deeper discount.

You worry that patients will be hurt if you do not come to a deal. Without a deal, you will miss your annual revenue target, headquarters will be disappointed in your ability to negotiate, and part of your team may be fired as a result. Headquarters will insist the case for your proposed price should have been easy to make and that the drug is hugely valuable. You believe it is, but you've also now sat through a meeting where every detail of the data has been picked apart and viewed in the most negative possible light.

The majority of high-stakes P&R negotiations unfortunately proceed this way—but the Payers also experience the same doubt and frustration as is illustrated here for Pharma. Both sides are in fact seeing their counterparties as irrational and untrustworthy. Let's rewind the tape and take a closer look with a more omniscient perspective.

6.1.2 A Typical P&R Negotiation (from an Omniscient Perspective)

Both sides greet each other cordially, confident in their position but anxious about how the meeting will unfold. As the Pharma representative puts forth his proposal, the Payer feels irritated. The values seem extremely high—and, just as bad, arbitrary. Perceiving to be in a position of power (as the single buyer), the Payer feels that his power status is being threatened and the Pharma negotiators are making illogical arguments and relying on best case scenarios to make their case. The Payers show how displeased they are. After all, they know Pharma representatives have historically been more likely to give discounts if they see real displays of anger and frustration.

Pharma feels slightly abused by the Payer's behavior and does not want to show fear, which they feel could invite more abuse. They keep composure and do not back down, in fact reinforcing their confidence in the proposal. The Payer feels frustrated that their views are not being heard. They reiterate their concerns, more loudly now, accusing Pharma of painting an unfairly rosy picture of reality, maybe even trying to trick the Payer by not interpreting all the relevant data in an unbiased way. The Payer exposes all the points where the counterparty could be trying to fool them, to show they have not succeeded. As they do this, they are testing Pharma's intentions. Were these just uncertainties? Or was the company trying to withhold and distort information, stealing taxpayer money from much-in-need hospitals to enlarge the already-huge profits of multimillionaire shareholders and Pharma executives who care nothing about health and only about profit?

The Pharma representatives hear the Payer and interpret their remarks as bargaining tactics to avoid paying a fair value for the product. There are always uncertainties in clinical data, because biology is not an exact science. Besides, you can't run clinical trials against all possible drugs and still be first to market, or do so in an economically feasible manner. But do they really want your company to run all possible clinical trials before actually letting the drug reach patients? Don't they care about patients? Don't they see the big picture? Or are they just picking on these things as an excuse to propose a totally unreasonable price?

The perception that the Payer is being deliberately unreasonable for negotiation gain fuels the Pharma representatives' frustration.

Pharma brings up that other countries around the world have already praised the drug. The Payer is irritated by the response and thinks: Is Pharma saying that these other countries' Health Authorities are better than ours? That is no defense. It is an insult! If Pharma doesn't want to discuss the data and details, then let's have it their way! The Payer is then direct and informs Pharma of the discount they believe is fair to compensate the Payer for the uncertainty in the product. The proposed price is not well-received and the escalation continues.

Unfortunately, even with the best collaborative intentions, both sides can still come across like enemies to each other and the negotiation can quickly slide into an emotional, reactive, and unproductive dynamic. The good news is that there is a way out of this all-too-common scenario. We can try one final replay of this conversation, using the strategies to come in the rest of this chapter.

6.1.3 A Win-Win P&R Negotiation (with Omniscient Awareness)

Both sides greet cordially given the time pressures, Pharma quickly thanks for the meeting opportunity and makes a clear opening statement about their willingness to work together with the Payer. Then, instead of exchanging proposals, they acknowledge that their product may be seen differently by them and by the Payer, and that before numbers dominate the conversation, they want to hear the Payer's perspective and concerns. In this way, they can clarify misunderstandings and take their input into account to make sure the subsequent proposal will be appropriate.

The Payer hears this as a gesture of goodwill but is not sure whether to believe it or whether it is a negotiation tactic. To be on the safe side, they refuse to "go first" and instead ask Pharma to be the ones to open the discussion of the product.

The Pharma representatives, prepared for this contingency, agree and quickly present a summary of the product, being as objective and neutral as possible. On uncertain points in the data, they are careful to explain why such uncertainty exists (e.g., sharing the limitations in trial design and the rationale behind their design choices). They are aware that everything they say is being met with suspicion, so they are very careful to provide appropriate context.

The Payer perceives Pharma's summary as transparent, not sneaky, so they relax a bit, as their fear of being fooled diminishes. In their turn to speak, the Payer raises a few new issues and expresses some disagreement on a few points. They conclude that because of these issues, a big discount will be required. Pharma takes careful notes, clearly showing they are listening attentively. At some points, they politely interrupt to ask more detailed questions to be sure they fully and correctly understand all Payer's concerns.

When the Payer is done, Pharma starts answering the Payer's concerns one by one. They acknowledge that the Payer is entitled to feel the way they do. Where possible, they add information the Payer did not know about. They ask for clarification from the Payer wherever they are still confused or in disagreement. Whenever the case, they admit they had not seen the issue from the Payer's perspective and try to make the difference in perspectives clearer between them. They acknowledge where there is uncertainty that could impact expenditures, such as an increased risk of off-label use blowing up the budget.

On more critical points, Pharma suggests that they work to find workarounds in the proposal, i.e., ways of minimizing uncertainty or clauses to minimize the impact of uncertainty. The Payer feels catered to as Pharma puts forth ideas that indeed address their concerns. The Payer stops envisioning the worst-case scenario and starts believing in Pharma's good intentions. They become less defensive and more open with information.

As the negotiation unfolds, the Payer realizes that their expectations for the discount may have been too high, and that with the clarifications and workarounds being proposed, the final discount is heading toward a number lower than they initially expected. They become a bit frustrated and nevertheless demand the large discount. From their perspective, they want to see if the collaborative Pharma representatives will accept that.

Pharma politely asks for the reasons behind such a large discount request. At this point in the discussion, the Payer does not have good grounds to ask for such a large discount, given how Pharma is willing to address their concerns. On the one hand, the Payer feels good to have its concerns attended to, but they are also frustrated because they still want the large discount. Perhaps they promised large discounts internally before the negotiation. Perhaps they were requested by higher political powers to show that they were shrewd negotiators and could secure low prices for the public. Perhaps their internal KPIs involve large discounts. The Payer does not reveal the reasons but tries again, this time pushing for the discount without having any reasons left to support it.

The Pharma representatives, keeping their collaborative and polite stance, calmly explain that they believe they are already satisfying the Payer's concerns and that an extra discount would not be legitimate or needed. They acknowledge that the Payer had prepared that request, or have internal stakeholders expecting that level of discount. However, instead of giving a discount, they propose to work together to calculate how the deal on the table is providing value, saving costs, and representing a significant total price reduction. They want to arm the Payer with the tools to explain internally that the high discount was a rough solution to their fear of uncertainty, and since the uncertainty has been handled in other ways, the high level of discount is no longer warranted. The Payer is getting legitimate discounts and their concerns mitigated, which they would not have gotten had they only pushed for the higher discount. From their side, Pharma gets their drug listed for reimbursement quickly and for a price in line with the Payer country's reality.

We anticipate that a few readers still do not believe that conversations like this are feasible. To some Pharma representatives, the Payers care only about discounts and budget impacts. To some Payers, Pharma representatives are sneaky and only care about profit and listing their drugs. Some may argue that they have already tried this approach to negotiation and it just does not work the way we have described. We understand the concern: There are many nuances that one needs to get right for the process to work well. In the rest of this chapter, we will explain how so you can do it too.

6.2 Before the Negotiation

6.2.1 Don't Pick a Fight with Someone Bigger than You

People negotiate in order to obtain good value for themselves. If, during the negotiation, it seems that their expectations of value are not going to materialize, they tend to become frustrated and see the counterparty as the obstacle. They try to use power to get the counterparty to give them what they want. That use of power comes in two forms:

- Hard Bargaining (explicit use of power): coercing, threatening, or intimidating
- Soft Bargaining (hidden use of power): tricking the counterparty (providing misleading information, perceptions, or expectations)

At first, using power seems like an efficient way of getting what we want. However, using power triggers fear or resentment, leading the counterparty to resist your power by using their power in return. This leads to each side trying to "one up" the other, increasing the amount of power they apply. After a while, the efforts of the negotiators are focused on applying more power: it becomes a power-based negotiation.

If the power of one side is vastly superior to that of its counterparty, then using power is indeed an efficient way of negotiating, for the powerful side. However, if that is not the case, using power has a strong chance of leading to ineffective, value destroying negotiations with impasses and breakdowns.

In the case of P&R negotiations, there are many ways the sides can use power on each other. Payers can:

- Threaten not to list the product (using the power of monopsony—i.e., being the only buyer in the market)
- Run "winner takes it all" tenders between a product and non-therapeutic equivalent ones, when it would be supposed to be priced on the product's value
- Use biased appraisals of the clinical value of the product or biased calculations of costs or cost-effectiveness to reduce Pharma's room to negotiate the commercial terms
- Use a biased negotiation process to push Pharma to lower prices
- Manipulate emotions and pretend to be offended if Pharma does not provide special treatment to their citizens
- Behave aggressively and disrespectfully
- Be positional (i.e., stick to a single price or "solution" and refuse to entertain others), using take-it-or-leave-it tactics
- Provide wrong or misleading information on the confidential prices of comparator or competitors
- Use the media to spread desired information (or misinformation)
- Enact new laws that change the negotiation playing field to their advantage
- Enact new taxes or executive orders to reduce/cap their costs or reduce Pharma's revenues/profits
- Make public announcements/commitments or budgets that tie their hands in the negotiation
- Take unreasonably long to evaluate and negotiate a drug, delaying entry of the drug and consequently its revenues, or threatening to do so.

On the other hand, Pharma negotiators can also use power if they:

- Distort or omit relevant information about the product, the clinical data, epidemiological data
- Lie about their internal constraints ("*Headquarters will not allow…*")
- Stick firmly to their positions
- Threaten to remove their product from the market
- Have supporting KOL (Key Opinion Leaders) put pressure on the Payer
- Influence patient groups
- Use political influence
- Use the media to spread desired information (or misinformation)
- Use loopholes in the laws or systems to act in legal yet unethical ways
- Sue or threaten to sue the government over abuse of power or other inappropriate behavior

Payers often have a power advantage over Pharma, making power-based strategies a risky choice for Pharma in P&R negotiations. We have accompanied many negotiations where Pharma "just used a little power as a precaution," triggered the Payer's fear and resistance, and initiated a power-based escalation that destroyed value and ended in a big loss for both sides, but worse for Pharma's side. These negotiators failed to appreciate our human tendency when feeling attacked to react with power moves of our own, many times before giving the counterparty a chance to prove us wrong.

Consistently, despite the Payer's advantage on average, Pharma can be quite powerful when they bring a new product that is unique and valuable. So there is enough ground for the Payers to feel fear and believe they have to preemptively attack to feel safe. Nevertheless, given the overall value destruction these negotiations bring, choosing power-based strategies is often also suboptimal for Payers.

The safer choice for Pharma is then, usually, to abstain from using power, even if the other side uses theirs. Not using power does not mean allowing power to harm us. In a boxing match, it is true that to win you have to punch sometimes. But in a negotiation, this is not the case. Better is to dodge their punches, resist the temptation to punch back, while trying to get the other side to stop throwing them, and hopefully solve your differences in a non-aggressive way.

6.2.2 How to Make a Plan and Not Regret It

Excellence in negotiation is often depicted as coming up with very smart tricks in the heat of the moment. The reality is not as glamorous. Excellence in negotiation is the result of careful training and preparation that will enable you to avoid unnecessary power moves, craft a trusting relationship, consider many relevant options, and find the best ways forward.

As part of this plan, it is important to have as much information as you can. In negotiation, large chunks of valuable information are impossible to learn before you talk to the counterparty. That does not mean it should stay that way. After a successful meeting, you should no longer ignore:

1. What the Payer thinks of your value dossier
2. what the Payer is particularly concerned about
3. the worst case scenarios the Payer is building in their mind
4. the mistakes and misunderstandings the Payer has about your drug and therapeutic area
5. KPIs the Payer is pursuing and being measured on
6. the roughly approximate net prices of competing or similar drugs the Payer is using as benchmarks
7. potential offers your competitors are presenting
8. financial, political, or interpersonal workplace pressures the Payer has internally
9. the personal goals of the Payer's negotiators

These topics will undoubtedly impact your negotiation, and assuming or ignoring them will undo your carefully crafted strategy. Instead, acknowledge what you don't know, how important this information can be for your negotiation success, foster an internal sense of genuine curiosity, and start preparing questions on each of the above listed topics.

Anticipate how to manage the counterparty's potential discomfort in answering your questions, and prepare what you would do with the answers if and when you learn them. These answers will reveal the negotiator's **interests**, the term we use to refer to anything and everything a negotiator values, including their wants, needs, desires, fears, or concerns. For example, anticipating or learning the Payer's worst case scenarios will reveal which scenarios they believe threaten their interests. Learning their KPIs helps understand what they value or feel the need to capture.

If you learn the other side's **interests**, you can then craft **options**, our term for proposals, offers, suggestions, ideas, or recommendations to satisfy both yours and the Payer's interests. Better still, the parties can co-create and exchange options to satisfy as many interests as possible, until a package of options has significantly high value to all and turns into a **commitment**, our term to describe the final deal.

6.2.3 How Does One Negotiate Without Using Power?

Let's give an example:

The label in your drug includes patient populations A, B, C, and D. Despite population D being the largest of the four (with 40% of the total population), you anticipate very few sales in D, as your clinical value for these specific patients is lower, and your competitors offer a strong competitive advantage in this niche. This is information you know well but the Payer doesn't. Hence, the expectation of your total sales breakdown per population is the following, in terms of packs of product:

Population A sales forecast: 30,000 packs

Population B sales forecast: 30,000 packs

Population C sales forecast: 35,000 packs

Population D sales forecast: 5,000 packs

You are proposing to the Payer a price of $100 per pack, across all patient populations. This is a price in line with the clinical value of your product across the four subpopulations.

The Payer asks you for your sales estimate, which you duly provide, and then expresses concern that your sales in D will be much higher than your estimate. Therefore, given that your volume will be larger, he wants a larger discount to minimize budget impact. More importantly, as you bring a lower clinical value for D patients, he wants a steeper price discount to reflect the lower average value. So he proposes a 40% discount across the board.

Some negotiators would try to move forward by claiming that their estimates are good and sound and that they really expect to have only 5000 packs in sales. They will stick behind their $100 **position**, what we call when a negotiator demands a single, inflexible solution for the negotiation and shows no intention to budge. Oftentimes, this solution is acceptable to the positional party but hard to accept for the other side.

Even if the negotiators remain positional, they will feel a bit trapped, because to support the 5000 figure it would be helpful to say that the competitors are strong and may bring more clinical benefit to patients, even if only in D. This would be criticizing their own drug, and most negotiators would avoid such self-inflicted move or getting into the details, and instead say they trust their forecasting teams. A bargaining process is likely to start, where they make some price concessions to the Payer, argue a bit more, wait for the Payer to make a counter-proposal and so forth. They may end up closing at an 18% discount, and feel very happy that they did not cave in to the 40% that the Payer requested. The Payer, however, would have been happy with 15% and now feels that opening at 40% paid off. They leave the negotiation thinking they should have asked for a 50% discount and maybe they could have gotten a 20% discount instead. They take note of that for the next negotiation.

Some other negotiators will fear how the 5000 sales forecast will acknowledge the low clinical value for their drug in population D, and will inflate this forecast for the Payer. They might change it to 30,000 and bargain from there. Even though they did not admit a lower clinical value, they will still have to provide a large discount to appease the Payer's concerns about the high volume (and also for the lower clinical value anyway, as the Payer won't change its mind about that just because of an inflated estimate).

Other negotiators will start by asking for a price of $120 instead of $100 to protect themselves from the bargaining game. However, it is unlikely the Payer would ask for only a 40% discount in that case. Maybe the initial request would be 60%.

As you see, there are plenty of ways for one side to try to mislead the other and position for advantage in the bargaining process. However, these moves create undesirable risks in the short and long terms, do not consistently lead to good results, and often generate distrust and harm relationships.

Instead of bargaining, you should look at **interests**. Interests can be positive (needs, wants) or negative (fears, concerns). In this case, a key concern expressed by the Payer is in spending a lot of its funds in D, the largest subpopulation with the lowest clinical value, already well served by competing products. To solve that, you should not dismiss the Payer's concern. Dismissing is not solving, and dismissed issues have a nasty habit of coming back to the table, louder and angrier! Instead, you should try to find an option that can address their concerns, while also respecting your interests. Some possibilities could be:

Option 1: Restrict your product to populations A, B, and C with a price slightly over $100, This option requires giving away the potential volume from population D, where your drug's clinical value is lower. On the positive side, the average clinical value of your product is higher for populations A, B, and C, which legitimately supports a higher price.

Option 2: If patient tracking is feasible, have a trigger in your deal to renegotiate price if your sales in D exceed a certain amount, and assume your forecasts are appropriate.

Option 3: If patient tracking is feasible, due to the lower clinical value in D, you could provide a rebate specifically for verified sales in D (but not for patients in A, B, or C, who should keep paying the relatively higher price).

Option 4: If patient tracking is feasible, you could provide a sales cap at 6000 packs (the sales estimate plus 20% as an error margin) for patients in D, in return for something more valuable to you (e.g., a higher price).

Option 5: If patient tracking is not feasible, and the costs justify this, you could undertake a sampling study to evaluate your share of sales in D in the short-term future. Depending on the result, you could incorporate option 2 above (renegotiate), or incorporate as a consequence of the sampling study the ideas in options 3 or 4.

There are potential criticisms to each of the options above, such as:

Option 1: Restrict a population? Why should we give away access and value like that?

Option 2: Renegotiate our deal downwards? What is the advantage of doing so?

Option 4: A cap? Why would one give away potential value like that? What if the sales in D are higher than expected?

Option 5: That's a lot of money and risk! Why run the study at all?

The criticisms are valid but also have something in common: they compare the worst-case realization to an alternative that doesn't exist. The Payer is unlikely to accept your initial and preferred position without any changes or discounts.

Let's assume, as an example, that not addressing the D issue will result in an 18% discount across all sales. The options above make it possible to accept a potential risk on 5% of the product's value (5000 packs in D, out of 100,000 expected packs in all) instead of a likely loss of 18%.

There are also a few potential process risks. You may fear that as soon as you offer one of the options above, the Payer will accept and still insist on the original discount request, so you will be safer holding firm. You may also worry about creating a precedent that these options are always available. These are reasonable concerns, but, again, do not outweigh the potential benefits, and you can always continue negotiating collaboratively to manage these risks. The lesson here is simple: promote different options to satisfy interests instead of being stuck in a single position, in order to find deals that preserve or increase the value for all sides.

6.2.4 Tips on Preparation

You may struggle the first time you start preparing the interest list for a negotiation, as you may focus on positions instead of interests. Positions are single, inflexible options. Interests are the concerns driving the positions. To move from positions to interests, ask yourself: *Why do I want this?* Be extensive, going beyond the obvious, think about short, medium, and long terms, financial and non-financial interests, individual, team, and organizational interests, the needs, the wants, and even the nice to have, the things you are afraid of, risks you want to avoid. Then flip the script and try to anticipate the same for your counterparty. The goal is to make a long list that raises your awareness to all value levers in this negotiation. This is the heart of your negotiation preparation.

When you prepare options, prepare many (having only one option is a position) to give you flexibility to find solutions if the negotiation takes unexpected turns. Be creative, and do not censor yourself. It is okay to include improbable or crazy options since they may lead you in a productive direction even if they themselves are not the answers. While interests are generic, it is during the options part of your preparation that you get specific and calculate numbers, prices, or other scenarios or packages. Go down the lists of interests (yours and your counterparty's) and create options for each and every interest.

6.2.5 The Explorer Role

Preferably, your options should be prepared before the negotiation meeting. Some negotiators would be wary of improvising options in the middle of a negotiation. If they were not carefully prepared before, one may run the risk of proposing something that does not work or that HQ may not agree with. Proposing on the spot, as you learn the interests of the other side, can have both benefits and risks.

Of course, to craft well-tailored options, you need to know the interests of the other side, which you may only find out during the meeting. How to solve this? We recommend hosting a first meeting to discuss concerns and wants before making a proposal. This way you can lay the groundwork for cooperation and prepare with fuller knowledge.

6.2.6 Legitimacy

Satisfaction of interests is not the only way to reach a deal. Many times, you cannot fully satisfy interests, especially if expectations are unrealistic. In any event, your options become more persuasive if you can demonstrate their **legitimacy**, the term we use to describe the arguments to justify why a proposal is or not fair, reasonable, appropriate, adequate, or the right thing to do to all stakeholders.

To be persuasive, it is advisable that legitimacy is based on objective, external, neutral criteria. Legitimacy is not the same as a smart justification or excuse to back up my preferred option, since any win-lose negotiator can do that as a dissimulated bargaining move. Instead, legitimacy is the reason that represents my *genuine belief* of why my proposed option is the way that allocates value in the more sensible way, for both of us, in our negotiation. Usually, Market Access conversations ignore this step and, without fair justification, lack legitimacy. For instance, the negotiation may proceed as follows:

- Pharma explains why the product is so good and, wanting an 11% premium over the comparator, proposes 15% to have some bargaining buffer.
- Payer says that the premium request is crazy, highlights all the reasons the product is not so good and proposes 1%.
- Pharma explains why 1% is ridiculous, defends the product, repeats the benefits, and proposes 12%.
- Payer explains why 12% is outrageous, says that Pharma is destroying the national healthcare service, and makes a final offer of 3%.
- Pharma explains how the 3% is unacceptable and offers a final deal from HQ at 9%.
- Payer makes a final offer of 4.5% to be taken to HQ.
- Pharma, three days later, offers 6%.
- Deal closes at 5%.

Without legitimacy, there is no way for negotiators to hold ground, prove the potential validity of their offer, convince the counterparty, or show that they are genuinely trying to find a good solution. But if you have legitimacy, you don't *have to* move. Be flexible to move, but only if given a good reason to do so. If your proposal is carefully done, you shouldn't need to move much. They may point out other aspects to be considered in the calculations, and then do so. But the goal is to find a legitimate option for all sides, not just to throw our preferred numbers back and forth.

6.2.7 The Same Negotiation, with Legitimacy

Payer: Let us finally talk about the price.

Pharma: Yes, I think it is a good idea. If we understand correctly, our price should be based on the price of our comparator while considering the differences in terms of clinical benefits. Instead of throwing out numbers for bargaining's sake, we prefer to explain carefully how we derived our price, because even if you disagree with it, we want you to see that we are honestly trying to find a number that makes sense given our product's perceived value. Then we are glad to discuss any concerns you may have as to our method.

Payer: OK, go ahead.

Pharma: Our comparator costs 10,000 euros per treatment and has a cure rate of 81%, with similar adverse effects to our product. We believe the safety profiles to be similar. Do you see it the same way?

Payer: Correct, we agree that the safety profiles are very similar.

Pharma: *The only striking difference between the two products, in clinical terms, is the efficacy, moving the rate of cured patients after treatment from 81% to 90%. This represents a little more than an 11% relative improvement over the comparator's cure rate. We used a rounded 11% improvement over their price of 10,000 euros to calculate our proposed list price of 11,100 euros per treatment.*

Payer: 11% premium? We don't pay those sorts of premiums. I can't give you special treatment. We need to be fair here.

Pharma: *We recognize your responsibility to treat all companies fairly. That is why we are asking for the 11% premium. Based on our research on products over the past five years, this price is very much in line with what has been paid before. That said, we could be missing some data, or how you are approaching your thinking. Can you please share more?*

Payer: 11% is a lot. We were thinking 2%.

Pharma: Can you explain where that figure comes from?

Payer: It is the value we are willing to pay.

Pharma: *If you do not mind sharing, how did you come up with 2% and not a lower or higher number?*

Payer: It doesn't matter how we got there. Our internal workings are none of your business. We are ready to offer 2%.

Pharma: We did a careful pricing study to be able to propose a price that could make sense to us and to you. We also attempted to transparently share our method. 11% is not just a number we are proposing to bargain, it is the number we believe makes sense given the market, other products, and the clinical value we are bringing. We know we may have missed something, so we are open to change our mind, but to do so we would need to know what we missed.

Payer: Y*ou are not taking into account the whole picture. In practical terms, 90% and 81% are more or less the same. We don't think it justifies paying 1100 euros more.*

Pharma: We see. Well, when we prepared for today's meeting, we looked at the 19% of patients who fail treatment under the comparator and found that our product reduces that number by almost half, to 10%. These unresponsive patients will be the ones responsible for a large share of costs and care. From this angle, we calculated the benefits and savings that our product can bring to the overall healthcare system and believe by this measure we could actually justify a premium of 23%.

Payer: 23%?? Are you out of your mind!?!

Pharma: *No, and that is why we are not proposing 23%, but showing how 90% and 81% are not, in our way of seeing things, more or less the same. Those 9% of patients make a lot of difference. Also, we hope you can see that we are not trying to justify the maximum price possible, but rather that we worked hard to identify a price that could make sense for both of us. Our research shows that 11% is one reasonable way to look at our case as it is within what similar products have received in the recent past.*

Payer: You are coming here with these calculations to justify large premiums. But given that new drugs only get approved if they are better than older ones, prices would always rise and we would go bankrupt! This makes it impractical to use calculations like these.

Pharma: Our experience is that prices don't increase permanently, as they are usually negotiated down every second year. When our comparator came to market four years ago, it cost 11,400 euros per treatment, which is more than what we are asking for now even without considering inflation or its savings to the healthcare system.

Payer: Yes, those 9% of patients are costly but those savings don't enter my budget, so I can't use that to justify a premium.

Pharma: Is there any way we can help redirect some of the savings we are bringing to your budget, given they are all inside the MoH?

Payer: Mmmm... Look, budgets are under extreme strain right now and we should not discuss previous deals. We are willing to offer 6%. Do we have a deal? We are meeting in the middle.

Pharma: Thank you for the offer. I appreciate your willingness to work with us to find a solution. We did not offer 11% to bargain and find a number in the middle, we tried hard to find a number that would also work for you. We are truly convinced that 11% makes sense. We are open to being shown where we may be wrong, in which case we may change our perspective and then our number.

Payer: I am being flexible. I moved from 2% to 6%. You should be flexible too!

Pharma: Our flexibility is about being open to hearing your perspective on what the appropriate price may be, and being flexible to think differently and change the price. I am doing that. I am not exchanging positions because I did not start with a high number to give you fake concessions after.

Payer: Are you accusing me of using fake numbers?

Pharma: No, I just said that WE are not doing so. You may have good reasons for your numbers, I just do not know what they are yet, which makes it hard for me to change my mind or my price. Or you may not, which would not be surprising, as unfortunately many other Pharma negotiators have been here opening with very inflated first positions. But I am not doing that. What is, for you, the most reasonable way to calculate the premium?

Payer: I was not prepared for this type of conversation. I will think about and respond to your premium offer and its reasons at our next meeting, when I expect you to come ready to negotiate down your premium request as well. By the way, I already don't think it is appropriate to use 11% instead of the absolute improvement of 9% efficacy.

Pharma: Thank you for accepting to find the proper number that makes sense for both of us and putting the effort in preparing. Much appreciated. About the 9%, is it that you think that we should get a premium proportional to the 9% point increase, not the 11% improvement?

Payer: No, I disagree with both methods, but between the two, I prefer the 9%.

Pharma: Why do you think that?

Payer: If we had a standard of care with 15% efficacy and you came with a new product at 45% efficacy, I could see a scenario for a 30% premium under the percentage point increase. But by your logic you would expect us to pay three times more than the comparator. Would that be reasonable?

Pharma: *This is a good example. Indeed, the difference between a 30% increase* vs. *a 200% one is huge. From our analysis, and we have some slides on this, if you are interested, I am happy to show them, or send it later, the equivalent three times approach from your example seems reasonable. In our analysis, it was dominant over the 30% approach. We just have to think about new drugs replacing ineffective generics and we get way above 200%, for example.*

Payer: *But that's different.*

Pharma: *Yes, some of the comparators (not all) are generic, but if we brought a 9% improvement over a generic, I could anticipate that you would not be very open to increase the price several fold, or am I wrong? In any case, I would love to learn more and, if I understand why the logic should be different, I will be happy to consider adjusting our price request. I also understand that you were not expecting our conversation would take this turn, so, as you requested earlier, I am happy to continue in our next meeting. Can I send you the analysis we did, so you know where I got my perceptions from?*

Payer: Okay. Yes, it will be good to have time to prepare. Please send me the analysis, let me have my staff look at it, and we can continue next time.

Carefully crafted legitimacy allows you to justify standing your ground while being flexible IF you are given a superior or complementary reason to yours. The goal is not to be positional on legitimacy, but to negotiate legitimacy to identify each side's different perspectives on a reasonable allocation to the value on the table and then help everyone converge on a rationale that works for everyone The parties can thus protect their relationship while claiming value, clearly explain the deal to internal stakeholders, and arrive at a solution everyone believes is the best they could come up with together.

Despite the benefits of legitimacy in negotiations, there are a few traps or poor practices. Some negotiators pick a preferred price, fall in love with it, attach meaningless though smart justifications as fake legitimacy just to push their position. Others believe and behave as if their legitimacy were symbolic of moral superiority and trigger angry responses from their counterparties. Many negotiators pile up several legitimacies behind a price, which do not sum up to a more persuasive conversation, as the weaker argument brings down the overall convincing power of legitimacy. Many others still use legitimacy as an instrument to convince others, but are not open to being persuaded by their counterparty's legitimacy.

Successful use of legitimacy hinges on a genuine collaborative search for an acceptable allocation of the negotiation value. If you chose to negotiate win-win and believe in legitimacy to persuade, instead of the win-lose approach of using power to coerce or trick your counterparty into your desired commitment, you must be consistent and remain open to persuasion if the counterparty brings superior legitimacy to yours. When preparing legitimacy, research as many as you can find to have something to help you allocate the value generated by whatever option you co-create with your counterparty. Then support your preferred option with one compelling legitimacy you genuinely believe in and that the counterparty is likely to embrace. Think about the chosen legitimacy being used "against" you, would you have accepted it if you were on the receiving side?

Preparing legitimacy, choosing a genuine one that aligns with the preferred options while anticipating counter-arguments, and mapping out the legitimacy conversation in advance can contribute to more successful market access negotiations. This exercise becomes particularly important given the unique legitimacy challenges within P&R negotiations. For example, both sides cannot share what would otherwise be valuable and persuasive data due to confidentiality constraints: the payer cannot share its local net pricing data on comparable medications, and pharmaceutical companies cannot share their international net pricing data for the same medication.

6.2.8 Alternatives

Another reason for people to accept deals is when they feel that these deals are better than their alternatives. **Alternatives** are the other potential courses of actions, deals, or solutions that *do not* involve an agreement by the current counterparty, that any party can pursue if the current negotiation fails to meet their interests. Examples of the alternatives for the Payer are:

- Do not reimburse your product
  - Stay with the lower quality, but probably cheaper, comparator, leaving the unmet need for your drug unsatisfied
- Reimburse only your new direct competitor
- Slow down the process enough to cause commercial pain on your side
  - by rejecting your application and waiting while you submit the value dossier again
  - by having you agree on a bridge program, for free, and then stall
  - by creating the need for additional evidence
  - by sending you back to the Scientific committee
  - by stalling and reducing your lead against your competitor who is behind you coming to market
- Create a law that goes against your drug and impedes potential revenues as a clawback law or a new tax
- Change the P&R process dramatically to their advantage, such as turning it into a competitive price-only tender

Looking at the Payer's alternatives can help you understand how likely they are to close the deal, or to walk away instead. If you had a strong scientific assessment recommending reimbursement, there is a strong patient group pressuring the Payer, with media coverage, and no competitor product in the market, their alternatives are not very good. Payers are less likely to walk away, especially if the options offered by Pharma are legitimate and satisfy their interests somehow. If, on the other hand, your product is trying to negotiate the same price as a competitor, with no clinical benefit, their alternatives are pretty strong.

When negotiators are planning on walking away, they tend to consider a few things:

- Is the BOOT (Best Option On the Table) better than my alternatives?
- What is the transition cost for me to leave this deal and move to another one?
- Will there be short- or long-term negative consequences if I walk away from this deal today?
- How will I explain to my stakeholders why I walked away?

The first three considerations are utilitarian questions or cost-benefit analyses. The fourth question is extremely important in organizations and it often supersedes the other three questions despite being less objective or concrete. Consider how your counterparty would justify walking away to their stakeholders. If you are clear on your commitment to keep working with them to craft a mutual-gain solution, and have put legitimate options on the table that satisfy their interests reasonably well, your counterparties will have a low willingness to walk away, unless their alternatives are really superb.

Words of caution about alternatives:

- Your perception of someone else's alternatives is not fool-proof. Underestimating their alternatives can mislead you into feeling overconfident, and lead the Payer to make efforts to increase its own power (e.g., the implementation of the W tax in France to fight the power of Gilead with Sovaldi as seen in Chap. 3.)
- Conversely, there is no need to become underconfident if the Payer has several alternatives such as having access to competitor products. The Payer's alternatives may never be acted upon as long as you don't initiate a power-based negotiation. Indeed, many Payers try to keep an even playing field between companies, try to reimburse several competitor products, and don't use their alternatives as a power tool to the extent they could, since they also need to protect broader social and healthcare interests and not just commercial or political ones. This exaggerated fear of having your product not listed has made many negotiators preemptively use power to "protect" themselves and inadvertently escalated the dynamic to worse results for all.

Do not use alternatives as a power tool by making the implicit or explicit threat of walking away, or by telling your counterparty that they don't have good alternatives and can't walk away, so they must take what you offer (or, in P&R lingo, that they "should think about the patients"). This can inadvertently start a power-based negotiation, and in fact mentioning alternatives is one of the most common ways by which people use power in a negotiation.

After listing your alternatives during your preparation, highlight the one(s) you would probably pursue first in case you do not make a deal. This is your Plan B or **BATNA**: the Best Alternative to a Negotiated Agreement. Then do the same for your counterparty's alternatives to see what their BATNA *might* be. Notice that the BATNA could be several alternatives bundled into a larger course of action.

6.2.9 Relationship

You should not underestimate how great your relationship with the Payer could become. Except for countries where Payers are openly aggressive, almost all Market Access Directors say they have "a very good relationship with Payers." We disagree. In our perspective—with the exception of the best Market Access negotiators—the majority of Pharma-Payer relationships are indeed cordial on the surface, but their bargaining interactions hardly reflect or foster productive negotiation dynamics.

On the one hand, many Pharma representatives describe their products only in the best possible light, without acknowledging the full reality. They argue that the clinical value is always above the Payer's evaluation, and some present prices without much legitimacy or supported by biased data to support the highest possible ask. Conversely, many Payers seemingly dismiss the positives of the scientific evaluations and twist it as negatively as they can. They only criticize, and even at times punish a drug for being too good (e.g., treating lots of patients), to avoid paying as much as it is worth. They try to allocate all the risk onto Pharma and request extreme discounts not grounded in any legitimacy.

While not all parties on either side behave that way, it is frequent enough that it creates and feeds into an adversarial bargaining pattern. Both sides argue in very biased ways and make proposals a third party would see as unfair, just to gain the upper hand or a better deal.

There are certainly times when the relationship is different, the Payer and the Pharma negotiators are friendly and avoid rough conversations, but the discussion of the value of the deal is conducted as a "goodwill gift." That is, the Payer asks the Pharma representative to show that they are truly being friendly by offering a very low price. They ask for financial value as proof of a good relationship, or even in return for keeping that good relationship. This is **manipulation**, as one side leverages their counterparty's feelings for unilateral substance gain.

Our idea of "a very good relationship" is different. It can be best described when the Pharma and the Payer negotiators work hard, together, to find an appropriate deal that can satisfy both sides' interests, even when they cannot find one. They respect that they see things differently and then focus on solving or minimizing the differences and uncertainties of the product/forecasts/sales/expenditure. They acknowledge that satisfying everyone's interests is a very hard challenge. They refrain from and are confident that the other party will not manipulate, play tricks, hide relevant information, be positional, biased, or refuse to appreciate their point of view, even when they disagree. Furthermore, they have a desire that the other does well in the negotiation and is perceived as having done so by their organization. These acts are genuine and not dependent on the negotiation outcome.

This is no easy task. To be able to obtain this kind of relationship does require quite a lot of preparation, focus, and skill. To understand how to approach the negotiation, from a relationship perspective, there are seven questions worth thinking about:

- What are our current behaviors to one another?
- Could the other party be annoyed, distrusting, or disappointed with me?
- What are their perceptions of me and my organization? And vice versa?
- How could this negotiation be important for them on an emotional level?
- What could be the points of friction in this negotiation?
- Which internal negotiations might they be involved as part of this negotiation? How may they be feeling about them?
- What can I do in order to move our current relationship to a relationship that is genuinely very good?

If your negotiation has relationship issues, you should actively solve those issues before moving on to anything else. Negotiations become much harder when there are relationship problems.

6.2.10 Preparing for Your Negotiations as a Team—and How that Leads to Miserable Failure

You've probably been there before: sitting in a "war room" jointly preparing for a negotiation. The idea was to bring together several heads and obtain the wisdom of the crowd. Soon enough, teammate #1, who may have spent a lot of time calculating what a fair and realistic asking price could be, proposes an asking price of €80. Immediately, teammate #2 says, "*What about €90? Our product delivers awesome value and it deserves a higher price tag!*"

Teammate #2 sees a room full of appreciative smiles. Conversely, teammate #1 is suddenly seen as not ambitious enough, not believing enough in the product's potential or, worse still, not working toward maximizing shareholder value. The groupish mood and the number escalate even further. Now **groupthink** has crept in, no one dares to challenge or bring data against high prices. Joint preparation tends to increase optimism and thus the asking price—but it can foster a rigidity, a groupthink that leads negotiators to believe that because they all agreed on something together, it must be right. Working as a team, negotiators usually start to develop an Us vs. Them attitude.

If preparing as a group, you must first avoid falling into the groupthink trap. Then, promote a brave space for diverse thinking, where individuals can say what they believe is helpful, even if risky or against the group, without fear of personal reprisals or judgments. Finally, agree that decisions should be made with a risk-and-reward perspective: some negotiation moves are risky but can bring higher rewards (e.g., bargaining for a higher price). People should not be seen as "achievers" and "losers" but rather pursue moves with various levels of risk. Ask:

- What is the potential reward of this move (what can I gain from it, and how sustainable will it be in the negotiation)? What are the odds that this move will work?
- What is the potential risk (what can go wrong and how will that affect the rest of the negotiation or even future negotiations)? What are the odds and impact of a backlash if this move does not work?
- How can we improve this move so that we keep or increase the rewards while reducing or managing the risks?

Next, create a map that accurately describes reality. Include the range of options, the possible moves and decisions, rich with details and possibilities and ways to respond to different scenarios. If you have a bad map, no matter how intelligent you are and how rational your decisions are, you are bound to rely on false or biased information and end up doing worse.

Making this detailed map is a high-return investment in improving the negotiation no matter where it turns. In one case, a co-author of this book was invited to help a market access team after a turbulent two-year long P&R negotiation, which greatly delayed the drug's access in that market. As they were about to negotiate over their next drug, equally if not more complex and expensive than its predecessor, they called for help. The assisted team spent 3 weeks creating a map rich in detail and possibilities, including ways to handle different turns. At the negotiation, the Payer started aggressive, and asked a difficult question. The team leveraged its preparation to remain calm, acknowledged the relevance of the Payer's concern, reframed it into interests, and shared a previously prepared option that satisfied the Payer. The whole negotiation took only 2 h and achieved a great outcome.

With the map ready, you can decide on your milestone moves. You do not have to—and in fact could not—plan the whole negotiation as this would require perfect foresight. Instead, take into account that you will learn a lot more during the negotiation meetings and you can iterate and refine your moves as you go along. Overall, we believe low-risk trumps high reward. Risk in a negotiation is often compounded (e.g., the risk of the second move multiplies the risk of the first, and so on), and even minimum-risk moves can jeopardize your deal. There is **no risk-free move** in a negotiation.

Once completing the map, you should role-play the negotiation with someone who knows the other side well, take the learnings from the role play and incorporate them into your plan. Once you are done planning, take a moment to imagine the negotiation is a failure. Ask yourself not whether it will fail, but rather why would it have failed? This may open up some more thinking that will help the preparation.

(Include here the 7-element preparation sheet of a Market Access Negotiation Role play Kadiximab)

6.2.11 Obtaining Internal Support

Many people find that their internal negotiations are even tougher than the external ones. Different audiences inside organizations may have different interests and opposing KPIs, even though they are supposed to be on the same side.

The internal negotiations between the Pharma HQ and its subsidiaries (a.k.a. Market Affiliates or just Markets) create a lot of tension. From each market's perspective, HQ may be imposing their views and demanding unrealistic goals without taking into consideration the specific difficulties of that market. HQ can afford to take more risks and push for higher prices, as they can meet their targets even if a few Markets don't list a particular product, compensating for these failures with successes elsewhere. The individual markets do not have this same portfolio of countries to buffer a failure. A market may in fact see its entire yearly revenues collapse or at least fall short of targets due to a single risk miscalculation. Thus, Markets may perceive their HQs as being more focused on supporting high prices than in securing access, increasing the risk of no deal or not saving patient lives.

From HQ's perspective, the market may not be taking into consideration the vast pool of knowledge HQ has from other markets, and may instead go for the simpler solution of lowering prices to secure access. If they do not try hard enough to reach the highest possible price, HQ worries extreme discounting could harm other countries through reference pricing and Payer gossip. HQs worry that Markets may be risking reimbursement in other countries and jeopardizing future R&D investment, and thus also risking not saving patients' lives.

Also, incentives differ depending on how each company splits their sales revenue. If revenues are higher than expected, most profits go to HQs, conversely, if revenues are lower than expected, profits, and thus HQ, are hit harder than the Market Affiliates. Meanwhile, the Markets have a more binary outcome (e.g., deal or no deal), where no deal can be quite disastrous and lead to downsizing the local office. On the other hand, an excellent deal may not be as good locally as Markets rarely keep most of its profits. Such incentive differences push HQ, but not the Markets, to pursue better deals.

Market Affiliate negotiators normally face some barriers when negotiating with HQ, namely:

- HQ wants to prevent complexity and keep things simple (e.g., just negotiate a price), as they have to handle multiple markets.
- HQ wants to reduce time going to legal and higher management with requests to do something different.
- HQ and Markets have conflicting KPIs.
- HQ is afraid of creating negative precedents.
- HQ, expecting a power-based negotiation, fails to understand what and why the Market wants what it wants.
- Cross-cultural issues.

Lack of time, attention, interest (e.g., for smaller Markets), or trust. How do you handle all this? *You negotiate in a value-oriented way with your HQ.*

Some tips for that negotiation:

1. *Be proactive and start early.* Don't wait until your HQ sends you negotiation instructions, and then criticize it or suggest a contrary strategy. Instead, start earlier than HQ in preparing the negotiation. Ask them for information, and proactively provide them with information about your market and specificities.
2. *Show you care.* Ask about their interests and preferences for this negotiation and try to empathize with and understand their challenges and pain points. Ask them how you can all achieve what you want and need.
3. *Avoid stereotypes.* You don't want to merely complain that your Payer is the worst and that the only solution is for HQ to lower your price floor. HQ hears that from every Market. Instead, explain the reasoning behind your deal and help them understand how it will satisfy all stakeholder interests.
4. *Know what everyone wants.* For you to properly negotiate win-win, you must know what value means for all parties involved. That is, you will want a mandate that gives you the opportunity to tailor your deal to your company's and the Payer's interests. The earlier you can find what type of deal all parties want and give that feedback to HQ, allowing them the time to negotiate internally on your behalf, the better. Some people may feel the opposite, as in: "If I wait until the very end, during the Payer negotiations, it will be harder for my HQ to refuse my request, because I will be up against a wall." That is true, but: (1) that is a high-risk strategy, meaning that if you get a no, there is not much you can do then, and (2) even if HQ caves in, they probably won't develop the best feelings for you, and this may hurt you in the future.
5. *Make their job easier.* Understand the internal negotiation process and how can you best tailor your message. Then assume they are super busy and you are not a priority, send your request in the highest quality package you possibly can, and describe your external negotiation challenge in ways that facilitate their decision-making and impresses them that you did your homework. Don't make them trust your opinions. Use data.
6. *Answer the question "Why you?"* If you are in HQ, you want to treat all affiliates in a fair manner, unless there is a significantly good reason to treat anyone differently. If you want to gain an exception, consider that at some point, they might have to explain why. So, help your HQ by giving a clear reason why to grant you an exception.
7. *Discuss the measures of success (your KPIs).* It sounds basic, but if one side is pursuing price and not opening any precedents, and the other is pursuing revenue or just reimbursement, this should be acknowledged, discussed, and considered throughout the conversation.
8. *Move the conversation from "right" and "wrong" to risk-reward.* Just as in your own group discussions, this can be very helpful. There is some caution to have in terms of different cultures. In risk-taking cultures, talking about risk

may sound cowardly or non-ambitious. In such cases, you may want to refer to risk indirectly, with comments and questions such as: "this move may decrease our expected revenue...," "more likely to lead to an impasse," "what would happen if it doesn't go exactly as we want?" "how does that impact our probability of achieving the higher/highest reward?"

9. *Be culturally sensitive*. With HQ, you will face different cultural obstacles: different nationalities, hierarchical levels, or negotiation approaches. Whatever you say will be interpreted through their own cultural lenses and may lead to very different interpretations, not necessarily your original intention. Be aware of prejudices and be very clear about what you mean and don't mean. Ask questions to fully understand their intentions.
10. *You may be the less cross-culturally aware*. HQ negotiators interact daily with many Markets, and thus more often become cross-culturally aware. Meanwhile, Market negotiators often meet the same HQ team, dominated by a single corporate or national culture. Foreigners in the HQ have acculturated themselves by learning the HQ's dominant national and corporate cultures. If you are from the Market, study, not stereotype, your HQ's culture and how to effectively negotiate within it.

6.2.12 Finding the Right Counterparty to Negotiate with

It can be very frustrating to have proposals rejected at the negotiation table because "*it goes against our policy/process*" or "*that is not how we do things*." What can be done?

We see two ways forward: One is to negotiate "*through*" the counterparty, that is, negotiate with the counterparty so they can negotiate inside their organization on your behalf. The other approach is to directly negotiate with someone else, at a higher or more appropriate position in the organization, who has the authority to negotiate what you want.

It can be quite hard to swap counterparties during a negotiation. If the counterparty is already in the power mindset, to propose something outside of their scope may come across as trying to trick them. Proposing to negotiate with their boss can be even worse, as this attempt to "go over their head" or bypass them may communicate that we are disrespecting them, making them irrelevant, or making them lose face toward their bosses. Establishing a collaborative relationship from the start can help counterparties escalate issues internally without being seen as caving into a power move.

A good practice is to try to negotiate access to the right counterparty *before* the official negotiation starts. Be judicious with this strategy, and pre-escalate a negotiation only when you believe that the case is more complex, risky, or especially costly to all parties. In such cases, the higher-ups are more likely to appreciate the early warning and access.

Answer these questions:

- Is this a case worth pre-escalating and thus pre-negotiating?
  - How likely is this case to be uncommon?
  - How likely is our favorite proposed deal to fall significantly outside of their negotiation boundaries or their mandated pool of possible solutions/prices?
  - How likely is it to generate conflict, antagonism, and strong negative emotions later in the process if we do not change something early?
- Who is impacted by this deal? I must make sure that all relevant voices are heard or a single one can destroy the deal.
- Who can change the process for the benefit of all parties? Do I already have some new process suggestions (not positions or single "perfect" solutions) to facilitate the conversation?
- How can my pre-escalating move be misunderstood as an attempt to gain power over the counterparty? How can I minimize such risks? Am I truly open to listening and engaging in a better process that differs from my ideal scenario?
- Who is my most likely opposition? How can I talk to them before they become a problem?
- If multiparty, how do I influence the influencers? I need multipliers and allies, and I must get them moving soon and fast.

After mapping the stakeholders in this way, we can better choose when to pre-escalate, who to talk to, and in which order.

In P&R negotiations, there are a few additional particularities. First, Payers are often concerned that closer relationships with Pharma representatives could look like warming up to Pharma at best and corruption at worst. Pharma negotiators have to be very careful to avoid doing anything that could create discomfort in the counterparty or risk their reputation as upstanding and honest officials. If you believe that pre-escalation could lead to any negative rumors, abide by the saying: "*Caesar's wife must be above suspicion.*" You should only pre-escalate when you are suggesting a correction due to a failure or anachronism in the system. Your request has to be to improve or modernize the existing suboptimal system and process, to help all, not just you.

Another particularity is, in some countries, the opacity of the Payer's internal negotiations, which makes it hard to know the best path to gain access to the parties you want to reach.

Once you decide whom in the Payer organization you are going to try to negotiate with first, you need to prepare for that out-of-process negotiation by being able to answer a few key questions they may be wondering about:

- *Why would I talk to you? What is in it for my organization?*
- *Why me and not the normal channels?*
- *Why should you be granted an exception and allowed to follow a different channel?*
- *How can I justify this to other people? Am I running a risk here?*
- *Do I feel like doing this? How much time will this cost me?*

It is important to craft a pitch that answers these questions. It might look something like this:

"We are asking for this chat because we believe our product brings some differences (namely ___) compared to usual submissions. This cannot be completely captured with the current process and risk placing us at a tough impasse later on. We have ideas on how these differences can lead to better deals and strongly benefit everyone (your agency, patients, and also our company), but we fear that the current P&R negotiation process could limit our ability to do so. We would very much like to briefly make you aware of these issues."

There are a few important aspects to the paragraph above:

- It says we already bring ideas (options) that can be valuable to them (interests).
- It explains why our product/situation is different (legitimacy).
- It says that the current process is not totally suitable for the product, thus justifying why we should not take the usual route (legitimacy).
- It states that the suboptimal process and its limitations could lead to a suboptimal deal, including to the Government, thus appealing to a potential mutual process interest to avoid suboptimal options.
- It talks about negotiating the process for the benefit of all parties, thus limiting the risk of unintentionally giving preferential treatment, making mistakes or tarnishing their reputation. You are suggesting negotiating a process before the official negotiation starts to make it fairer (not biased) to all parties. That includes competitors who may in the future bring drugs with similar characteristics. It shows that you are not seeking special treatment, but rather that you have found a flaw in the system and are inviting the Government to fix it for the benefit of all involved. (process option, interests, and legitimacy)
- It asks only for a small time commitment ("*briefly*" and "*make you aware*" instead of "*negotiate*" or the like) so that the Payer knows they are in control and can decide to continue this conversation or send you back to the normal process. By asking the Payer for a short time only, you lower the costs and risks of saying "yes" (commitment).

Hopefully, by hearing or reading such a paragraph, the Payer will feel curious and safe, and maybe even feel a responsibility to hear you out. Of course, there is no guarantee of having the meeting or getting an agreement to discuss it further, but at least you are maximizing your chance of getting the negotiation onto the right path.

If you receive a positive reply, the game is on. It is a different game from a P&R negotiation; at any moment, the Payer can think the conversation is no longer safe, ethical, valuable, or interesting and send you back to the normal channels of negotiation. How should you handle such a tough conversation?

1. **Be mindful**. Start by being thankful, express gratitude for their time, and directly move to explain how you expect to create value for all.

2. **Assume you can be kicked out at any moment**. Prepare a carefully scripted succinct speech to deliver the important information quickly, and give more details later if the meeting keeps going.
3. **Focus on the topic that justifies talking to them and not someone else**, making clear for them why this case is special and different from the usual process. Do not introduce topics you could properly negotiate through the normal channels, since that risks the meeting immediately coming to a close.
4. **Listen very carefully whenever they speak**. Understand clearly what they say and what they don't say, and ask for more details or clarification when you are not sure. Answer any questions clearly and honestly. If they interrupt, do not force the script, but rather stop and listen.
5. **No early commitment requests.** Beware of asking for early commitments, as those may seem like too much, too fast.
6. **Make everything easy for them**. Bring some *short* documentation that you can leave with them to read, remember, and negotiate on your behalf with others. If you absolutely need to ask them for something urgent, try to make it so that they have enough understanding of the consequences of their decisions.
7. **Be flexible**. If you are bringing presentation slides on a laptop, bring them only for support (graphs, visuals, etc.) and be prepared to abandon them if you do not have enough time.
8. **Always be productive**. Remember that they do not need to grant you the time to talk about what may look like an exception. Do not react to an aggressive or rude tone, since this may just be an early knee-jerk reaction where they are misunderstanding your points. Positively reframe the message and answer the question they are asking, even if their posture seems overly aggressive.
9. **If all else fails**… If they decline to continue talking to you, ask them for recommendations of what else to do or who to talk to. Ask if they want to be informed of the outcome of conversations with others. Thank them for their time and opportunity to discuss your issue.

6.3 During the Negotiation

6.3.1 Starting Off on the Right Foot

Most people enter negotiations following a *wait & see* strategy. That is, they are willing to be collaborative with the counterparty, but only if the counterparty is collaborative in return. People fear being perceived as naïve, weak, or stupid, against someone who is trying to take advantage of them. To be seen as tough is often much preferred to being seen as a "sucker."

This is especially true for Payers, being responsible for taxpayer money and the health of citizens. Their fear of being taken for a fool or seen as corrupt makes them extremely risk-averse. They also worry because they are negotiating with a counterparty who knows much more about the product and had much more time to prepare for this particular negotiation. The Payer negotiators split their time among dozens of negotiations or have the negotiations be an add-on on top of their "day" jobs as physicians, academics, or other. As such, they do not have the time to go through all products in as much detail. Plus, drug prices abroad are confidential, making it hard for Payers to check how good their deals are. As Payers distrust Pharma's trustworthiness, they often see no alternative than to act defensively.

It is also helpful to take the Payer's identity and perception of Pharma companies into account. Payers and Pharma negotiators do not meet for the first time as a clean slate, but come to the negotiation bringing their prejudices and stereotypes about the counterparty. Pharma's negotiators see Payers as focused on prices and budgets, and not caring about a drug's value or positive impact on patients. Payer negotiators see themselves as qualified professionals who many times, unfairly, make a fraction of what Pharma executives make, while dedicating their lives as protectors of the public good. Payers see Pharma negotiators as people who only care about profit, only use health arguments when it works in their favor, have historically taken advantage of their pricing power, and are willing to do whatever it takes to reach their KPIs. How can this not feel like a fight between good and evil?

Some of the worst deals we have seen in Pharma were the result of a negotiation where the Pharma negotiators were perceived as trying to trick or outsmart or outpower the Payer. Trying to play tricks on the Payer, such as presenting biased estimates of prevalence, is a very risky strategic choice in P&R negotiations, even before considering the long-term impact on the relationship, the ethical concerns, and the tarnishing of a company's reputation.

Looking into this good vs. evil picture is a very narrow, black-and-white way of looking at negotiation strategies. Instead, begin by trying to dispel the "good vs. evil" story. Invite the Payer into a new story, where both are qualified and competent negotiators, devoted to improving health, who need to collaborate to find solutions, often not easy ones to find, that will be affordable to the public and produce a return to shareholders at the same time. Being on separate sides of a negotiation often means differing interests between the parties, but not necessarily that they are adversaries.

A proactive relationship approach can rewrite the good vs. evil narrative from the start, and show our collaborative intentions, thus making it safer for the other side to reciprocate.

Most negotiators do begin by saying that they have the most collaborative intentions. Even or maybe especially those that are intending to play tricks on the other side. All that means is that you have to work harder to convince others of your true positive intentions. Words are cheap, but by negotiating in this collaborative manner, consistently abstaining from using power, you will earn the trust of your counterparties and rewrite your story.

6.3.1.1 The Opening Statement

Negotiators who want to create the appropriate environment to negotiate win-win believe that they must build trust. Trust is not necessary but helpful for win-win strategies. The challenge is that trust takes time to build and few have the luxury to wait until trust is fully built before starting to negotiate. Robust win-win strategies allow negotiators to build a conducive negotiating environment without the pre-existence of trust.

Our suggestion is to start with an **opening statement,** your first sentences of real impact in the negotiation, to create a feeling of *mutualism*: that both parties will be better off working collaboratively than "fighting" each other. With mutualism, it is in the other's self-interest to be collaborative, since they will obtain more value that way. To create mutualism, consider this question:

- *How can I move their perception of me as their adversary to instead as a member of their team, pursuing a common goal or facing a common challenge?*

Craft your opening statement only once you are done with the rest of the preparation and have a good idea of what the issues may be. As you identify the biggest common challenge that both of you face, frame it in broad terms in your opening. Suppose, for example, that your drug got a very negative scientific assessment, not in line with the assessments in other markets, and that this is not due to the drug potentially not having a great clinical value but from a technical issue in the clinical data. Consider further that challenging that assessment is not an option you wish to pursue. To match that scientific assessment with a straight rebate would require a discount way beyond the floor price Headquarters gave you.

The difference between the scientific assessments in different markets can thus be the common challenge. Show the Payer that you want to work with them, *as a team,* to jointly solve the problem you both face, which is how to reimburse this product with a particularly negative scientific assessment that binds the Payer to achieve a strong price reduction, but that the Pharma HQ will surely disagree to avoid affecting other markets. You could say:

> *Thank you for the invitation and for your time. I am happy to be here and having this opportunity to work with you.*
>
> *The Scientific Assessment caught us by surprise. It was quite different from my company's expectations, which may create some extra difficulties in this negotiation. However, I look forward to working with you to find a way to secure reimbursement that satisfies the scientific assessment directives, your views, and our own constraints.*

Notice how we did *not* say that the problem is that this market's assessment is different from other markets, which would be an attack on their assessment.

Mutualism changes the dynamic most people assume going into a negotiation. But the opening statement is not enough. You need to act consistently with it, treating the Payer as a team member. That may involve trying to sit at a 90° angle from them if possible, instead of facing each other; taking time on coffee breaks to socialize with them, if possible; not having the posture of someone who is hiding information from them, etc. When the negotiation gets tough, it is often helpful to put the disagreements into context, and remind everyone that it is indeed a difficult mutual challenge. For example, in this same negotiation:

Payer (in semi-aggressive tone): As I said, we want a 50% discount to match the scientific assessment. Give us that discount so that we can reach a deal.

Pharma: I agree that we should comply with the scientific assessment and that if we were to meet it with a straight discount, that would be 50%. I am also aware that for this negotiation what matters is the scientific assessment of this market, and I am not arguing against it. What I hope you also understand is how our company has reasons to be surprised by that assessment and how such an assessment creates a problem for me, when we have our product on its path to higher prices in other markets.

Payer: But that is your problem, not ours.

Pharma: Unfortunately, because of the large difference between the scientific assessment versus *other countries, our HQ disagrees with our country's scientific assessment and thus with the proportionate discount you requested. Furthermore, the risk that your requested discount negatively impacts our prices in other markets becomes much larger. And while you can argue that this is only my problem, I believe it is our joint problem because I still think it will be beneficial to list the product in our country, if we find a deal that can work for us both and respects the assessment.*

Payer: Are you saying that the scientific assessments in other countries are right and we are wrong? If not, how could such a deal be if not a 50% discount?

Us: Not at all. I don't have the competence to assess which ones are right and wrong, or even if there are wrong or right ones. Our market issued the more negative assessment, rightly or not, and this generates negotiation problems. I want to work with you to solve these problems in a way that respects the assessment, as well as your views and my constraints. I hope it is clear why giving such a large straight rebate is not a solution that I can propose or accept. Given that the scientific assessment opens the possibility for us to address the flagged uncertainties in many ways, shall we think of different ways to mitigate them, which we may combine with a discount, albeit a smaller one?

This conversation, if not framed within a mutualistic perspective, could easily slide into a conversation where Pharma would argue how wrong the scientific assessment was, with the Payer taking this as a matter of national pride and sticking to how binding the scientific assessment is for this negotiation. The job here is to avoid getting locked into the good vs. evil or Us vs. Them perspectives, especially because the Payer does not have the mandate to override the scientific assessment even if you could demonstrate how wrong it was.

6.3.2 How to Develop Great Relationships While Negotiating

6.3.2.1 Trust

A good negotiation relationship is not only about having sympathy with each other, sharing commonalities, or a cordial attitude. It implies trusting each other and being individually committed to helping the other succeed. Each side should feel that the other is honest, reliable, competent, and cares.

If this seems totally incompatible with a negotiation, it is because you are confusing a negotiation with a bargaining process. A bargaining process implies misleading the other about how much you can pay, when you will walk away, etc. If you only bargain, it is extremely hard to develop and maintain a truly good and trusting relationship. Most P&R negotiators, from Pharma or Payer, carry a substantial amount of fear, distrust, animosity, tricks, and misdirection beyond the formal and cordial respect.

How can you develop a good relationship?

1. By being honest. Do not lie, distort facts, or be biased about presenting your data.
   (a) Question: Won't we be taken advantage of if we are totally honest and transparent?
   (b) Answer: Maybe, so be translucent, not transparent: don't lie, do present all data that is relevant, but you should not share information that is not related to the value in the negotiation, but instead gives your counterparty negotiation power over you. If asked such power-transferring questions, such as: "*What is your floor price?*" Answer "*That is a question I am not comfortable answering, as the answer would put me in a vulnerable negotiation position. Plus, it already hints at you wanting me to close the worst possible deal I can, which I hope you can understand is not my interest here. Conversely, I am not interested in taking every cent you have or asking what maximum budget impact you could accept. I prefer to refocus on what could be a good deal for both of us.*" This is different from any questions wanting to assess, for example, the clinical value of a medicine. Those questions are assessing the value in the deal for them, and you should answer them clearly, even if it means a worse deal for you.
2. *By being reliable*, always delivering on what is promised and acting in a consistent manner
   (a) Question: If we depend so much on Headquarters, how can I always deliver on my promises if I do not control what HQ decides or does, and I am even limited on what the company allows me to do?
   (b) Answer: Under-promise and over-deliver. Promise what you can control, and be transparent about what you do not. Be sure to transmit to the Payer all the work that you and your HQ colleagues have to do when approving something, so they see the challenges and delays not as lack of concern or respect. Don't speak about your HQ as if it were a bad, capricious, or unreliable party.
3. By showing you care for them and for the well-being of others
   (a) Question: But we care for the well-being of patients—isn't that enough?
   (b) Answer: No, that is not enough, first because the Payer doesn't truly believe that you care about them. The argument that you want our patients to have access to your medication can easily be heard as "I want to sell more!" Show by actions, not words alone, that you care for others, including patients,

healthcare staff, and the Payer. Show concern for the pressure they are under. Think about how you can help them achieve their goals.

4. By resisting rationalizations and preemptive power moves
   (a) Question: But what if they are planning on a power move against us? Aren't we supposed to defend ourselves?
   (b) Answer: Not so fast. First, we may have misunderstood them, so ask more questions instead. Besides, we often rationalize our power moves based on our fears of what the other side may or not do. This means we are negotiating with something that hasn't happened yet or may never happen if we avoid a negative dynamic. If you do not want power moves in your negotiation, don't start out assuming or acting as if they are coming. Take responsibility for your own actions, avoid quick reactions, and proactively promote a win-win dynamic.
5. By reducing suspicion and misunderstandings
   (a) Question: How do we do that?
   (b) Answer: When we don't know what is going on, we tend to create worst case scenarios in our head, especially if trust is not there. It is safe to assume Payers will interpret everything you do quite negatively, because of their negative prejudice about Pharma. So, if you are doing something that may be negatively interpreted by the Payer, anticipate and explain why you are doing it to clarify that there is no ill-intention or untrustworthy behavior going on.

Will these efforts sacrifice potential value in order to obtain and maintain trust? No, what they may do is forgo undeserved value that you could have captured unethically through power moves. But in the larger picture, you will obtain much more value. The best deals we have seen in Market Access have been struck by people who had developed long-term trustworthy relationships with Payers and resisted easy temptations to take advantage of the Payer's blind spots. By having this level of trust, the Payers no longer needed to over-ask or needlessly act tough to protect themselves from potential tricks. Instead, they became open to working together to create innovative deals that brought broader, quicker access with more value for all involved.

6.3.3 Outsmarting the Payer?

It is a widespread misunderstanding that negotiation is about outsmarting the counterparty. This can be somewhat true in bargaining or power-based negotiations, though it often boils down to a pyrrhic victory: you may win the battle, but at a great cost today and in the future. We have unfortunately seen, heard, and read about a few negotiations where the Pharma negotiator tried to outsmart the Payer. Sometimes it works, many times it backfires badly.

As an example of a usual temptation Pharma negotiators face: the normal negotiation relationship between prices and volumes suggests that lower volume drugs will command higher unit prices, while large volume ones challenge the budget more and incentivize Payers to demand more discounts and lower unit prices. Pharma may be tempted to provide lower volume estimates for their benefit. However, Payers are already schooled in such tactics. If the volume estimation from Pharma seems inflated, the Payer uses that high volume to ask for higher discounts. If, on the other hand, the volume estimation seems underestimated, then they will use that volume to demand a sales cap over which products are free or almost free.

Even if not for this counter-move from the Payer, presenting misleading information at the negotiation table is a risky strategy. Even if Payers don't spot that your numbers are inflated, you will be stuck with those numbers for the rest of the negotiation, even when they work against you. All along you will feel anxious and risk being exposed.

And, if you negotiate based on tricks, counterparties are more likely to reciprocate. Then, of course, there is the situation when they are using their tricks on us. Yet, there is a big difference between falling for their tricks and tricking them back. We only need to protect ourselves, not attack the other side.

6.3.4 Discounts for Goodwill

Does giving discounts demonstrate trustworthiness? We make the case it does not. We can offer Payers lots of things to build our relationship: more data, more information, more documents. But offering a lower return on the investment of our shareholders, or securing less money for R&D and lower bonuses for our colleagues are not friendly or relationship-building gestures. These are unilateral transfers of money from your pocket to theirs. Real relationships are built, not bought. Do you ask the Payer for a premium, so that they can demonstrate that they value your relationship? Of course not. If Payers ask it is because they have power. Asking money to build "relationship" is manipulation.

What do you do if they ask for a discount as a demonstration of goodwill?

Payer: I believe you value the relationship with this Agency. Obviously, we expect that to be reflected in your discount to us.

Pharma: Indeed, we do value our good relationship. I am putting all my efforts into crafting a deal that specifically addresses your concerns and interests, to make it as valuable as we can for you.

Payer: I appreciate it. But now we are stuck. We agreed to what a fair price for your product could be... but that price, even though it makes sense from your arguments, is higher than we can pay. So I would like to ask you, in the name of your concern for our Agency and taxpayers, to lower the price to a level I can pay, which is 10% lower than your last offer. 10% is not too much. I expect it should not be a problem given our strong relationship.

Pharma: I am sorry to hear that your budget does not allow you to close a deal that we both find appropriate. I am assuming that this is as frustrating for you as it is to me. Unfortunately, I don't think I can comply with your discount request. I can instead work with you to find ways around your budget limitations. For example, if I know until when your budget is valid, we may be able to tailor a deal around it. Alternatively, is there any way you could consider renegotiating that budget internally? How about (...)

Payer: No, no.... We want a straight 10% discount for our relationship's sake, not to find ways around the problem. Thanks for that the effort, but let's stick to the discount.

Pharma: Regarding the extra 10% discount request, we have already achieved a lot more than a 10% increase in value on the deal so far, compared to a simple list price deal. Your request for another 10% on top of what we already created for you is quite a large discount request at this stage. Let's find other ways to improve the deal and overcome your budget limitation.

Payer: Other companies seem to believe that our relationship is worth 10%...

Pharma: I hope you can see I value this relationship from the transparent way we interact, for all the concern and respect I have for you and your agency, and our effort in finding the best deal for all of us whenever we can. Giving away money beyond the appropriate price, when it is not even mine to give... does not seem like a healthy path for a good relationship.

Payer: Other companies do that... And you seem to not want to help us with the discount...

Pharma: On the contrary, I am committed to finding solutions that improve this deal. My focus is on being open and trustworthy so that together we can find solutions that others may overlook. I don't use any tricks to try to pull the price up to give fake discounts afterwards. I am always willing to go the extra mile to find the best deal for us and I will never ignore a request from you. And I have a fiduciary duty to my company and shareholders to close deals that are fair for all, bringing public value, and making a profit at the same time. That is why I am proposing to look into the issue of your budget limitation, to try to find a solution that can work for all of us.

Payer: (still a bit skeptical) *Okay, so what do you suggest we do, specifically?*

The Payer does not know what else you have up your sleeve. So it makes sense that they would still ask for an extra discount for the relationship, just in case that would work. Seeing that it doesn't work, they can check that box from their bag of moves and move forward with the negotiation.

What if they declare an ultimatum: either give us a discount or we will not reimburse your drug? This is a slightly different game, but only slightly. In the above example, the Payer pushed your guilt button with the implicit message that if you did not give the 10% discount, you would be the one causing a relationship deterioration. Here they are pressing the fear button, saying that if you do not give the discount, your drug will not be listed. Both cases are manipulations and in both the advice is to avoid giving in while trying to find other ways, not penalizing for yourself, to satisfy the Payer's interests. Separate the two conversations: "*Is our relationship a good one and how can it be improved?*" and "*How can we get the reimbursement through without that extra 10% discount?"* and explain in more detail why the 10% won't work for you.

In the case of not listing, you can always add: "*Why would you not list my drug if we already recognized that it brings good value to the market, we already found some solutions to increase value to both sides and, while we are facing a price obstacle, I am still here trying to find solutions with you? Why is the discount the only possible answer if we have not yet explored other possibilities to bridge this gap?*"

6.3.5 Understand and Improve Their Internal Negotiations

Imagine you are sitting at the negotiation table and the Payer comes with something different... an odd proposal or a suggestion to negotiate in a different way than what you are used to. As they explain it, what goes on in your mind? Probably something along the lines of: *"How will my HQ react to this? What might be the problems? How will I tell them about this?"*

Even if the Payer has "total authority to close a deal," that usually means total authority within a pre-specified scope of deal, which may or may not include what you would like the deal to be. As you negotiate focusing on value, you will expand the pie and include topics not measured by the Payer KPIs or not considered in its internal negotiations.

Payers may just react by saying "*no, not interested,*" and stick to their position despite you clearly showing how your proposal would be better for them. How can you overcome this hurdle?

1. *Be aware* that you are negotiating both with the Payer and their internal stakeholders—without knowing who some of these stakeholders are!
2. *Ask questions early* about the Payer's internal processes and stakeholders: "*What can I do to facilitate your internal conversations?*"
3. Ask questions about the *Payer's internal measures of success* (whether they are pursuing KPIs on percentage-based discounts over the initial price offer, absolute price, budget impact at the end of the year, budget impact predictability from the start, etc.) in a way that does not seem you are probing for sensitive information, but rather that you are on the same side and want to help them succeed in their KPIs.
4. *Help them negotiate internally* by providing them with visual support and information (charts, slides, etc.) for the information you bring to the table, so that they can easily communicate internally the value of the deal and how together you solved your differences in opinion and conflicts of interest.
5. *Share information on your internal negotiations*, what your HQ appreciates, what internal steps are needed to obtain what you brought to the table, what kind of information may help you change your mandate, etc.
6. *Send them minutes of the meetings*, after each meeting, in a format that is helpful for them to bring to their internal stakeholders. Especially for complex issues, be

careful to make things clear in the minutes and make sure that the Payer negotiators come across in the minutes as being good negotiators and doing their job well.

Many times, Payers will open up and share with you the intricate internal negotiation hurdles they must face, so that you can help increase their chances of success. You will then be able to jointly find solutions for both sides' internal negotiations. This exercise, especially when done early, can have an interesting side effect: it may demonstrate a true sense of care and commitment to the Payer negotiators' success and thus strengthen your relationship.

6.3.6 Negotiate the Negotiation

Substance negotiation is what most people usually call negotiation: the negotiation of everything that goes in the contract (e.g., price, volume, payment terms, etc.) and that is usually converted into financial terms plus different rights and duties.

The Communication negotiation is what happens when the parties negotiate how they will negotiate the substance: What should be talked about when? In which order? Who shall speak, when, and how? How should the negotiators address differences? How do we make decisions? Who needs to be involved in the decision-making? What procedural steps should we take in the clinical evaluation and in the commercial negotiation? How much time do we have? What communication means do we use? Are there chances to appeal? How do we proceed?

These are connected. When a negotiation follows a clear, consensual, productive and fair **process**, there is a very high chance of the negotiation going smoothly, with little value destruction and with both sides achieving what they want. As an example, consider the work of a mediator when a conflict goes to mediation: the mediator's sole job is to instill a productive process on a previously chaotic negotiation. In many cases, mediators do not negotiate the substance, but mediate the process so the parties can best negotiate the substance. This process focus dramatically increases the chances of solving the conflict and reaching a deal.

In the same way, a good win-win negotiator is one that can take both roles: negotiator and mediator. Be the negotiator when negotiating substance and the mediator when negotiating process. Negotiate the best you can for yourself on the substance, while pursuing a productive, fair, and unbiased process for all.

6.3.6.1 What Does a Productive, Fair, and Unbiased Process Look Like?

When there are relationship issues, they are solved respectfully and productively (to the extent possible) before negotiating everything else.

- The negotiators agree on the agenda, the time and number of meetings, the scope of the deal and conversations, the authority each side has to commit or each other's internal approval processes.

- Negotiators learn about each other's interests (including wants, needs, and concerns) before making proposals.
- The deal is crafted by the two sides to address all parties' interests. Instead of exchanging proposals, the sides should work together to build the deal. They should start from a broad sketch and progressively define the details and only then include preferred yet legitimate numbers.
- The authority of all negotiators should include room to explore at least a few solutions for the negotiation, instead of being limited to a single position. If not, you need to negotiate that authority internally as well.
- If the negotiators feel the negotiation is not progressing as it could, the negotiators should "park" the substance negotiation and discuss the process: how it is going, what may be the problems and how to follow a better process.
- Negotiators should make definite commitments on the substance only when the deal is about to close. That is, they should not commit on some parts of the deal without knowing the full deal, such as committing on the price before knowing all the conditions.

This can be challenging in P&R, as the proposal often must be submitted in advance and the meeting is booked to discuss the proposal. Also, the Payer's concerns are often those provided by the Scientific Assessment Body. So how to proceed in P&R? By having a process negotiation first. Here is how this might go:

6.3.6.2 Example of a Process Negotiation

Payer: What is your proposal?

Pharma: Before sharing a proposal, I would like to discuss the agenda for today's meeting to make sure that we will be using your scarce time as productively as we can. I sent you one agenda proposal via *email/letter. Did you have a chance to read it? Would you mind if we briefly discuss it?*

Payer: OK, go ahead.

Pharma: Do you have a proposal for the agenda yourself?

Payer: No, I don't have proposals for agendas. Do you have a proposal for your product instead?

Pharma: Sure, we will get to a proposal soon. I understand that this is the main point for you today. For me, it is important to know what you care about so I can provide you with a proposal you will appreciate. [Moving to the agenda:]

1. *I propose that we start by learning your concerns about our product and dossier, so we can address them or clarify any potential misunderstandings.*
2. *Then, we can discuss the type of deal that would be more appropriate to your concerns and our limitations.*
3. *Finally, we can discuss price and other numbers toward a specific proposal.*

Does this sound like a productive way forward? I think we can save a lot of time by tailoring the proposal to your concerns.

Payer: Actually not. That seems like too much time wasted on less relevant things. I want a proposal.

Pharma: I could give you a blind proposal, completely miss the mark and waste our meeting fighting over something that is just wrong to begin with....

Payer: Just give me a proposal with your best price.

Pharma: If I were to offer my best price, we might miss out on other ways to create value. If you dislike it and ask for discounts, I would not be able to offer more. You would then be frustrated and demand things I cannot provide. We would risk losing a viable deal.

Payer: That works for me.

Pharma: I hear you, but it does not work for me. I want to give you the best deal we can and close a deal we both like.

Payer: The only thing you can give me is price, so stop wasting my time.

Pharma: It is not my intention to waste your time or mine. Could you quickly tell me what you dislike about our product so I can give you a price?

Payer: Well, since I still do not know your net price proposal: I found your submission price proposal outrageous, the scientific committee criticized your drug's efficacy in the subpopulation B, and I want a 50% discount over the list price, plus a quick negotiation.

Pharma (taking notes): Let me see if I got your main points so I can address them properly: share net price proposal, high submission price, criticized efficacy in subpopulation B, and quick negotiation. Rest assured I will share a net price today and I am trying to get there as quickly as productively possible. Anything else that you are concerned about or where you think we may disagree?

Payer: I disagree with your estimates of cost-savings for our healthcare system.

Pharma (taking notes): Thanks for sharing. Anything else?

Payer: That's all. I generally dislike your product and, without the 50% discount, I see no reason to reimburse it.

(example to be continued)

This successful process negotiation example shows how it can be hard to negotiate the process with a Payer, who often:

- Prefer to follow biased but familiar power-based bargaining processes where they have an upper hand
- Distrust anything that comes from Pharma, so they will assume that every new move you are trying is an attempt to take advantage of them through the process
- Are in a hurry or feeling insecure
- Believe that the only negotiation lever to pull is price

If you follow this book's approach, they will be wrong in these four beliefs, because:

- They will obtain a better deal if they let you craft the deal with them instead of bargaining against you.
- You will not try to take advantage because you will also realize that choosing fair and efficient processes is mutually advantageous.

- The process will be on average quicker than the typical bargaining process and one where they'll have greater visibility and feel more secure.
- You will be able to customize the deal you propose to them, beyond just lowering price.

Their beliefs are based on their past negotiations, so it is understandable that they think as they do. Sometimes you will have to wear your "mediator hat" to argue resiliently for a more efficient, value-focused negotiation process.

Most negotiators never negotiate the process, so you will be doing something new and your counterparty may become suspicious and defensive. Hence, you must **transparently** explain why your process suggestions benefit all parties and the negotiation. Beware of becoming positional on process. Remember to be open to persuasion if your counterparty suggests a superior process to yours as the goal is to negotiate the best possible process for all.

But if the Payer can set the process to their advantage, why would they accept a process that is even or balanced? This is an obstacle, but not an insurmountable one. Let's continue the negotiation:

Pharma: I assume that your discount request is based on the lower value in subpopulation B. If so, we understand that the clinical value in that population is less evident than in subpopulation A, and probably lower.

Payer: There is hope for you after all.

Pharma: Thanks, we believe this is a legitimate reason to give you a discount. We could keep our price for subpopulation A, and match our comparator's price for subpopulation B, where we demonstrated only similar clinical value to them. Even though our trial was not intending to show superiority across different subpopulations, we relate to the scientific rationale which questions our results in subpopulation B. If we tentatively apply your 50% discount suggestion to match the comparator's price on subpopulation B, which represents 30% of the target population, we get a 15% discount overall.

Payer: Good move, but 35% more to go.

Pharma: Our submission price was calculated to reflect our drug's superiority vs. *the comparator, as explained before. The efficacy within subpopulation A is even higher if not averaged down by the results in subpopulation B, and yet we are not raising prices for subpopulation A. Could you comment more on why you still find our price too high?*

(to be continued)

In our experience, most Payers are not as tough and one-sided as the one depicted here. We don't want to imply that all Payers are like this, but rather demonstrate that you can negotiate the process even when meeting tough Payers. Many Payers dislike the hassle and frustration of usual bargaining and, if feeling safe and transparently convinced, will agree to follow a better and fairer process.

6.3.7 What If My Payer Has Many Limitations on the Type of Deal They Can Accept?

You may have heard the following lines in a previous negotiation:

- "To pay a different price per indication? That would be great, but the law says it should be the same."
- "To pay less for longer periods of treatment? Wonderful idea but we can't track patients as people have complained it creates an administrative burden."
- "Give us a rebate plus another discount mechanism? Wonderful, but that is not accepted in our system. It has to be all in rebate."

Many P&R systems are rigid, and work reasonably well if the drug is standard. However, when the drug presents more than average complexity (e.g., different patient populations with different clinical values, different indications, uncertainty in some aspects of the data, to be used in combination with other drugs, etc.) the process rigidity makes it very inadequate. This is especially worrying as many of the innovative breakthrough drugs of our time will have most if not all of these features (Eichler et al. 2020). The concept of "patient population" is becoming more and more granular, such as "diagnosed with hormone receptor-positive (HR+), human epidermal growth factor receptor 2-negative (HER2-) early-stage cancer (Stage I or II)," which means that the number of subpopulations with different clinical values has been dramatically increasing, as has the specificity of treatments, their accuracy, benefits, and thus the complexity of the negotiations surrounding them.

It is important to be aware that if your drug clearly does not fit the original administrative process, Pharma and Payer are in for a tough negotiation. Something must give: either you obtain an exception, you find a workaround such as averaging between subpopulations, you reduce some of your initial ask, you accept a terrible deal or maybe your drug won't enter the market at all. None of these scenarios are ideal. By accepting and following a maladjusted anachronistic process, the P&R negotiations are bound to be suboptimal, if not altogether disjointed and unproductive.

If you can anticipate that there is something unusual about your product that will benefit from exceptional treatment, our advice is to start discussing the process with the Payer early as described in section "6.2.11 Finding the Right Counterparty to Negotiate With." Do this even before submission, sometimes, because during the P&R substance negotiation, it is harder to convince any counterparty that a new process suggestion is not a trick to gain power or a better price. If done early, it is easier and clearer to separate the mediator hat (process) from the negotiator hat (substance). You are much more credible if you try to negotiate the process for the P&R of your future drug before and separately from its price and then adapt your submission to follow the Payer's suggestions.

6.3.8 Escaping the Price-Only Focus

6.3.8.1 The Bargaining Process

"Bargaining" (not to be confused with "Negotiating") is the simple and widespread process used in shops and bazaars around the world. It relies on an exchange of each party's preferred prices (aspiration price) as positions starting far from each other. They then proceed to exchange concessions, interspersed with threats to walk away, and, if successful, they converge to a point somewhere in between, often close to their bottom lines (reservation price).

Bargainers make concessions, which reduce their positional demands in exchange for nothing, on the hopes of preventing the other side from leaving the negotiation. The frequency and size of each side's concessions signal willingness to move, and what price they are expecting to land. In theory, if one negotiator values reaching its aspiration price more than it values closing a deal, they will move less. If, on the other hand, they are more concerned with not losing the deal, they will take larger steps toward the counterparty's position. To do better than your counterparty in this negotiation approach, there are a few things that a negotiator can do:

1. Start with extreme positions ("anchoring"). Share them decisively or add fake legitimacies to back them up.
2. Make smaller and less frequent concessions than your counterparty.
3. Clarify that you are unable or unwilling to make concessions to force them to choose between losing the deal or accepting your proposal.
4. Fake negative emotions, bluff that you are close to your financial or emotional limit, and threaten to walk away if the counterparty stops making concessions.
5. Disguise that you are trying to fool them so that your counterparty does not reciprocate with equally extreme moves.

Most P&R negotiations follow this bargaining dynamic, where the parties waste months throwing numbers at each other. Unfortunately, because of its simplicity, bargaining has many drawbacks, such as:

- Reduced value creation. Value creation requires the sides to share information to craft options that maximize the satisfaction of interests. Instead, the parties take turns making concessions, starting from desired positions and decreasing in value until a compromise is reached.
- A key goal of the communication is to mislead the counterparty, thereby damaging relationships and preventing meaningful learning.
- It is easier to bargain over one or few variables than over a complex deal. So bargainers separate the variables (namely, price) into isolated discussions, which reduces exchanges, synergies, and value creation even more.
- A key bargaining move is to convincingly threaten to walk away, without actually doing so, to extract concessions from the counterparty. That is quite difficult to pull off for a Pharma country affiliate negotiating with the single payer system representative. The only instances where walking away would be a relevant

power lever is with drugs of extraordinary relevance—but in that situation we believe it to be unethical, and highly risky, to make that threat.

With all these disadvantages, are there any advantages to bargaining in a P&R negotiation?

Well, for the Payer there are. It is a method that does not require much preparation and that can be quite quick if the powerful side wants it to be quick and the less powerful side caves in. Also, the least prepared side runs fewer risks of being fooled by the other side, without the possibility of being taken advantage of by the more complex deal structures that arise from a value creating negotiation.

When the Payer is negotiating with Pharma negotiators they distrust and who will nevertheless bow to its demands, it is a good strategic option to choose bargaining. They will dictate the terms and the Pharma representative, after more or less of a struggle, will likely renegotiate its proposal with HQ until meeting the Payer demands. The outcome will be a value destroying or value wasting deal, but often acceptable for the Payer. Besides, without much experience with win-win negotiations, Payers are unable to compare their bargaining results with and thus remain ignorant of what could have been done better.

For the Payer to trade the bargaining game for a more complex value negotiation, they will need to feel:

1. **Safe:** they are not going to be tricked or run other risks.
2. **Interested:** there is more value for them (higher satisfaction of interests) in the value negotiation than in the bargaining process.
3. **No easier way**: using power on the Pharma representative will not likely give them comparable value.

A pharmaceutical product is what it is; the negotiation cannot change or customize it. So the Payer tends to see it as a standard good and only wants to negotiate on price. However, while the product is indeed fixed, the deal is customizable. In customizing it, far more value can be obtained beyond price. For instance, you can consider the specification of the patient population, how to price the drug, the structure of the deal (e.g., Pay per performance, Price Volume Adjusted, etc), curbing or estimating off-label use, eventually a sort of cap, and so on and so forth. If nothing else, you can provide great legitimacy for the Payer to internally justify the deal.

6.3.9 Alternatives in P&R: Use of Power, Safety Net, and Walking Away

In P&R, alternatives shape negotiations. A case in point, despite single-payer systems increasing the potential purchasing volume for Pharma and the eligible discount for Payers, the strongest source of discounts comes from the Pharma's inability to walk away to alternative buyers. From a national perspective, Pharma has no alternative for selling their product, increasing the power of the single Payer in a country due to its monopsony status.

On the other hand, Pharma has patent laws to ensure that few similar drugs are available to the Payer, so when negotiating patent-protected drugs, the Payer's alternatives can also be very unappealing. If a drug has been approved by the scientific bodies and brings a noted improvement to patients, or if a drug already has patients using it (such as when renewing a deal), not reimbursing a drug can create a lot of backlash against the government.

Alternatives in P&R are also special because they deal with people's lives and health. As we have seen, if left unregulated, Pharma can price its drugs on the patient's willingness to pay, which is abnormally high when someone is trying to get rid of pain or stay alive. Willingness to pay is the pricing version of negotiating based on the other's alternatives, as it means: *"How much more are you willing to pay for my drug, before it becomes worse than your alternative?"* The alternative can be a replacement medicine, if there is one, or the unacceptable loss of health/life, if there isn't.

Resorting to alternatives in P&R is especially dramatic: it can mean loss of life or health for patients, loss of popularity for the government, and no revenue on a product for Pharma. Playing a game of chicken with such high stakes is definitely not how we would like our healthcare systems to be working, even if it happens sometimes.

In some countries, the Payer may threaten not to reimburse a drug to force the Pharma negotiator to accept a perceived illegitimate proposal or be blamed for leaving patients untreated. On the other hand, a Pharma HQ may choose not to address the Payer's concerns, stall negotiations in an impasse, and leave patients untreated.

In other industries, negotiating using alternatives in this way is often value-destroying, and while some people may see it as unethical, most do not see a problem. However, in P&R, this negotiation approach is considered unethical by most. We deeply respect the people on all sides and know that in large majority, they are doing the best they know how. So why is it that such important negotiations sometimes unfold in this ethically questionable manner?

6.3.9.1 No Choice?

In our view, what happens is that people feel they have no choice.

Pharma negotiators of innovative life-saving products may see themselves in an ethical dilemma when the Payer threatens not to allow access to its product unless the company makes a perceived illegitimate and extreme concession. It would be easy to rationalize the situation, as this: *"If the Payers, who supposedly should have patients as the first priority, do not care, why should I have to cave in instead?"*

However, one has to prevent the "fight or flight" mindset to take control in that moment. The Payer is also under extreme pressure and probably feels it has to disregard individual patient impact as a way to follow through with its duty: *"The money I save on this drug can help more patients elsewhere,"* they reason. Plus, they fear that if they demonstrate their concern for patients, the Pharma negotiator will take advantage of that. So, in this moment, it is important to avoid the blame game.

From an ethical perspective, one cannot say that the ethically appropriate solution should be to always cave in and give the Payer what they demand. In such a scenario, the Payer would hold absolute control over setting prices and conditions for life-saving drugs, regardless of how unreasonable or inherently unfair the terms may be. Any country could free-ride on the more balanced negotiations conducted by other nations, leading to reduced or no investment in such drugs if this trend were widespread. What is then the ethical thing to do?

Our suggestion is to ask the following question: *"What else can I do to get us out of this situation, without using patient lives as a bargaining chip and without being motivated by pride?"*

There are usually plenty of things to do before caving in or walking away. There may be several mistakes or misunderstandings in the negotiation leading up to the impasse; maybe there are emotional reasons, such as the fear of being taken advantage of; or an ill-adjusted process.

6.3.9.2 Alternatives as a Safety Net

The high stakes of walking away without a deal are why having alternatives as a safety net can be so important—and in fact minimize walking away from occurring.

Preparing beforehand, then having our BATNA in mind during our negotiation will help us negotiate better by not being so afraid to fail, in the same way that trapeze artists can perform better and be more relaxed knowing there is a safety net to hold them in case of a fall. In the same way that a trapeze artist does not want to use its safety net so should a P&R negotiator try to avoid using its alternatives.

In P&R negotiations with a Single Payer system, the alternatives for Pharma are usually not very appealing, as entering a market without reimbursement is almost pointless. So we need to look at the alternatives in a bit more detail. Instead of asking ourselves: *"What is my alternative if this negotiation process fails and my product is not reimbursed?"* we propose to ask: *"What is my alternative in case this negotiation goes really bad, we get into an impasse or there is a breakdown, assuming I will do as best as I can to prevent that from happening?"* Usually there is something you can do before losing the chances of reimbursement. As an example, consider the following scenario:

You are negotiating a high-profile drug. Your company has ethically and very positively negotiated with the reimbursement agency on this and other drugs, so you have a sound reputation. However, the Payer is engaging in aggressive bargaining, and despite your positivity, out of the blue, they make another demand such as:

> *Either you give me* [some outrageous thing] *or you will be out of the market and I will publish a press release saying that your company was unreasonable and blackmailed us, tarnishing your company's reputation, here and abroad.*

If we have no safety net, we may be so afraid that we may feel that there is no choice but to comply. But if we had thought about alternatives, we would have already considered what to do in a similar situation. We would have considered what other relevant governmental bodies we could write to, what kind of press release we could craft, and even how to act if the Payer took this path. In doing this, the dreadful scenario we are being threatened with would lose a bit of its impact. Being less afraid, we could then try to negotiate out of that situation.

6.3.9.3 The Alternatives Conversation

When your counterparty pushes you to talk about what will happen if you don't reach a deal, we recommend that you collaboratively and calmly reframe the alternatives conversation back into a value-focused one.

What you will do depends on the situation's specifics. For instance, they may be so angry that they are willing to lose as long as you lose more. This can be a bluff but it can also be true. You should try to understand if the Payer actually thought you had done a bad thing (e.g., being unreasonable, blackmail, or other negative behaviors) and work hard to solve any relationship issues or the frustration of the Payer, in case it is not a bluff. If you do those properly, it will get increasingly obvious if it is a bluff, in which case the Payer will probably want to get out of the corner it has placed itself in. Help them do that by allowing the tension to dissipate and not mentioning the threat again.

Other times, the Payer will threaten to use an alternative they claim will be better for them. Take the following example: *"If you don't give us* [extreme demand] *we will then prefer to go to arbitration."*

The idea here is that they think or bluff that their alternative is better than the deal you have proposed and that they will happily pursue it. In this case, it is a good choice to discuss that possibility in a very collaborative manner. Why very collaborative? Because the human temptation will be to dare them to pursue their alternative, which is a high risk move that incites them to follow through not to lose face.

Pharma: OK. I understand that you think our last proposal is unfair, and therefore you believe arbitration would give you a better deal.

Payer: Of course it will.

Pharma: Well, it is not my intention nor do I see myself pushing for an unfair deal here, but maybe I am not seeing things well enough. Can you tell me where you feel the deal is unfair or inappropriate?

Payer: The price you are asking is clearly unfair! It is too high!

Pharma: I understand the price is high and that it will create some budget impact. We have shown you our way of thinking and why we believe it makes sense. We have also worked on your calculations and pointed out a few issues we felt were not totally correct. Why do you feel that arbitration would be different? Is there anything we are overlooking?

Payer: Common sense. You are overlooking common sense.

Pharma: How is that?

Payer: You will find out in the arbitration...

Pharma: Can you tell us now? If we are overlooking something, we would prefer to learn and save us all the time and hassle.

Payer: You will find that out in the arbitration.

Pharma: Can you tell me how is that good for you?

Payer: I will get all I want.

Pharma: That is unfortunate, since most arbitration are not so one-sided, and we believe we have a good case as well. I understand you don't want to reveal your full-arbitration case, neither do we. I'm asking where our current proposal is so clearly incorrect that an arbitrator can see the flaws, but I can't. Once and if I see that, I can adapt my proposal. If, on the other hand, it is you that may be overlooking something, maybe I can clarify that.

In this example, the Pharma negotiators tried to understand how the Payer perceived their BATNA (e.g., arbitration) as better than a potential deal. Had they found out, they would have used that information to adjust its proposal to better satisfy the Payer's interests, making it better than their alternative.

The Payer could also be overestimating the value of the alternative, in which case having a conversation about its advantages and disadvantages could make the Payer less interested in pursuing it. Yet another possibility would be that the Payer was just bluffing. In all these cases, it is beneficial to openly and collaboratively discuss the alternative that the Payer brought into the conversation, as misunderstandings can be clarified and the negotiation can be protected. Even if it was just a bluff, by discussing it rationally we remove a bit of its power.

6.3.9.4 Word of Caution

A big mistake people make in negotiation is to anticipate that their counterparties won't walk away or make aggressive moves because "it would not be logical" (famous last words!). Thus bargainers corner their counterparties, trusting things will end up well.

The mistake is that our logic is built from our perspective, not theirs. As we do not know their point of view fully, we may simplify it into the financial cost/benefit of the deal. And yet, there are many reasons why negotiators may make moves that lead to outcomes with lower objective value (e.g., walking away to a worse alternative or pursuing a very high risk strategy), such as:

1. Miscalculating the risk-rewards of their moves or the cost-benefit of the deal.
2. Out of anger, pride, or not to lose face.
3. To create a reputation of not caving in, to help them in future negotiations.
4. Because of organizational internal constraints, rules, or fear of precedents.
5. To follow their boss's orders or peer's desires.
6. To improve on their personal KPIs.
7. For personal reasons (lack of time, etc..).
8. To blame someone else for the bad result (the counterparty, the arbitrator, etc.).

Given so many reasons why people act in ways that decrease value for themselves, it is very risky to assume we can anticipate how the other side will act. It is much better to foster open communication with them, obtain and share as much information as possible, and collaboratively steer toward solutions that make sense and work for everyone—especially when we are dealing with people's health and lives.

6.3.9.5 When the Payer Does It

One problem you may face is when the Payer offers you a non-legitimate deal that is just marginally better than not being reimbursed, money-wise. In such cases, the Payer may be counting on you being afraid, and rushing to secure a deal that is at least better than not being reimbursed at all. In these cases, the Payer may be thinking: "*This deal is better than your alternative, so you will accept it. You will complain, whine, and take time, but I will stay still and wait, and you will accept it.*" This is simply using power to force you to take a deal they know is unfair.

Complaining about the deal not being legitimate won't help, because the root problem lies in them thinking only about alternatives, not legitimacy. What you need to do is change their perception that their proposal is better than your alternatives or that you will take it just because it is better than your alternatives. Some suggestions:

Pharma: "For me, your proposal is not recognizing, even the slightest, the value of our product. And I cannot ask my headquarters to accept it without knowing how to justify why your proposal could be fair. That would ruin my career and therefore I am not willing to pursue this path."

Payer: "Failing the reimbursement will be worse for your career!"

Pharma: "Not really. Not reimbursing is financially bad. Your proposal is also financially bad. Rejecting a very bad proposal will not be badly seen internally. I guess it is the same with you, right? Would you be blamed if you rejected reimbursement, had I made only extremely high price proposals?"

Payer: "Well, internationally it will look bad if you failed reimbursement here!"

Pharma: "It is possible, and we see another possibility as more likely. It is not that we got a negative scientific assessment, is it? So, other Markets will see evidence that we did not agree to a price that doesn't recognize the value of our drug. That can be a good thing. In fact, accepting your offer could hurt our prices in other markets more than not accepting."

Payer: "Prices are confidential, so there is no concern there."

Pharma: "Headquarters fears that some European Payers have been sharing information through non-official channels. Also, other healthcare systems do not prevent 100% of prices from being published online. Altogether, HQ would prefer to reduce large price fluctuations between different markets. We can nevertheless adapt to each Payer preference and perspective, propose to solve differences with Managed Entry Agreements, and agree to different prices when based on good legitimacy. So we can still tailor great deals for Payers, which is why I am asking repeatedly for the legitimacy behind the proposal you made. However, just accepting prices we dislike without a good rationale has become even less acceptable than before."

Payer: "Are you insinuating that I would not keep confidentiality?"

Pharma: *"Not at all. Unfortunately, more and more markets have started exchanging information, and while I do not doubt your word, we cannot rule out that someone in your organization, in the future, could share more information than we would like. I think this should not be a concern, as we should be able to converge on a deal we both are happy with. I just wanted to explain to you why this proposal, that you have not yet explained the rationale for, won't work for us. I did not want you to think that my refusal was based on stubbornness or a negotiation trick."*

Hopefully the clarification above should make the Payer reconsider. Caution, do not confuse this Payer's power play with situations where they are genuinely and legitimately dissatisfied with your offer: "*This price is what my internal stakeholders agreed to pay, it is what we think it makes it worthwhile for us to pay, and if your HQ doesn't want to meet this price, we prefer to not reimburse the drug.*" Here, it is advisable to revisit interests to attempt to tailor new and legitimate options superior to their BATNA, and still good for you.

6.3.9.6 Walking Away from a P&R Negotiation

There are, however, a few instances where one may need to walk away from the negotiation. It can have terrible consequences, as it negatively impacts the health/lives of the potential future patients, result in drastic job loss for people employed in the local affiliate (including the negotiator), as well as cause international reputation damage. Therefore, it should be considered carefully and as a choice of last resort. But if it is so bad, why even consider walking away?

For a good reason: because a common power-based tactic is to push the counterparty to the limit, and only stop pushing when the counterparty walks away. And then, once they do, to call the counterparty back to the table.

Unfortunately, there are a few Payers that engage in this sort of behavior. They exhaustively use power moves and block your every win-win attempt (e.g., they refuse to discuss other options, to solve disagreements, or to improve the negotiation). They continue making positional demands, seeing how far they can push you. You have no more discounts to give, and your last proposals seem too far apart. When these conditions happen, it is time to seriously consider walking away. Your goal should be to walk away from the table in a manner that increases the chances of them closing a deal with you. How can that be done?

- Make it very clear to them why you are walking away (to be sure there are no misunderstandings between the two sides).
- Make it clear how and why you have absolutely no way to improve on your proposal for them.
- List all the efforts you have made in trying to find a solution and why that did not work.
- Express your disappointment in reaching this impasse and express your willingness to do things differently, if they are interested.

- Leave the last proposal on the table, valid for a reasonable period to account for the time they need to reconsider their decision
- Leave the door open for them to come back, without feeling like they are losing face if they do.

Declare all of this in writing. Sometimes people are very stressed in these moments and only listen to half of what you are saying. A document clarifies that you are not bluffing and allows them to use it in their internal negotiations and it protects you in case the situation goes public.

What is the chance of the Payer coming back to the table after this step? It is not great. It is a high-risk strategy, only advisable when your chance of closing a good deal for you while staying at the table approaches zero. In this case, by walking away, while keeping the door open to be brought back in, you are actually increasing your chance of closing a deal.

From an ethical perspective, before walking away, you should consider whether your drug is life-saving or unique, in which case it could be argued that you shouldn't take the responsibility of leaving the table, even if that increases the chances of closing a deal. Other factors to consider are whether patients can get the drug through other sources (e.g., abroad), whether there are any programs to get access to the drugs, and what the process in place is for cases where negotiations break down. Anticipating this issue in your internal negotiations can help you make a superior and ethical decision in each case.

6.3.9.7 Could You Be Wrong?

It may happen that the behavior of the Payer will be so extreme as to make you think they are doing the power play described above, demanding lower prices until you leave the table only to call you back or they leave just to come later.

However, there is a significant chance that, despite seeming like they are pushing for lower prices beyond what is reasonable, they are in fact not. Misunderstandings and wrong assumptions are the staple food of negotiations. Maybe the Payer got surprisingly good prices from similar drugs and believes you can offer them similar prices. Maybe they have an overly negative projection of costs or on the clinical value. Or maybe you are the one with an optimistic view, an inflated appreciation of your product's benefits, an HQ price miscalculation, or a misguided push for improved results. Maybe the Payer inadequately got some backdoor information on prices from other markets or maybe you are the one operating under wrong assumptions from competitor prices.

There are a lot of reasons why the two sides could come across as making unreasonable demands even if they themselves don't think they are doing so. In these situations, the tension between the two sides is already high. Walking away would be throwing fuel onto the fire.

Just the fact that it seems like the Payer is doing the above-described tactic is not enough for you to gamble that they are. What you should instead do is double your efforts in collaboratively trying to learn and then understand where the potential misunderstandings may be coming from, with the Payer and with your HQ.

6.3.9.8 Bridging Programs

As P&R negotiations can last up to a couple of years and to ensure early access to patients in need, Pharma often create bridging programs where they temporarily supply the drug for free or at a price to be decided during the protracted negotiation. Bridging programs reduce the pressure for the Payer to close the deal quickly, as patients are not held hostages waiting for the drug. While these programs decrease Pharma's bargaining power, we applaud their negotiation ethicality since patient lives should never be used as bargaining chips. Conversely, Payers abuse of the power imbalance inherent in bridging programs, when they postpone reaching an agreement to extract more value from a prolonged bridging program or threaten to do so if they do not get a discount knowingly underserved.

Bridging programs can become financially positive for Pharma, when they help increase market share, awareness, brand value, or convert paying patients once the program ends. In terms of power, even though the Payer is not in a rush to close a deal when having a bridging program, it can become harder for the Payer to walk away from the negotiation if many patients and healthcare providers have become acquainted with the product and developed expectations of it being reimbursed.

Our recommendation is to establish a reasonable duration for the bridging program, ensure that it contributes to a delimited and clear negotiation process, and carefully consider when to start charging for the product. If possible, these issues should be negotiated with the Payer at the beginning of the negotiation instead of sending a positional bridging proposal.

6.4 Handling Competitive Pressure

Competitive pressure is a very strong source of power in negotiation, and it often favors the Payers in P&R negotiations. It increases the Payer's BATNA and thus their ability to walk away if they find the pharmaceutical company's BOOT (Best Option On the Table) to be inferior to its competitors. Given this improved BATNA, Payers have increased credibility when they threaten to walk away unless the pharmaceutical company gives further discounts.

Competitive pressure also creates information asymmetry to the Payer's advantage. While list prices are public, only the Payer knows the confidential net prices of competitive products. This information asymmetry allows Payers to bluff about how low competitors' net prices truly are to create fake legitimacy when demanding more discounts from the pharmaceutical company.

Most procurement negotiations insert competitive pressure in their processes in the form of a request for proposals or bidding processes, which pitch suppliers against each other for the buyer's benefit. Each supplier has the incentive to propose a superior option than its competitors to increase its chances of closing the deal.

Pharma is different. In many cases, except for generic products, drugs do not have therapeutic equivalence to one another. They are not exact replacements and thus they are not really competing with each other in the P&R negotiation, just in the market after reimbursement. Even MDs do not want drugs treated as exact replacements, so that they can still make decisions on prescriptions. One reason a win-win, power-free negotiation approach works so well in P&R negotiations of innovative products is because patent protection reduces competitive pressure. Different competitors can all be reimbursed, and not just the tender winner, providing diverse treatments in a market and the most adequate one to each patient's condition.

In other industries or in Pharma without patent protection, a tender involving five potential providers gives the buyer a strong power-based belief that it can secure a great deal exclusively through win-lose value claiming moves (e.g., pitching competitors against each other, lying about their prices, going back and forth among them for increased discounts, threatening to walk away, etc.) that it discourages value creation efforts. Negotiators default to the lowest price without exploring or securing other value drivers. In some tender types, the lowest-priced winner gets the full market and the others get nothing, preventing patients from medications that could have been best to treat their particular conditions.

Even with patent protection, Payers try to leverage competitive pressure, and related win-lose threats or information asymmetry when they say: "Your competitor has now lowered their drug X price to Y. I expect you to match that price."

When this happens, the first step should be to clearly assess the situation. A few questions you can ask yourself are:

- Where are we really competing head to head and where is it that we are not?
- Is there an official therapeutic equivalence or not? Can the Payer really influence my sales?
- Could the Payer genuinely expect that prices should be matched between competitors?
- Would the Payer feel cheated if we disregard the competitor threat?
- What is the goal of my competitor? To maximize market share or revenue? Why would they do such a competitive move? What would they expect me to do afterward, in return? What would they do after that next move?

These questions can make you see the situation from different angles. The first two questions are about alternatives. In a way, we are asking ourselves: "Is my competitor drug a real alternative for the Payer in our negotiation? Can they really move our sales to our competitor?" While Payers make this threat regularly, in most cases it is either an empty threat or a threat that would have a large cost for them to fulfill, as they would get into problems with other stakeholders.

The third question is about legitimacy. The Payer may see no valid reason why your drug should cost more than a similar one, and that may feel unfair to them. It is important that you have thought in advance about the reasons for a price difference. Our suggestion is that you don't brush away this topic, have a thoroughly prepared answer, and learn more how the Payer sees the two products before sharing your views.

The fourth question is on relationships. Payers may expect free-market competitors to engage in a price war, and may feel cheated if it does not happen or prices do not come down. The price war expectation is mostly misplaced in markets with very few competitors, who can compete on other dimensions. Also, there is not much fairness in a process that sets the prices of original branded drugs based on their clinical value, and then expect huge price drops due to price wars. But Payers may get stuck in wishful thinking and, even if you disagree with their perspective, they might feel cheated.

It is really important to clarify your specific situation. A branded drug ethically resisting to drop prices despite branded competitors on the Market is very different from when companies, after the loss of patent exclusivity for their drugs, make unethical moves to diminish the number of generic competitors in the Market to maintain prices.

The final question for you to consider is what will be the dynamic in case you drop vs. not drop the price. How will your competitors react? What will the Payer do next to your competitor if you drop the price? Consider the different scenarios and which ones lead to better outcomes for all, not just for you nor just for the Payer. Why? Because if you consider a scenario with a terrible outcome for any stakeholder with a say in the negotiation such as: "I will undercut my competitor's price and increase my sales dramatically and the Payer will be happy with me," there is a high likelihood that such a stakeholder will not stay put under that very negative outcome and reacts. It is therefore not a stable outcome.

6.5 Conclusion

We hope that this chapter can help you establish a better relationship with Payers and implement a win-win negotiation that maximizes value for you, while justifying to your internal stakeholders that you are indeed trying to maximize value and not just caving to the power of the other side. We have troubleshot what we believe are the main difficulties most negotiators are likely to face. We wish you huge success in implementing win-win in your P&R negotiations!

Reference

Eichler H, Pignatti F, Schwarzer-Daum B et al (2020) Randomized controlled trials versus real world evidence: neither magic nor myth. Clinical Pharmacology & Therapeutics 109:1212–1218. https://doi.org/10.1002/cpt.2083

7 Conclusion

At first look, healthcare and negotiation may seem only distantly related. We naively expect healthcare to be exclusively guided by science, best medical practices, and prioritizing patient welfare. However, as it hopefully has become clear by now, nothing could be further from the truth. Healthcare has been a system forged by the aggressive negotiations between its main stakeholders.

Negotiation is a great way for stakeholders to interact, solve problems, or create value. However, different negotiation strategies blossom under different settings and deliver different results. When the parties opt for win-lose negotiation strategies, based on the use of power in any of its forms, unless one is significantly more powerful than the other, the deal is doomed to be subpar. If one party does happen to be sufficiently powerful to push through any deal they desire, the weaker party is left merely licking their wounds, with nothing to feel good about, and that is hardly a sustainable scenario. In the case of P&R negotiations, where no one party is sustainably much more powerful or independent than the other, value is consistently destroyed as negotiators battle it out seeking the elusive ideal of the all-for-me outcome.

While that does not sound like the goal to pursue in healthcare, that is too often the reality we see. Different countries have devised different systems of healthcare to provide different levers and levels of power to different stakeholders. In some systems, those that pay for care have more power; in others those that deliver care are in a better position. Our healthcare systems have become the most comprehensive and effective we ever had in the history of humankind, but no system can be said to have found the optimal solution yet. Not for lack of trying, of course. As we have seen, there are challenges and trade-offs on the Government and Pharma sides, which won't go away or be fully solved by any one party on its own. While some remaining stakeholders are outside of the focus of this book, we assure you that the same would be the case for them.

The healthcare systems of today work and deliver care well in developed countries, and even reasonably well in many developing ones, especially if we compare

H. Falcão et al., *Pharma, Prices and Power*, Future of Business and Finance,
https://doi.org/10.1007/978-3-031-93933-4_7

them with what they were just 50 years ago. Healthcare systems still can improve significantly, but we believe they are likely to get worse given their current and future challenges, unless we start doing a few things differently. Focusing on Pharma alone, let's look at the positives of Pharma's integration into current healthcare systems:

- New cures are being developed at a high rate, historically speaking.
- Payers don't absorb the risk of failure in developing new cures, at least not directly.
- Pharma and Payers are aligned through some of their incentives to develop the best possible cures.
- Each country decides how it wants to evaluate clinical benefit and is able to set their own rules and reimbursements.
- Countries don't have to agree between themselves on how to allocate the effort or arbitrage the cost in supporting innovation, as pharmaceutical companies do that by negotiating with each Payer individually.
- Innovation spreads relatively cheaply to poorer countries after the loss of patent-protected exclusivity, providing broader access to poorer populations around a decade later than in wealthy countries.

It is important to consider these positives, as often we focus so much on the negatives that we fail to appreciate what we have. By doing so, we risk losing what works. That said, we can review a summary of the current challenges:

- Some patients don't have timely access to the best therapies: for example, patients in poorer countries before patent expiration; patients who are uninsured or which their plans don't cover them; patients in wealthy countries and good healthcare systems waiting in line; or patients where the system did not agree to reimburse a needed drug.
- Value-negative activities suck value out of the system, leaving the rest of us poorer and with worse care, including value-negative practices from all stakeholders that can harm the health or wealth of tens of thousands of individuals.
- Investment is channeled to me-too drugs or expensive drugs aimed at "wealthy-country" diseases, rather than innovating in new areas or in areas of broad need in developing countries.
- Minimal patient choice: patients have no access to clearly presented data that enables them to compare different therapies and different doctors. Every other stakeholder in the system either distorts or hides data from patients.
- Clinical trials do not provide the clearest data, with manufacturers having an incentive to run the quickest trials showing most effect, not the most revealing of how the therapy will fare in clinical practice.
- P&R processes are suboptimal and, in some important countries, fail to deliver the impartial assessments and negotiated outcomes that we believe they should.

7.1 Where Should we Go from Here?

Left on their own, systems of stakeholders using power against one another tend to enter downward spirals, instead of "healing" on their own. In good times, when resources abound, and everyone is growing—as in the West after WWII—problems are less notorious. Conversely, when resources and growth become a concern, as seems to be the case now globally, everything becomes harder, people and institutions become more afraid, and negotiations become more reactive, desperate, power-based, and aggressive, ultimately leading to more value destruction. If there is indeed less value to go around in the current climate, then we should tolerate this vicious cycle of value destruction even less.

Innovation may help solve our healthcare problems. With better drugs and better AI helping to deliver drugs to patients in an improved manner, we may be able to supply healthcare cheaply and to a much larger set of patients, especially in poorer countries. Unfortunately, it may also lead to more costs, as innovation may extend the life of very old patients and increase the financial burden to weaker economies under a demographic downturn. This innovation dichotomy could lead us to consider a few tough questions: Should we accept the current innovation trade-offs and just try to tweak the system? Should we start prioritizing some innovations over others? For example, should we focus on cost innovation over life-extending efforts? Should we consider accepting lower investment on innovation overall in exchange for lowering the cost of the medications we already have? Should we instead continuously increase taxation or health plan contribution?

If nothing else is done, we may have to start collectively making some very tough choices that we would prefer not to make. To avoid such choices, we can try first to obtain more value where we know it is being destroyed regularly. One example is when healthcare stakeholders approach P&R negotiations with win-lose strategies, reducing them into a power competition, and trampling the search for value creation, jointly tailored solutions, or fair outcomes.

To get out of this cycle is not easy. After all, while some value is being destroyed, what is not destroyed is being mostly captured by those with more power, who have few incentives to change the system. The more we engage in power battles, the more we frame the system into competing groups, such as Pharma vs. Payers, and the more we become groupish. As groups knit more tightly together to protect themselves from power moves from competing sides, they ignore in the process who they are truly pairing up with. As a result, we see interesting behaviors emerging when Payers who free-ride on other Payers propose alliances for mutual defense from Pharma. Or when Pharma acts as a block irrespective of the fact that value-negative players are creating problems or destroying value for the value-positive actors. Or even when we see hard-working and extremely competent physicians protecting others who are… not like that.

The solution for win-lose P&R negotiations should not be to give more power to the weaker side, but rather to increase collaboration and undermine the role of power, which will lead to more value in negotiations.

7.1.1 Transparency

One proven way to do so is to increase transparency. By transparency we do not mean Payers and Pharma sharing their agreed-upon confidential prices. Transparency needs to go beyond this to include transparency in our social choices toward healthcare, the pricing and incentive structures, negotiation processes and behaviors, the value created by different stakeholders, the benefits and risks of each therapy, and so on.

Transparency allows other stakeholders to see the unfairness and the value destruction in the current system. It makes people want to take sides and interfere and, in that way, increases the collaboration against power abuses. Not coincidentally, those in power try to prevent transparency in every way, be it by increasing secrecy, distorting information, controlling the channels, or increasing complexity to prevent understanding and facilitating misinterpretations that can be exploited. As we increase transparency, we see the areas for improvement together. For example, transparency over the lack of standardization and simplification of data and its presentation reveals that we can make it easier to comprehend and debate without distorting or manipulating information, leading to better understanding, conclusions, and ultimately decisions.

As a society, we have been highly successful at doing this in the scientific assessment stage of P&R negotiations, and that is laudable. However, this transparency does not continue in the remaining steps of price negotiations. How would citizens react if they saw the coercive, aggressive, and dismissive ways in which some Payers negotiate? How would they react when seeing a pharmaceutical company being reimbursed based on their trial data, when that data later fails to materialize in patients themselves? Expanding away from P&R, how would citizens react if they understood the tactics of healthcare plans to refuse treatments to patients, and if they could differentiate value-positive from value-negative approaches when choosing a plan for themselves? What would patients' informed choice look like if the risks, costs, and benefits of different pharmaceutical therapies were clearly explained in impartial ways that most people could actually understand? (Gigerenzer and Gray 2013) How would patients choose if they could assess their doctors' historic biases in prescribing certain therapies or the average post-surgery satisfaction of previously surveyed patients? There are ways to make this happen (Gigerenzer and Gray 2013; Porter and Teisberg 2006), but little interest in investing in it. Finally, how would patients respond to seeing exactly how their politicians decide on public health? Actually, we know the answer to that last one (e.g., on the British Lockdown Files), and it is not positive! (The Telegraph 2023) This leads us to the second step.

7.1.2 Reward Good Faith and Disincentivize Bad Faith

We need to punish ill-intended moves (sometimes called "bad faith") and reward the positive ones ("good faith"). We need to punish deception, misrepresentation, and other nefarious behaviors. By a strange quirk, it seems that behaviors that would be considered unacceptable in most other social environments are considered okay in negotiations. As it is today, the risk-reward of unethical moves in negotiations often favors those who commit them. Unethical negotiators stand to gain a windfall if they get away with their unethical or power moves, but nothing much happens if they are caught, unless two rare conditions occur: (1) negotiators demonstrably break the law and (2) there is someone interested in prosecuting them. The imperfections in our system's ability to control unethical behavior unjustly increase our healthcare costs without delivering any corresponding value, unlike the benefits we gain from paying doctors and nurses' salaries or purchasing value-adding drugs.

Instead, we can create negotiation processes or negotiate as we demonstrated above in ways that reward those who collaborate and prevent those who take unethical advantage from repeating their approach time after time. Similarly, we should create incentives for better behavior. Transparency is one lever to do so, but we should create more.

The concepts of negotiating in "good faith" and "bad faith" were created to evaluate the negotiator's intention behind their behavior. As it so happens, these two concepts evolved restrained by a bargaining frame (win-lose), and have not yet evolved to reflect win-win strategies. While the distinction in win-lose is already laudable, the concepts could be drastically improved to incorporate the win-win frame and yield better practical applications.

7.1.3 From Us vs. Them to Value Positive vs. Negative

Thirdly, we should break down the Us vs. Them mentality. We should avoid grouping stakeholders into opposite camps. Payers are right on some points and wrong on others. Pharma is right on some points and wrong on others. Some Payers are doing many things right, and some are not. Some may actually be taking advantage of other Payers. The same happens inside Pharma and with the remaining stakeholders.

Therefore, we should move beyond forming groups based on class, often done to increase power, to forming groups based on whether we are contributing or taking advantage of the system. Stakeholders who are bringing value to the system should want to work together to fight abusers. Instead of supporting everyone in their class, they should fear being grouped with value negative stakeholders, not to jeopardize their reputation.

Won't this make value negative stakeholders join forces? Yes, but they already do! Purdue Pharma had no trouble finding the 1% of value-negative Doctors.

7.1.4 To Better Define Value

Fourth, we need better regulation that properly measures, identifies, and promotes value by companies competing in the market. The rules and institutions encourage, enable, or nudge competitions, businesses, and overall activities to be either positive and value-generating for society or part of a value-destroying, parasitic jungle.

Historically, countries with proper rules and institutions have thrived. Those without, or where the rules don't apply to the powerful or those setting the rules, have not. The same happens on lower levels of the organization ladder.

In the context of P&R negotiations, a few healthcare systems established very objective value definitions, such as the UK's QALY, which could provide predictability to investors and Pharma and Governments in making choices for the most valuable and needed treatments. As seen above, the system is far from perfect, with QALY not capturing all the nuances of clinical value (Lakdawalla 2024), and NICE's negotiation bias defeating the purpose of objectivity. However, it is a step in the right direction.

Many healthcare experts support the development of a more accurate definition of value across the entire healthcare system, not only pharmaceuticals, as another big step toward a better optimization and valuation of resources across the board (Porter and Teisberg 2006; Lakdawalla 2024).

7.1.5 Be Inclusive

Fifth, we should create the right forums and environments for people from all of these groups, including patients and patient representatives, to find solutions. Most people, when placed in the right environment and under the right incentives, can collaborate. There is a whole field of knowledge on how to create such processes. However, this knowledge is usually ignored. We either make official, across-the-table negotiations between association representatives, which are a simulation of a nineteenth-century battlefield, or we offer chaotic panel discussions without any incentive to collaborate or find pragmatic solutions. Or we create commissions, without being careful enough as to their processes, constituency, power, or support, and thus they also end up not producing all that much.

In this book, we shared advice on how to improve P&R negotiations as a window onto how this and other processes can collaboratively tailor superior solutions. Larger groups require a very carefully crafted process management, but collaboration and win-win are also possible and yield great results.

7.2 Conclusion

Powerful stakeholders will counter moves that diminish their negotiation power. Most of the points above are sticks for which to counter such power: Transparency brings more people collaborating against power abuses. Rewarding good behaviors and punishing bad deeds allows good actors to thrive while reducing the number and impact of bad actors. Regulation can directly forbid moves to increase power or abuse power, thus nudging the parties toward collaborative and practical solutions. Breaking down the Us vs. Them mentality exposes value-negative actors. Better defining value permits the allocation of resources as a function of value to patients instead of negotiation power.

Then there are the carrots. The current system destroys value—so a big carrot is to retain all of that value instead of it going to waste. Also, many healthcare professionals and people working in healthcare organizations are disappointed with their careers and would love to be able to contribute more on behalf of patients' well-being. Imagine the system destroying less value and allowing healthcare workers to perform better and to act in a more ethical and less "defensive" way. That is a big carrot.

When information is clearly laid out to be understood, misrepresentation and deception are actively combated, people don't have to dumb down to groupthink, regulation incentivizes value-generating competition, and negotiators understand each other's limitations and KPIs to jointly manage them, P&R negotiations will gravitate toward win-win and we will all benefit. Stakeholders can interact through positive negotiation processes that enable them to work collaboratively to find solutions. They will find solutions to problems at a small scale, and the best solutions will shine and expand, bottom-up.

Changing entire healthcare systems is a huge endeavor. As such, we suggest instead testing different approaches on pilots at hospital or regional level, or on a single therapeutic area. In that way, we can measure costs and improvements and perfect different initiatives.

Better ways are possible. We should not normalize power use and abuse as the way to define one of the most important elements of life. We can negotiate our way to better healthcare, one negotiation at a time.

References

Gigerenzer G, Gray JM (2013) Better doctors, better patients, better decisions: envisioning health care 2020. Mit Press

Lakdawalla D (2024) Ensuring affordable and valuable pharmaceutical innovation for Americans. USC Schaeffer. https://healthpolicy.usc.edu/research/ensuring-affordable-and-valuable-pharmaceutical-innovation-for-americans/. Accessed 1 Jan 2024

Porter ME, Teisberg EO (2006) Redefining health care: creating value-based competition on results. Harvard Business School Press

The Telegraph (2023) The lockdown files

The manufacturer's authorised representative in the EU is Springer Nature Customer Service Centre GmbH, Europaplatz 3, 69115 Heidelberg, Germany. If you have any concerns regarding our products, please contact ProductSafety@springernature.com

Printed and bound by CPI Group (UK) Ltd, Croydon, CR0 4YY

17/09/2026

02218431-0003